Who was HIRAM ABIFF?

Who was HIRAM ABIFF?

by

J. S. M. WARD. MA., F.R.Econ.S., F.S.S., P.M.

Late Scholar and Prizeman of Trinity Hall, Camb.
Fellow of the Royal Anthropological Institute
Member of the Royal Asiatic Society
Etc.

Lewis Masonic

First published 1925
Reprinted as paperback 1986
This facsimile hardback reprint 2017

ISBN 978 0 85318 553 6

Published by Lewis Masonic

an imprint of Ian Allan Publishing Ltd, Addlestone, Surrey KT15 2SF.
Printed in England.

Visit the Lewis Masonic website at www.lewismasonic.co.uk

CONTENTS

PREFACE

In this book I have endeavoured to solve the problem which has puzzled Freemasons for many years. It seems to me strange that many anthropologists, who are Masons, have missed the opportunity of applying the principles they have learnt to use, when studying the customs of primitive races, to our own ceremonies and traditions.

The Dying God has for many years been a subject of study, and yet in the very heart of London, on almost every day of the week, His tragic story, only thinly humanised, is being enacted. If I have read the facts aright, Hiram Abiff is one of the Priest-kings of Tyre, the living incarnation of Adonis, who was offered up as a Consecration Sacrifice at the completion of the great Temple at Jerusalem.

In the course of my work I have received much kindness and help from Dr. Haddon, Professor of Anthropology at Cambridge, and Mr. Sidney Smith, of the Assyrian Department of the British Museum, both of whom are Masons and authorities on their respective subjects, also from Mr. G. E. W. Bridge and Mr. N. M. Penzer.

With regard to the books I have consulted, these are indicated in the notes, but there is one man above all to whom I must express my deep sense of indebtedness. Sir J. G. Frazer has been an inspiration in all his books, and to him more than to any other author I owe a deep debt of gratitude.

In conclusion I sincerely hope that my readers will find this book as interesting to read as it was for me to write, and that it will lead them to have an even higher veneration for our great Masonic Hero.

J.S.M.W.

Who was Hiram Abiff?

CHAPTER I

OUR PROBLEM

Every thoughtful Mason must have asked himself the above question time after time. To most it will be clear that the legend has a striking affinity to the theme of the Ancient Mysteries, and students have usually compared it with the legend of Osiris in Ancient Egypt.

To the author, however, it seems a mistake to go to Egypt to find the origin of our legend when the ritual itself indicates Palestine and the Near East as the true source whence it is derived. The very fact that the Bible, as we now have it, makes hardly any reference to the chief character in our Temple legend, and gives barely a hint of any tragedy, is alone sufficient to show that whatever be the case with other parts of our ritual the legend itself was not derived from any extant version of the Scriptures known to Englishmen in the 18th century.

The obvious field for research is therefore Palestine, not Egypt, and we must study not only the Jewish records as set forth in the Bible, but also profane history, and the beliefs and customs of the heterogeneous group of races who inhabited Syria and Asia Minor at the period of the building of the first temple, and during subsequent ages.

By the time my readers have finished this work, they will, I trust, have realised that Hiram Abiff is a far more tragic figure than even our legend represents. He stands for something greater, vaster, nobler and more terrible than a mere man of honour who, rather than betray his sacred trust, laid down his life. As the story unfolds, my readers will perceive that we are spiritual eye-witnesses of a vast, soul-shaking tragedy, whose grim and all-embracing character reveals the unplumbed depths of cruelty and folly from which, in the course of ages, mankind has slowly emerged, guided by that Light which is from above.

Hiram, indeed, may be a real man of flesh and blood, who, like thousands before and after him, has been sacrificed in the false belief that thereby the corn will be made to grow and the building to stand firm for ever. One of that long line of Prophets, Priests and Kings whose blood has stained the flower-bespangled earth that the Great Mother may be fruitful and

1

multiply. Vain, yet heroic victims who, at the call of duty, went down unfalteringly into the valley of the Shadow of Death.

That Hiram was not the last architect who was sacrificed at the completion of the building on which he had toiled these pages will show, and even to-day in the dark corners of the earth humble, yet valiant, representatives of our Master still follow the same blood-stained path that he once trod.

The road which we shall follow in this book is like the Masonic pavement, checkered with black and white, and like that used in the R.A. it is flecked with crimson. We must descend into the black night of the Abyss itself—the Abyss of savage ignorance and fear, and the lower we descend, the further back in time we venture, the blacker becomes the darkness, lit only by a glimmering ray—the unfaltering faith and quiet heroism with which men accepted the high office and the grim fate which savage and primitive ideas had assigned to them.

We shall not reach the lowest depths of the abyss; fortunately we can content ourselves with imagining what lies beyond in the far-distant and dim-red dawn of man, when we shall have seen enough to realise how long and painful has been the journey by which civilised man has climbed to his present state. But as we follow the path back from darkness to light we shall find new hope and salvation in the evidence we shall gather up as to the way in which, amid the darkness of primitive magic, men have arisen, inspired from on high, and seizing the ancient grim magical ceremonies, have transformed and ennobled them into things of beauty, proclaiming to all a message of hope: " The dead die not, for as the corn dies to rise transformed and beautified, so shall mortal man shed the husk he calls his body and, soaring upward like an eagle, shine with the stars for ever and ever."

Later came the Mystic who, taking the ancient legend, again transformed it into a symbol of the inner strivings of man's soul, the High Quest of God: a revelation that even in poor sinful man there resides a Spark of the Divine Being with Whom we can achieve union and At-one-ment, the Beatific Vision, the end of the age-long Quest. Thus we shall perceive God working in a mysterious way, in strange places. We shall see that the long-drawn agony of man, inflicted by man himself, has after all not been entirely in vain. Perhaps above all we shall acquire a new and more genuine admiration for the stern old prophets of the Jewish faith, fighting desperately, often hopelessly outnumbered, against the adherents of a lower conception of Divine things.

On the other hand let us recognise that not only in Palestine was the Light of Lights at work leading men on from the Lower to the Higher, but in far-distant lands other prophets of the Most High, using similar Rites and customs, ennobled and transformed them into a means of conveying to mankind, by allegory and symbol, profound spiritual and moral truths. In the course of our work we shall trace the origin of such peculiar features as the Lion's grip, the Eagle's claw, the two pillars, the sprig of acacia, stepping over an open grave, and of that bright Morning Star whose coming brought Peace and Salvation to the multitude but death, stark and terrible, to one lone man. In review there will pass before us initiation Rites of Death and Resurrection which exist in all parts of the world, and from them we shall learn much which will help us in our study.

When investigating primitive beliefs we must remember that the savage is far from logical. He is perfectly capable of holding at one and the same time beliefs which *we* can see clearly contradict each other. Even to-day amongst civilised races the same phenomena can be witnessed and quite intelligent men will honestly maintain two or more beliefs which are mutually destructive. Logical thought, indeed, is of very modern growth, and we must therefore not be surprised if we find that our primitive ancestors and the modern savage attach to a mythological being the attributes of the Sun, the Moon, and the Earth at one and the same time.

Another factor which is apt to confuse the beginner in anthropology is that various races and cults, particularly in the Near East, have constantly borrowed details and incidents from each other, while we, who wish to probe deep into the working of the human mind in its journey towards the light, must be prepared to find not only an abysmal ignorance of the most elementary facts of life, but often a lack of sound logic, made the more surprising by flashes of genuine inspiration and real knowledge.

In this work we shall perhaps discover even more important facts than the answer to our original question. We shall traverse vast regions of time and space; we shall walk amid the primeval jungles of modern Africa, and follow the solemn procession which mourned for Adonis slain. We shall see the bodies of men hanging from trees which were never planted on the hill of Calvary, and, in the spirit, witness the bale-fires of Moloch blazing from end to end of the ocean-wide Empire of the Phoenician race.

We shall see tragedy after tragedy flit past us on our journey from land to land. The rolling of the death drums and the shrill tune of magic flutes will blend in our ears with the wailing of a countless host which will follow us even into the sacred precincts of the Temple of King Solomon, and the still more sacred threshold of the inn at Bethlehem. Amid heathen temples and Gothic churches, from the palm huts of New Guinea to the ornate Lodges of modern London, we shall follow the foot-steps of our Master Hiram, as he treads the pathway of sacrifice, dyed red with his own blood.

Let us then roll up the curtain on the grim tragedy of the divine men, be they kings, priests, or architects; let us follow the shadowy figure of the Master Architect in particular, back through the ages to his home on the mountain of Lebanon where, according to the Scriptures, Adoniram presided over the levies in the days of Solomon, King of Israel. Let us trace the tragic end of Adoniram himself as given in Holy Scripture, and let us learn the meaning of the name Hiram—He that Destroys—and discover the grim cause which made him a widow's son.

CHAPTER II

THE FIVE HIRAMS IN THE BIBLE[1]

Let us follow the Master's footprints
   Adown the darkening years,
Back to the dim red dawning,
   Through the valley of blood and tears.

.   .   .   .   .   .

Let us walk by the side of our Master
   Amid the gathering gloom,
Where the conch shells wail to the Heavens
   And the solemn death-drums boom.

.   .   .   .   .   .

On through the darkness of anguish
   Where the stricken God-man dies,
To the hour when the corn seed burgeons
   And the souls of the dead arise.

.   .   .   .   .   .

    In considering who Hiram was I shall assume that my readers know by heart the form of the legend given in Emulation working, and shall only, from time to time, add thereto such variations or additions to the ceremony as survive in the Provinces or overseas, and form important links in the evolution of our ceremony.
    The first place to which we shall naturally turn for information is the V.S.L. which, however, tells us little, nor must we be surprised thereat if, as I propose to indicate later, Hiram represented a popular Syrian God, against whom the champions of Jehovah strove unceasingly.
    There is no doubt among Biblical critics that in the time of Josiah, B.C. 624, not only were many abuses swept away, and important reforms carried out, as indicated in the V.S.L.[2], but that the previous volumes of the Bible were carefully revised, and anything which might be considered to indicate the slightest toleration of the old indigenous beliefs was deleted. For all that, we learn that the shrine of Astarte (or Ashtoreth of the Sidonians) which had been built by King Solomon[3] was still standing in the time of Josiah, and that it was he who had it broken down.[4]

---

1.   I shall adopt the following emblems to indicate notes :—A number, e.g. 1, to indicate the origin of the fact stated or a reference to a book which confirms it. A letter in ( ) to indicate a note of general interest to the reader.
2.   II Chron. 34. v. 1. and II Kings 22. 1.
3.   See I Kings, 2.5.
4.   See II Kings, 23.13.

All these reforms Josiah did, because of a book which the priests discovered when they were restoring the Temple of King Solomon, and the critics are agreed that this book was Deuteronomy, which dates from this period[1] and was fathered on Moses by a legal fiction, of which English history also supplies numerous examples.

Throughout history Reformers have found it necessary to pretend that their reforms were really old customs which had been forgotten, for otherwise the people would never have accepted them. In England it was Edward the Confessor who was thus made responsible for reforms instituted by Henry II, and even by later Kings, whilst among the Jews it was naturally Moses.

The new and strict code of moral laws and monotheistic teaching thus propounded, naturally necessitated a careful revision of the older books, lest the lax party in the Jewish state should quote from them in support of the view that, after all, some toleration of the old faith was permissible, since Solomon, or some other Jewish hero, had undoubtedly worshipped Astarte or Moloch, and yet had been beloved by Jehovah. Therefore, where any such facts could not be deleted, care was taken to show that these acts of the hero were strongly disapproved of by Jehovah.[1] Nevertheless, we can detect evidence that heathen customs were carried on despite Jehovah's wishes, and sometimes such heathen customs are mentioned without any mark of disapproval at all. In these cases no doubt the fact slipped the notice of the reviser. One example here must suffice:—Jephthah[a] offered up his daughter, his only child, as a burnt offering despite the supposed prohibition of human sacrifices indicated in Genesis 22.[2] Jephthah may also be regarded, in a sense, as a masonic hero, as my readers will remember. In the Bible, be it noted, there is no mention of disapproval by Jehovah, and so evidently this human sacrifice did not revolt public conscience, or the Priestly historians would have recorded it. If Jephthah could thus sacrifice his own daughter, is it unthinkable that a mixed body of Jewish and Phoenician craftsmen should, 150 years later, sacrifice a man ?[b]

---

1. Frazer, " Adonis, Attis and Osiris." Third ed. Vol. 1., pp. 26.
   W. Robertson Smith, " The Old Testament in the Jewish Church," pp. 395 sq., 425.
   Encyl, Bibl. II. 2, 708, sq., 2, 633 sq., Vol. IV. 4, 273.
   Principal J. Skinner, Introduction to Kings in The Century Bible, pp. 10 seq.
2. Judges 12, v. 31. sq.
(a) There is of course an alternative explanation, namely that Jephthah's daughter is mythological, a Syrian Persephone, but the more human story does less violence to Biblical tradition and is quite as probable. The mythological explanation, however, would prove the survival of " Heathenism " even more effectively than that I have adopted.
(b) The usual date assigned to Jephthah is c. 1143 B.C. and Solomon's temple is supposed to have been consecrated c. 1004 B.C.

Fortunately, however, there was one piece of evidence which the revisers could not entirely eliminate without destroying all their previous history, namely that supplied by certain professedly personal names and these, reinforced by inscriptions which belong to the avowedly non-Jewish precursors of Solomon, the Jebusite Kings of Zion, indicate clearly enough the survival of " Pagan ideas " in the Holy Land. The anxiety of the revisers, however, to delete as far as possible all references of a pagan nature may explain the mysterious disappearance of several former books of the Bible which are now only known to us by a brief reference.[1]

These preliminary remarks are absolutely essential in order that my readers should disabuse their minds of any preconceived notions they may have had, that the worship of Jehovah, the only God, was universally accepted throughout Israel at the time of Solomon, or even that the Wise King himself was a strict mono-theist. The most that we can say for Solomon is that probably he regarded Jehovah as the supreme God, but had no qualms about offering propitiatory offerings to other local and popular Gods when it seemed desirable. He was certainly not, like Josiah, eaten up with devotion to Jehovah, and therefore, among the mass of less spiritually evolved people whom he employed to build his new temple, we naturally should expect to find many who were devoted worshippers of the local God Adonis, one of whose great sanctuaries seems to have been Mount Moriah.

Let us now see what the Bible says about Hiram Abiff. We learn that Hiram, King of Tyre, sent Hiram Abiff to help Solomon build the Temple,[2] but from the accounts he appears to have been not so much an architect as a smith, a worker in brass. Too much stress, however, should not be laid on this fact, as in olden days many kindred building trades were grouped round the Masonic Guild. Even in the Middle Ages the Comacine Masons of Europe included among their numbers painters and sculpturers as well as masons, and we must not overlook the fact that it is specifically stated in II Chron. 2. 14 that Hiram was skilful to work in stone.

The two versions in the Bible do not agree as to his mother's tribe: Chronicles stating that she was " of the Daughters of Dan," while Kings says she was a " widow woman of the tribe of Napthali." Both accounts agree, however, that his father was a man of Tyre, and it is significant that Tyre was one of the centres of the worship of Adonis. The conflicting testimony regarding his mother's tribe may be explicable on the grounds that she was not a real Jewess at all, but rather one of the old race to whom it was difficult to allot a tribe, but that, in the eyes of historians, it seemed desirable to indicate that the great Architect of the

---

1. See II Chron., 9.29. etc.
2. See II Chron., 2.13, also I Kings, 7.13.

Temple had some Jewish blood in his veins. It is, however, possible that the real explanation is that she belonged to the tribe of Dan. Dan was divided into two sections; a small section being separated from the main body and having their location on the desert side of the tribe of Napthali, which latter tribe had the territory East of Lebanon, and bordering on Phoenicia. If a woman of the tribe of Dan had for any reason come into Phoenicia to settle she would probably have to pass through Napthali, and among her Phoenician neighbours might be considered to belong to the border tribe, through whose territory she would have passed, and who were one of the tribes of Jews best known to the Phoenicians. We are at any rate clearly told that his father was a Phoenician, and from the son's skill, which included work in the famous " purple " of Tyre, it is clear that his upbringing was in that city. He can hardly therefore have been a worshipper of Jehovah, and it is clear that the bulk of his fellow workmen were Phoenicians, for Solomon wrote and asked Hiram of Tyre to send him men.

We also learn that King Hiram promised him cedars and firs from Lebanon, and the Mountain of Lebanon, as we shall see later, was the Holy Mountain of Adonis of Byblos, where lay his most holy sanctuary. Moreover, we are specifically told that, later in life, King Solomon did worship Ashtoreth, the goddess of the Zidonians, and Milcom, the abomination of the Ammonites,[1] and that he built " on the right hand of the Mount of Corruption " a high place for Ashtoreth, and for Chimosh, and for Milcom. These were still standing 350 years later,[a] when they were destroyed by good King Josiah.[2]

Ashtoreth is the same as Astarte, the goddess whose love proved fatal to Adonis, and as late as the time of Ezekiel, c. 594 B.C., we find this prophet denouncing the Jewish women because they wept for Tammuz[3][b] at the North Gate of the Temple. He also denounces the men because within the courts of the Temple itself " with their backs towards the Temple of the Lord, and their faces towards the East . . . . they worshipped the sun towards the East."[4]

Thus we can see that the Jews at the time of King Solomon were far from being strict monotheists, and even the wise King himself not only did not serve Jehovah with a single eye, but took

---

1. I Kings, 11.5 seq.
2. II Kings, 23. 13.
3. Ezekiel 8. 14.
4. Ibid. 8. 16.
(a) Tradition says that Solomon reigned from c. 1014 B.C. to c. 975 B.C. Josiah commenced his reforms c. 624 B.C. and from the accounts it is clear that during the whole of this period worship had been going on at these and other " Heathen Shrines."
(b) Tammuz is the Syrian name of Adonis and from it comes the Jewish name for the month of June—July, Tammuz, which they still use.

care to build shrines for other Gods, perhaps fearing that otherwise they might be offended. We learn from the Bible itself that he was actually a worshipper of Astarte, and that, despite Josiah's herculean efforts later, her worship was not eliminated, for 28 years afterwards the ceremonies connected with the slaying of Adonis were still taking place.

As we shall see later, the " Song of King Solomon "[1] is undoubtedly a fragment of the ritual connected with the Rites of Adonis, and the sublime chapter 12 in Ecclesiastes, which tradition asserts was written by King Solomon seems to be connected with the death of Adonis.

So far as we can judge from the Bible the High Priests and the Priests of Jehovah did little to denounce these rival, or possibly partner, gods. Policy, may be, forbade it, and it was the prophets, and the prophets alone, who in the main fought with fiery zeal for the conception of one God and one God only. It was amid this atmosphere of easy tolerance of other Gods than Jehovah that King Solomon set to work to build his Temple, and for the task gathered skilled workmen from Tyre, one of the centres of Adonis worship, while he sent levies to Lebanon, which was the principal shrine of that God.

The next factor to be considered is the name of Hiram. It has, of course, a very definite meaning, and one of deep significance. The more so as it is borne by two men, namely the King and the Builder. Hiram means " Exaltation of Life," " Their liberty," or " Whiteness," " He that destroys."[2]

The above meanings apply to the King and the Builder, but the latter is distinguished by the addition, in the Hebrew, of the word " Abiff," which means " Father." In the authorised version of the Bible no reference is made to the title " Abiff " in Kings,[3] but in II Chronicles[4] the phrase is translated thus—" I have sent a cunning man . . . . of Huram, my Father's." This seems to imply that Huram was the name of the father of the reigning King of Tyre, and that this " cunning man " was one of his servants, and therefore his name is not given at all, but as I Kings 4, 40 clearly states that " Hiram made the lavers, etc.," it is evident that the name of the " cunning man " was, after all, Hiram. Literally the words are " Hiram's father," or " Hiram, his father,"[5] the *his* being the old possessive *his* which replaced for a time the Mediæval English possessive, e.g., " Christes sake," " Christ His sake," and to-day, " Christ's sake." Thus the

1. " The Song of Songs." A Symposium delivered before the Oriental Club of Philadelphia 1924, especially the paper by T. J. Meek, University of Toronto.
2. Major Sanderson, " An Examination of the Masonic Ritual " (Baskerville Press, Limited), p. 47.
3. I Kings, 7, 13.
4. II Chron. 2, 13.
5. Major Sanderson, " An Examination of the Masonic Ritual," p. 47.

meaning would be "Hiram's father," and as Hiram was the King of
Tyre who was sending him, this suggests that the architect was the
father of the King, a point to which we shall refer later in the book.

But we ought not to translate the one word without translat-
ing the other, for the whole phrase is one, a view which is considerably strengthened by the existence of another Hebrew name,
which, though written differently, is in reality precisely the same,
namely Abiram.   Abiram was the Prince of Israel, who, with
two others, was swallowed up by the earth when fire came out and
consumed his supporters for daring to claim the right to burn
incense before the Lord.[1]   His claim and his fate are of peculiar
importance to our research, for he clearly represented a rival cult,
and claimed that its priests were just as much entitled as were
Aaron and the Levites to offer prayers to Jehovah if they wished.

" Ab " means " Father,"[2] and is the same word as " Abiff,"
but when used as a prefix the second syllable, for the sake of
euphony, is omitted.   The " H," in Hiram, which in any case is
almost silent, is naturally omitted as well, and so we have another
Hiram Abiff, who according to the Bible suffered a tragic fate.
No one, however, has ever suggested that his name should be read
" Hiram, his father."   If, therefore, we treat the whole phrase
as one name and then translate it, most of our difficulties vanish.
In that case Hiram means " The father of him who destroys," or
possibly, " The father who destroys," or, less accurately, the
" Father of destruction."   Its next meaning is " The father of
their liberty—the father (or source) of their whiteness."   The
third meaning is " The father of the exaltation of life," or " The
source of the exaltation of life."[(a)]

Now, in the story of Abiram, he clearly was the father who
destroys, or the cause of the destruction of his children and of his
supporters, who perished through his presumption.   This fact
suggests that we are indeed on the right track.   Further there is
another Abiram, the eldest son of Hiel, who was offered up as a
foundation sacrifice when he rebuilt Jericho.[3]

Let us now consider the man Tammuz, for whom the daughters
of Jerusalem wept, because he too suffered a tragic fate.   It
was because there was a divine spirit in Tammuz, or Adonis,
that the man part was inevitably destroyed, as we shall see
later, while all the above titles are not merely appropriate to
Adonis, the God-man and his human representatives, but accurately indicate certain aspects of his nature, whereas for an Architect, the title " *He who destroys*," is hardly appropriate.

Further, we must not overlook the *King* Hiram, whose name
also means " He that destroys," etc.   Was he then in any way

1.   Numbers, 16, v. 3. & 31.
2.   See Frazer, " Adonis, Attis, Osiris," 3rd ed., Vol. I., p. 51.
3.   I Kings, 16, 34.
(a)   The phrase Exaltation will be familiar to R.A. Masons.

representative of Adonis ? The answer is emphatically " yes,"
and he was recognised as such in profane history, for subsequent
evidence will show that the Phoenician Kings claimed to be
incarnations of Adonis, and Ezekiel actually denounced the
King of Tyre because he called himself a God.[1] The actual
words are, " Thou hast said I am a God." Thus we see that this
name with all that it implies belonged to an earthly King, who
was the human representative of Adonis. How comes it that a
mere ordinary architect also possessed such an exalted title ?

There was, however, a third Hiram, contemporary with the
other two, and, like them, engaged on the Temple. This man
according to tradition was the successor of Hiram the Architect,
and his name was a compound consisting of Hiram and the word
" Adon," or Adonis, instead of Abiff. He was Adoniram, and
strange to say we know a great deal more about him from the
Bible than we do of the other two. Adoniram is the same name
as Adoram, the latter being merely a variation of the former. We
first meet with him in the time of David, who set him over the
tribute.[2] This was about 1022 B.C., and we next hear that
Solomon appointed him to the same office,[3] the name used this
time being Adoniram, not Adoram, where we also learn that he
was one of the great Princes of Israel, of whom ten are named,
and that his father was Abda. Ab, of course, means " Father of,"
and da is the same as Dod, or in full " Dodo." Dodo is the
true Hebrew form of the name " David " and means the Beloved.
Dod was the regular title of Adonis or Tammuz, the beloved of
Astarte, while Dodah was the title of Ishtar herself.[4]

Thus Abda would mean, " Father of the beloved of Ishtar "
i.e. " Father of Adonis," a most significant fact.

In connection with this, my readers should remember that the
regular form of lamentation for a King of Judah at his death was
most peculiar, and unquestionably had been adopted from the
form of lamentation used by " The women who wept for Tammuz."[5] According to Jeremiah, as translated in the authorised
version, it was as follows :—

" Therefore . . . . they shall not lament for him saying,
Ah, my brother, or Ah, my sister! they shall not lament for him
saying, Ah, lord! or Ah, his glory! "[6] Prof. T. K. Cheyne considers that the mysterious sister was none other than Astarte, and

1. Ezekiel, 28, 2.
2. II Samuel, 20, 24.
3. I Kings, 4, 6.
4. Frazer, " Adonis, Attis, Osiris," 3rd ed., Vol. 1, p. 20 note 2 etc. seq.
   Brown Driver and Briggs, " Hebrew and English Lexicon of the Old
     Testament," pp. 187, seq.
   G. B. Gray, " Studies in Hebrew Proper Names," pp. 60 seq.
5. Ezekiel, 8, 14.
6. Jeremiah, 22, 18.

that the word translated " glory " should be " Dodah," which he
contends was a regular title of Astarte, just as Adon was of Tammuz, hence his Greek name Adonis.[1]

In Hebrew, the words were " Hoi ahi! " meaning, " Alas, my
brother! "   " Hoi Adon! ", " Alas, Lord! "

We thus see that for some strange reason the Kings of Judah
had taken over the lamentations and even the title of Tammuz,
(Adonis) and that Adoniram also used this title, and, moreover,
was the son of the " Father of the Beloved."   As " Beloved " was
another title of Tammuz, we see that this Prince of Israel had
attached to himself two of the attributes of Tammuz, and we have
already learnt that Hiram, which forms part of his name, means
exactly the same as the name of the King of Tyre, who claimed to
be a God, and also that the word Hiram was attached to the chief
architect of the temple.   Finally, this word, meaning Exaltation
of life, etc., was far more appropriate to Tammuz than it could
be to a mere ordinary mortal.

Adoniram's high official rank and his title of Prince seem
strange if he were merely an important overseer of masons, and
nothing more, but if he himself represented a line of divine Kings
there would be nothing strange about his title, rank or name,
although we might wonder whether he was really a mason.   It
will thus be seen that we have learnt many curious facts from a
careful study of just one or two verses of sacred scripture.

The date of this second mention of Adoniram is c. B.C. 1014.
The next reference is of the same date, and relates how Adoniram
was set over the levy that cut timber on Mount Lebanon.   Now
Lebanon was *the* great sanctuary of Adonis in Syria.   Cinyras,
who, according to legend, was the first King of Byblos and father
of Adonis, is said to have built a sanctuary to Astarte at a spot
on Mount Lebanon, a day's journey from Byblos, or Jebal as it
is called in the Bible.[2]   This was no doubt Aphaca, which stood
at the source of the river Adonis, and the ruins of which still
remain.   It was destroyed by the Emperor Constantine because
of the licentious nature of some of the Rites which occurred there.[3]

Legend informs us that it was here that Adonis met Astarte
for the first time, or according to other versions, for the last time,[4]
and here his mangled corpse was buried.[5]   To this day, amid
crags and precipices, can still be seen monuments of the Dying

1.   Frazer, " Adonis, Attis, Osiris," 3rd Ed., Vol. 1, p. 20.
     Renan, " Histoire du Peuple de Israel," Vol. iii, p. 273.
2.   Lucian, " De dea Syria." 9.
3.   Eusebius.   " Vita Constantini," 3, 55.
     Socrates, " Historia Ecclesiastica," 1, 18.
     Sozomenus, " Historia Ecclesiastica," 11, 5.
     Zosimus.   1. 58.
4.   Etymologicum Magnum.   S.V. APHAKA. p. 175.
5.   Melito.   " Oration to Atonius Caesar " in W. Cureton's " Spicilegium
     Syriacum.   (London, 1855.) p. 44.

God, and from this spot the river each Spring runs red with his blood[a] to the purple sea.

Thus a man whose name means " The Lord who destroys " or " The Lord of the exaltation of life," the son of the " Father of the Beloved," presided over the levies which cut down the trees on the mountain sacred to him, whom the Syrians called " The Lord," " The Beloved," " Adonis," " Tammuz "; in short, the god of vegetation. If then Abda means " The Father of the Beloved," and he was the Father of the " Lord who destroys," it is evident that Adoniram himself was " The Beloved," and so a Jewish Prince ruled over the Sacred Mountain of Adonis and was known by the title used for that god.

It begins to look as if Adoniram was going to be even more interesting than the King of Tyre, whose name, Hiram, means " He who destroys," or the Architect, whose name indicates that he is the Father of " He who destroys." But let us see what else the Bible tells us of this great Jewish Prince who, from the time of David onwards, presided over the tribute, and who had charge of the levies on Mount Lebanon, a place which did not belong to Solomon, or to any of his successors, but to the Phoenicians.

There is one more record; the great Prince died a miserable death, for he was stoned to death by the Israelites when they revolted against Rehoboam.[1] This was about B.C. 975, and so although we do not know the year of his birth, or his age when David appointed him to have charge over the tribute, we have a glimpse of the last 47 years of his life. And what a miserable death for so great a Prince to die, knocked on the head by a mob of angry peasants! But as we meditate upon the fact, we recollect another mob consisting of Temple workmen, and another brave man knocked on the head. Strange that the successor should perish like his immediate predecessor, and stranger still that two Abirams should also have come to a violent end.

Thus of the five Hirams, three, according to the Bible, suffered violent deaths. Of the fourth all know the fate, and we cannot help wondering whether a like tragedy marked the close of the life of the King as well. Perhaps so, although Jewish tradition says he lived for hundreds of years. It may be, however, before we have finished this work we shall have come to the conclusion that there was something fatal about having the name of Hiram.

Concerning King Hiram the Bible also gives us some interesting information. We never hear of him until David has taken Jerusalem, when we find him sending messengers and gifts.

---

1.   I Kings, 12. 18 and II Chron. 10. 18. where the name is written " Adoram and Hadoram respectively."

(a)   Modern science which destroys so many pretty legends explains that the red matter in the river at this time of the year is merely red earth.

" And Hiram, King of Tyre, sent messengers to David and cedar trees, and carpenters and masons, and they built David an house."[1]

Now why should the King who ruled over Lebanon, the sacred fane of Adonis, hasten to convey his friendship to David, whose name means " The Beloved," immediately he had taken Jerusalem ? Why did he send him skilled masons and cedars and build him a house ? There is no mention of payment, neither is there any hint that David had threatened to conquer Tyre. If there had been even the possibility of suggesting the latter cause, we may be quite sure that the patriotic Jewish historian would have stressed and underlined the fact.

Perhaps we shall find the reason if we study the character of the old Jebusite Kings of Jerusalem. We learn in Judges that one of these early Canaanite Kings was called " Adoni-bezek,"[2] and in Joshua we learn that the King of Jerusalem was called Adoni-zedec,[3] which means " Lord of Righteousness." It thus very closely corresponds, strange to say, with Melchizedek—the King of Righteousness. This character is of peculiar interest to us and so we will consider the passage rather carefully.

" And Melchizedek, King of Salem, brought forth *bread and wine* and he was the priest of the most High God. And he blessed him and said, ' Blessed be Abram . . ."[4(a)]

The important fact here is that Abram recognises Melchizedek as a Priest-King and admits that he worshipped God. Thus we see that Jerusalem had a dynasty of Priest-Kings, and that some of them used the divine name Adonai and others Melch, which word means King, but more especially the King of the City, or god of the City, e.g. Melcarth, the name given to the Baal or God of Tyre, concerning whom we shall have to learn more later. Now, the title of the later Jewish Kings of Jerusalem was " Adoni-ham-Melech," " My Lord the King," which Frazer[5] considers indicates that they had taken over the titles of a line of Priest-Kings of Tammuz (Adonis), who originally reigned in Jerusalem, and it was because of this fact that David was so anxious to take the city, and transferred the then seat of his Government thither from Hebron.[6]

---

1. II Sam. 5. 11 sq.
2. Judges, 1. 5.
3. Joshua, 10. 1.
4. Genesis 14. 18.
(a) Abram is the same as Abiram and he nearly destroyed his son, by sacrificing him. Afterwards God changed his name to Abraham and perhaps the change explains why, unlike his various namesakes, he did not come to a tragic end.
5. Frazer, " Adonis, Attis, Osiris," 3rd Ed., Vol. 1., p. 20.
6. Ibid. p. 19.

Professor A. N. Sayce[1] considers that David only adopted that name, which should be written Dod or Dodo, after he had captured Jerusalem. Dodo means "The Beloved One," and according to him was one of the titles of Adonis (Tammuz) in South Canaan, and in particular among the Jebusites of Jerusalem, where Adonis was the supreme Deity.

These facts explain why Hiram, who himself was a Priest-King and a living representative of Adonis, should be anxious to propitiate the new Priest-King of Jerusalem, for such, of course, he would regard David. That David himself deliberately went out of his way to transfer the old sacred tradition to his own house, and even to his proposed Temple, is clear from a perusal of the account of the purchase of the threshing floor of Araunah, who we are carefully, yet apparently pointlessly, told was a Jebusite and a king.[2][a]

Now Adonis or Tammuz was the god of vegetation more especially of corn, and so a threshing floor would be particularly appropriate as a sacred place. As the corn was said to represent his body, during the period when the death of the god was celebrated it was customary not to eat corn, and the threshing floor, where the corn was beaten, in a sense depicted the martyrdom of the God. What place more appropriate as a spot for a shrine to Adonis, and therefore what more politic than for David to purchase it and on it build his new temple of Jehovah, thus grafting the new faith on the old ?

In this he would only be doing what Christians at a later date constantly did. For example, St. Paul's replaced an old Roman Temple, probably dedicated to Diana, who to some extent represents Astarte. Thus the site of the temple was converted from what had been a sacred place of Adonis, and no doubt this in part explains why the women still wailed for Tammuz at the North gate of the temple in the days of Ezekiel. As a matter of fact there is little doubt that the full ceremony of the death of Adonis was still enacted and re-enacted on the same spot, despite the nominal change of cult.

We thus see that Hiram of Tyre not only bore the titles " He Who Destroys," " Their Whiteness," etc., but ruled over one of the most sacred shrines of Adonis, and was most anxious to do all that he could to please a King who had just obtained control of another spot sacred to Tammuz. We shall see later that he was himself a Priest-King representing the god of his City, Tyre, and

---

1. " Lectures on the Religion of the Ancient Babylonians " (London and Edinburgh, 1887) p. 52—57.
2. II. Sam. 24. 18 seq.
    I. Chron. 21. 22 seq.
(a) Verse 23 in II. Sam. 21 significantly says " All these did Araunah, a king, give unto the King." A passage which can only mean that Araunah himself was a representative of the old Priest-Kings of the Jebusites.

that he sent Hiram Abiff to help David's son to build a temple to Adonis. At any rate, King Solomon did not hesitate to raise a second shrine close up against the Temple in honour of Astarte, and, as we shall see later, the very Temple of Jehovah seems to have been copied, in part at least, from the great shrine to Astarte-Adonis at Paphos, which was then standing. Perhaps Solomon felt some amends were due to Astarte and Adonis for converting their sacred spot into the site of Jehovah's temple.

There still remains one point in connection with the name of the Architect. Some scholars consider that the word Abiff should read Abib, a word which means " Ears of corn or green fruits."[1] If this reading be accepted it is a further confirmation of the view that Hiram Abiff is in some way connected with Tammuz. Neither can we overlook the significance of the gift of bread and wine made by the old Priest-King Melchizedek, and the very general uses of bread and wine to provide a sacramental meal in connection with a ceremonial ritual of death and resurrection.

Let us now turn from the Bible to profane history and see what we can learn therefrom concerning Adonis and the claims of certain Syrian Kings to be Priest-Kings, and incarnations of the God, but before doing so let us collect the meanings of the names of the different Hirams, for it may be that later, when we come to study the story of Adonis, they may prove more significant than they do at present.

Adonai means " Lord," originally the Lord God, and in this sense it was used by the Jews to replace the word Jehovah when the tradition had arisen that the holy name must not be uttered. At an earlier period, even in the time of David, no such idea seems to have prevailed, for there are many personal names which incorporate it, at any rate in part, as, for example, Adonijah, which means the " Lord God Jah,"[2] or " Jehovah," truly a strange name for a mere man to bear.   Incidentally, like so many others who bore a divine name, he was put to death, in this case by orders of his own brother.[3]

Adonis is merely a Greek form of Adonai, which was the title most often used by the Syrians when speaking of Tammuz. Although originally a divine title, owing to the fact that it was often borne by all descendants of these supposedly divine Kings (since they too were divine) it may have tended towards the close of the pre-christian era to have become less a divine and more an honorific title, but if so this was long after the time of Solomon. The Phoenician Kings in Cyprus and their children all bore the

---

1.   Maj. Sanderson, " An Examination of the Masonic Ritual," p. 47.
     See also Sampson, " Progressive Redemption," p. 172.
2.   I Kings, 1. 5. seq.
3.   I Kings, 2. 5.

title of Adonis[1] down to the time of Aristotle, or even later, and according to Cypriote legends Adonis was at one time king of Paphos in Cyprus.

We are now in a position to understand more fully the meaning and significance of the various names which occur in our legends, and we will deal with them seriatim, commencing with Hiram:

HIRAM means, (1) He that Destroys.
(2) Their liberty.
(3) Their whiteness.
(4) The exaltation of Life.

King Hiram therefore needs no further explanation.

AB or ABIFF means, " Father " or " Father of," and the alternative reading Abib means " Ears of Corn " or " Green Fruits." Therefore

HIRAM ABIFF means,
(1) The Father of Him who Destroys.
(2) The Father (or source) of their Whiteness.
(3) The Father (or source) of their Liberty.
(4) The Father (or source) of the Exaltation of life.

It will be recognised that several of these titles are peculiarly appropriate to Tammuz. Thus number (2) clearly indicates his nature as the God of Corn, and surely teaches that through his death men are made clean, neither can we altogether forget the fact that the destructive side of the Deity in India, called Shiva, is always represented as white and is called " The Great White God." In a similar way number (3) also suggests the vicarious sacrifice whereby the rest of men are saved and set free. Finally number (4) is a peculiarly apt phrase to denote one who is sown in corruption and raised in incorruption. One who exchanges mortal life for eternal and divine life, and thereby gives men the hope of a similar resurrection.

ABIRAM means exactly the same as HIRAM ABIFF, and it is interesting to note that the earlier man perished because he claimed to be a Priest of the Most High, a claim precisely similar to that made by Melchizedek, which claim, strange to say, was admitted by the Jewish writers without question, in spite of the fact that he was not even of the lineage of Abraham. The later Abiram was a foundation sacrifice and so very similar in his fate to Hiram Abiff, who was a consecration sacrifice.

ADONIRAM means,
(1) The Lord God Who Destroys.
(2) The Lord God of Whiteness. (The God of the Corn).
(3) The Lord God of Liberty. (The God who brings men liberty from mortal suffering and the terror of death).

---

1.   Frazer, " Adonis, Attis, Osiris," 3rd ed., Vol. 1, p. 49.

(4) The Lord God Who is in Himself the Exaltation of Life. (The God of the Resurrection).
ABDA means " The Father of the Beloved One." A title
of Adonis and a phrase which indicates that Adoniram is the
Beloved one. (i.e. of Astarte).

Great titles are these, indeed, for mere mortal men, and yet
four at least of these God-like beings perished miserably; one by
fire and earthquake, two at the hands of a mob, and one as a
sacrifice. In like manner perished Adonis and his earthly representatives, as we shall see, for now we will leave behind us the
Bible and see what additional knowledge can be gained from a
careful study of the profane history of the Near East.

Let us first learn all we can about Adonis and his divine
lover Astarte. Let us learn of the Priest-Kings, his representatives and their tragic fate. Let us compare the great shrine of
Astarte at Paphos with the temple which King Solomon raised to
the Most High with the assistance of Hiram, King of Tyre, Hiram
Abiff and Adoniram ben Abda. We shall begin by following our
master on the path which he trod in days of old, when rose that
bright morning star whose coming brought hope and salvation to
a multitude, but death to one lone man.

Let us learn also something of the bale-fires of Melcarth, the
Divine King of the City of Tyre, whose altar Solomon set up beside the temple he builded to Jehovah. Then perhaps we shall
understand that the tears which the women of Jerusalem shed
outside the North gate of the temple were not mere ritual tears,
at any rate originally, and in the process we shall realise whom the
Queen of Sheba really represents.

CHAPTER III

ADONIS AND ASTARTE IN BABYLONIA

The waxing and waning of the seasons, the growth and decay of vegetation upon which he depended for his food, filled primitive man with alarm, and he endeavoured to facilitate the resurrection of plant life by certain magical ceremonies.

As civilization advanced he supplemented his primitive ideas by a religious conception, in which he conceived of the earth as a great Goddess of Fertility, who in Autumn grew old and feeble and was in danger of death: for primitive man made the gods in his own image, endowing them with his own attributes, thus he believed that they were born, married, had children and could die. The thought that even the Great Mother, the fertile earth, was in danger of death and therefore he himself of starvation, filled man with abject terror, and carrying forward his old magical ideas of the past, he thought it desirable to perform certain ceremonies based on sympathetic magic to assist her over the dangerous period of winter. He explained the phenomena of Autumn, Winter and Spring as caused by the old age, death and resurrection of a Divine Being, but there was always present in his mind a terror lest some day that Divine Being would not rise again, and that the subsequent destruction of the whole world would follow.

Thus it came about that most primitive races enact a drama in which someone represents a God who is slain and comes to life again, but whereas to-day in most cases it is play acting, in the early dawn of man the one who acted the part of the God was really slain, in order that the Divine Spirit, which was supposed to be in this representative, should enter into another younger and more vigorous body.

The procedure by which this transference of the Divine Soul took place will be described at a later point in the book, and we shall now direct attention to a careful study of the stories connected with Astarte and her lover Adonis. Astarte, under varying names, was worshipped throughout the whole of the near East in pre-Christian days. In Syria and Palestine she was known as Astarte or Ashtoreth, in Cappadocia and Asia Minor as Cybele, and in Babylonia as Ishtar, while the same great Mother Goddess in Egypt was known as Isis.

The earliest form of the Adonia myth comes from Babylon. In these records he is named Dumi-zi-abzu,[1] usually called, however, Dumu-zi, from which form of the name is derived Tammuz, under which appellation he was known in Syria. In

---

1. P. Jensen, " Assyrisch-Babylonische Mythen und Epen " (Berlin, 1900).
   P. Dhorme, " La Religion Assyro-Babylonienne " (Paris, 1910).

19

the latter country he was usually spoken of as the Lord, Adon, and the Greeks, taking this for his proper name Hellenised it into Adonia.

In the literature of Babylonia Dumu-zi was the youthful lover of Ishtar, the great Mother Goddess who embodied the reproductive energies of nature. The references to the tragedy are very fragmentary, but we learn that every year Dumu-zi died and passed into the subterranean world and that his Divine Mistress sought for him " in the land from which there is no returning, in the house of darkness, where dust lies on door and bolt."[1] This, of course, was the Winter season during which animals and plants cease to re-produce their species. So serious was the position that the God Ea sent messengers to the Under-world and demanded from the Queen thereof, Allatu, the return of Ishtar. Meantime Ishtar had passed through the seven gates of the Underworld, at each of which she was compelled to pay a fee to the Warden of the Gate, which consisted of one of her garments, till at length she appeared before the Goddess of the Underworld stark naked. Despite these sacrifices, the Goddess refused to release Dumu-zi and poured contempt on Ishtar.[2]

It was at this point that the Messenger from the Gods arrived and compelled Allatu to sprinkle Ishtar and Dumu-zi with the Water of Life, so that the two might return together to the Upper World and nature revive.

Fortunately we have a number of Babylonian hymns which were used at the annual lamentation which the people of Baby-lonia made, which clearly indicate his close association with plant life, and particularly with the corn seed, which is buried in order that it may come forth to life and bear a goodly yield. Dumu-zi, in short, is the Spirit of Vegetation and particularly of the corn. These dirges were " chanted over the effigy of the dead God, which was washed with pure water, anointed with oil and clad in a red robe."[3] The flute was the instrument chiefly used, and there seems no doubt that here and in other parts of Asia the ancients had the secret of producing music which intoxicated the brains of the worshippers and worked them up into a state akin to frenzy. The secret rests in the use of eighths and quarters of tone and has recently been re-discovered in Mexico. By its use it is claimed that the musicians can arouse any sensations they choose in the human heart, a very dangerous power and one which explains many of the wild and fantastic scenes we shall presently describe.

This version of the story depicts Ishtar as the faithful, loving and sorrowing Mistress, but there is another side to her character which we shall consider in a moment. Her attitude of

1.   J. G. Frazer, " Adonis, Attis, Osiris." 3rd ed., Vol. 1, p. 8.
2.   Rev. W. A. Wigram, D.D., " M.S.S. Transactions," Vol. 2, p. 20.
3.   Frazer. " Adonis, Attis, Osiris," 3rd ed., Vol. 1, p. 9.

affection and solitude for the human race is also brought out in
her lamentation when the great flood almost obliterated the
human race, in which she says, " Did I of my self bring forth my
people that they might fill the sea like little fishes ? "[1]

But there is another, a much grimmer and more unpleasant
side of Ishtar which is set forth in the tablets which contain the
Epic of Gilgamish. Therein she asks him to be her lover, and
Gilgamish, in words which might have been spoken by an old
Hebrew Prophet, denounces her in no uncertain language. He
starts by giving a list of the calamities and misfortunes which
have befallen those who have been so unwise as to become the
lovers of the Goddess, and says, " What lover didst thou love
for long, which of thy shepherds flourished ? I will describe the
calamity which goeth with thee." He accuses her of having
caused the death of Dumu-zi and adds that every creature who
falls under her sway suffers mutilation or death, even the beasts
or birds, concluding with the words, " Dost thou love me and
would'st thou treat me as thou did'st them ? "[2]

When Ishtar heard this reply she was filled with wrath and
ascending to Heaven complained to Anu, her father, and Antu,
her Mother, that Gilgamish had proclaimed aloud all her in-
iquitous deeds. Anu thereupon created a fire-breathing bull
and sent him to devastate the fields around Erech, but Gilgamish and his friend Enkidu went out against the bull and
slew it. When the Goddess learnt of the death of the bull she
came out of the battlements of the city and cursed Gilgamish for
killing it, at which Enkidu " tore off a portion of the bull's flesh
from the right side and threw it at the Goddess saying, ' Could
I but fight with thee I would serve thee as I have served him.
I would twine his entrails about thee.' Then Ishtar gathered
together all her temple women and harlots and with them made
lamentation over the portion of the bull which Enkidu had
thrown at her."[3]

I cannot help thinking that the right side here, as in many
other accounts of a similar incident, is an aphorism for the virile
member, and if so the significance of the incident is perfectly
clear. The Great Mother before she assumed a human form was
represented under animal shapes, one of these being the Queen
Bee, an emblem constantly associated with Astarte and her
classical representative, Artemis. In the case of " Diana of
Ephesus " the bee[4] even appeared on the coins of the city, and the
survival of this attribute even in Speculative Masonry is proved
by the constant use of a bee-hive on 18th century certificates,

1. The Babylonian Story of the Deluge. British Museum, 1920, p. 36,
        1.1—3.
2. Ibid. p. 46, sq.
3. " Epic of Gilgamish." Published Brit. Mus. p. 48.
4. Encl. Brit. Vol. 2. " Artemis," p. 665.

tracing boards and the like. At that late period the presence of a
bee-hive is described as an emblem of the hard work and industry
which should characterise masons, etc., but this is a late explanation of the meaning of a symbol whose original interpretation was
very different. It is a pathological fact, known to all keepers of
bees, that the unfortunate drone is killed as the result of the
marriage flight, its male organ being torn out and left permanently
in the Queen. Thus the bee's husband is automatically destroyed, and yet without such destruction the Queen would be un-
fertile and the community of bees die out. Such a peculiar fact
would certainly not have escaped the notice of observant savages
who also, no doubt, were aware that certain female spiders after
a similar incident consume the male. The similarity of these
incidents with what happened when the corn was planted would
naturally strike the imagination of a primitive race, and that this
was the cause of the death of the lover of the Great Earth Goddess
is made abundantly clear by the legend of the manner in which
Attis died, which we shall consider a little later. Thus the lover
of the Great Mother dies and from the fruits of their union comes
forth a son, who again becomes the lover of the Great Earth
Mother, dies, and is the parent of another son, who goes through a
similar cycle. The corn is planted in the womb of the earth, and
dies, but from that dark place comes forth the young corn, which
grows to maturity, is reaped, and again placed in the womb of
Mother Earth.

We now perceive why it was that in the kindred rites of
Cybele and Attis, her Priests, in memory of Attis, mutilated
themselves, sacrificing their virility that the Great Mother might
be fertile. These ceremonies, which took place at the " Day of
Blood," were repeated annually in Rome, at the Vatican, which
was the Great Mother's shrine, well into the third century
A.D. There is not the slightest doubt that the original cause
of the death of Tammuz, or Adonis, was the same as that of Attis,
and the later legends were invented at a period when men were
becoming more fastidious. It is significant that one of the forms
of Diana was a bear, and at the great shrine of Astarte at Aphaca,
at the Source of the River Adonis on Mount Lebanon, is a great
rock sculpture in which we see figures of Adonis and Aphrodite
(Astarte). The former " is portrayed with spear in rest awaiting
the attack of a bear, whilst she is seated in an attitude of sorrow."[1]
It will be noted that the animal is not a boar, whose appearance
in the Greek form of the legend is undoubtedly very late, and
the occult significance of the bas-relief is that the unfortunate
man is destroyed by the Goddess in her animal form. This
ancient, and to our mind horrible, idea has nevertheless been
commemorated in Masonry by a certain peculiar incident in

1. Frazer, " Adonis, Attis, Osiris," 3rd ed. Vol. 1. p. 29.
   E. Renan, " Mission de Phénicie," pp. 292-294.

our ceremonies which persisted, not only among the operatives, but among the Speculative masons in Wales up to the last quarter of the 19th century, as we shall explain later, although it was robbed of any tragic or painful consequences.[1]

This apparent digression was essential to enable us to understand the true character of Astarte or Ishtar, the real cause of the death of her series of lovers, and the vehement denunciation, backed by the insulting conduct, of Enkidu, whose attitude might be summed up in the words, " You wanted *that* from my friend Gilgamish so I have given you a substitute."

The use of similar substitutes, which at a later date were offered to the Great Mother in the form of cakes made in the shape of the male member, to which we shall refer in the chapter dealing with the secret Adonis rites of Judah, indicates an amelioration of the ceremonies which were annually performed in her honour at the time of the weeping for Tammuz.

We get a still earlier representation of the Great Mother in her animal form in the Babylonian legends of the Creation.[2] Here she is called Tiamat, the Womb of the Abyss. To the populace she was represented as foul and abominable: " she was, nevertheless, the Mother of everything, and was the possessor of the Tablet of Destinies."[2] This monster apparently resented the attempt of the Gods to bring order out of chaos, and the result was a struggle between the Gods of Light, and the semi-animal creatures of the pit. One human-shaped being, however, was on her side, namely one named Kingu, whom she called " her husband." Tiamat appointed him to be her leader, and fastened on his breast the tablet of Destinies saying, " *Whatsoever goeth forth from thy mouth shall be established.*"[3]

The high Gods in Heaven were in panic, they could find no one valiant enough to overthrow Kingu, whose power had thus been established by Taimat, but Marduk, who is a form of the Sun God, came forward as the champion of the High Gods and agreed to do battle provided they acknowledged his supremacy.

" Marduk approached and looked into the " Middle," or " Inside," or " Womb " of Tiamat, and divined the plan of Kingu who had taken his place therein."[4]

In an important note the author of the British Museum pamphlet on " The Babylonian Legends of the Creation " says " The Egyptians distinguished a portion of the heavens by the name of " Khat Nut," i.e., ' the belly of Nut,' and two drawings of it are extant." He attaches thereto copies of these drawings, from which it is perfectly clear that the portion of the anatomy referred to is the womb, and in the second example a God, or

1. A. Heiron. " Ancient Freemasonry and Old Dundee Lodge," p. 153.
2. " The Babylonian Legends of the Creation." Brit. Mus. p. 13.
3. Ibid, p. 17.
4. " The Babylonian Legends of the Creation." Brit. Mus., p. 20.

human being, is depicted in it in the pre-natal position. The same authority states that Kingu " is Tammuz."[1]

We also learn from this text that Tiamat had had a previous husband, Apsu, who was slain by one of the older Gods, Ea. We thus see that Kingu reproduces the essential features of a later Tammuz, and the significance of his taking refuge in the womb of Tiamat becomes clear at once.

Marduk defeated Kingu and slew Tiamat with his spear, which latter emblem throughout all the transmutations of the Adonis theme plays its important part. It lingers right down to the days of the Holy Graal legends in Mediæval Europe, and it was with this weapon that in certain primitive areas, even in the classical period, human representatives of Adonis were slain. It must be carefully borne in mind, for again and again it will turn up associated in some way with Adonis.

Having slain Tiamat, he formed out of her, heaven and earth, and after creating a new race of animals, made men in the likeness of the Gods. In order to endow them with a spark of the Divine Nature he beheaded Kingu and " created man out of the blood of the God mixed with earth." The actual words he used are significant, for he said he would create man out of " blood and bone—Dami Issimtum."[2] The similarity of this word to Damu or Dumu-zi is most significant, and the words of Ea, " Let one brother God be given, let him suffer *destruction* that men may be fashioned " summarises the full import, not only of this one incident, but of the age-long story of the sacrifice of man for the sake of man.

In this very early Babylonian record we obtain the first and most primitive conception of the Great Mother, and the prototype of the Monster who in so many initiation rites is supposed to swallow the initiate, and then bring him forth re-born to a new life. To this day in the forests of New Guinea the initiates are swallowed up by a great monster (really a house built in that shape); they spend some time in the belly of this mythical dragon, and are restored to life as *men*. As we shall see later in the legend of Jonah and the great fish, a similar ceremony was still carried on in Judea in the 8th century B.C.

In the course of time the Babylonian religion developed gradually towards monotheism, although it never actually reached that stage; we find, however, in the later writings a growing tendency to claim that all the Gods are but forms of the one true God, Marduk. We also notice that the number of Gods is gradually reduced, and in particular that Ishtar absorbed into herself the attributes of a whole host of lesser Goddesses, especially those of the Great Mother Goddess. Another important development is the grouping of the Gods into Triads, Ishtar being associated with

1.   Ibid, p. 17.
2.   Ibid, p. 27.

Sin, the Moon God, and Shamash, the Sun God. It is therefore not surprising to find that she and Tammuz tend to take on the attributes of the sun and the moon, although she never entirely loses her original aspect of a fertility Goddess. Strictly, she was the Goddess of the Star Venus, both as the Morning Star, when it rises in the East, and of the Evening Star, a fact which explains certain incidents associated with the *Morning Star in the East* in the later rituals. It was at Antioch that the crowd raised their eyes to " That bright and morning star whose rising brings peace and salvation to the faithful and obedient of the human race." [1]

On two seals of about 2,500 B.C., now in the British Museum and illustrated in the Babylonian Legends—are depicted two scenes which, although officially described as " Shamash the Sun God rising and setting," are more probably a representation of the descent of Dumu-zi into the underworld and his subsequent coming forth by day. In the first the God is seen sinking into the underworld amidst what seems to be pine cones, one of his emblems, out of which grave springs up a young tree. Over the dying God stands the Goddess, who is dropping into the open grave an " ear of corn," for so the Museum authorities describe it, but to my mind it is much more like a pomegranate, the well-known emblem of fertility and—" Plenty." In either case she is clearly planting the seed. An attendant God is releasing an eagle, which among many Syrian nations was released at the emblematic burning of the God, to signify the ascent of his soul to heaven. Near by stands a God holding a bow in his hand, one of the best known emblems of the Great Mother, behind whom is a lion, another of her emblems, one under which she was constantly worshipped in Asia Minor. Opposite the lion is the bull, another regular emblem of the fertility Goddess and one which, as we have seen in the account of Gilgamish, was peculiarly associated with Ishtar.

The other seal, which is of about the same date, depicts Dumu-zi (or alternatively Shamash) rising from the Underworld. Two attendant Gods are supporting two pillars, or possibly doors, which are surmounted by lions. In either case the pillars or doors no doubt represent the gates of the Underworld being withdrawn. The lines of fire suggest the funeral pyre of the God to which we have already referred, while the eight pointed stars are the recognised emblem of Ishtar. The fact that there are two of them reminds us that she was Goddess of Venus, both as the Evening and as the Morning Star, and it was when Venus rose in the East, i.e., in the morning, that the time for the proclamation of the resurrection of Tammuz had arrived.

It may interest some of our readers to know that the symbol

---

1. Frazer, " Adonis, Attis, Osiris." 3rd ed., vol. I., p. 258.
   Ammianus Marcellinus, XXII. 9. 14.

of the God Nabu was the mason's square, which in Babylonia consisted of a right angled triangle, and a picture of it will be found on page 25, Register 3, of *The Babylonian Legends of the Creation.*

Before leaving the Babylonian accounts of Ishtar and Tammuz it seems desirable to say something about Enkidu, the great friend of Gilgamish. He was a mysterious being, not born like ordinary man but especially made by one of the Goddesses. He clothed himself in leaves and lived in the forest, where he established a sort of rulership over all the wild beasts. When the hunters came out to trap them Enkidu broke their traps and prevented them capturing the wild animals. These men appealed to Gilgamish, King of Erech, who sent out a temple Prostitute, who acted somewhat the part of Delilah. In the end she lured Enkidu away from the forests to the haunts of men in Erech.

It is clear from the above that Enkidu represents the untrammelled spirit of wild life. The Temple Prostitute was one of the women dedicated to Ishtar, and, to some extent at any rate, represents her. After the insult which Enkidu cast at Ishtar the Goddess brought about his death, but exactly how we do not know. It is after he has thus lost his friend that Gilgamish sets out on his great journey in quest of the secret of Eternal Life. This journey, as I have shown in Vol. 2 of " The Hung Society," is really an allegory of the journey of the soul through the Underworld, and we cannot help suspecting that Gilgamish is the other self of Enkidu. The similarity between the fate of Enkidu and Persephone on the one hand, and the journey of Ceres and Gilgamish on the other, is too exact to be accidental. It almost seems as if in this story we have an attempt to " reform " the old legend of Tammuz and Ishtar in which the Goddess appears in a very unpleasant light. It must not be forgotten that Ishtar, like all the great Fertility Goddesses, has a series of lovers who each in turn come to a tragic end, although in reality each is a reincarnation of the previous one, and before we have finished with our theme we shall find that there is, as it were, a link which connects the old lover with the new and transfers the soul of the dying God to his successor. That link is nearly always a sprig of Acacia, or some similar tree, which grows from the grave of the dead God and into which his soul temporarily passes before it once more becomes incarnate in human form. Even in the story of Gilgamish this magical plant, which secured to its happy possessor Eternal Life, appears. In order to obtain it, Gilgamish dived to the bottom of the sea and ascended with it back to the boat from whence he had come. The name of this plant is " The old man becometh young," and Gilgamish declared that he would " Eat of it in order to recover his lost youth." Unfortunately, however, a serpent stole the plant and thus deprived Gilgamish of Eternal

Life, just as the serpent similarly caused the loss of immortality to Adam and Eve.[1]

The twelfth and closing tablet of the Epic is sad reading. In desperation Gilgamish invoked the spirit of Enkidu from the Underworld, and the Ghost appeared and described conditions therein from which we gather that the Underworld was a sad and dreary place.

We thus see that the lamentations of Ishtar, even according to the Babylonians, were crocodile tears, and that the death of her lovers was the natural and inevitable result of mating with her, which fact explains some of the cruel and unpleasant features which disfigure the worship of the Great Mother in Syria and Asia Minor. We perceive that the simile of the Queen Bee, who destroys the drone by emasculating it, exactly describes the early conception of the Fertility Goddess. As a symbol of the processes of nature this analogy was perfectly correct, for Dumu-zi represents the corn, which by being planted in the womb of Mother Earth dies, but thereby a plenteous harvest is produced and through the sacrifice of the corn spirit mankind is saved. The children of Mother Earth thus begotten, i.e. the ears of corn, become her lovers, year by year, and suffer the same fate by being planted in the earth again. Since savage men believed they could assist the forces of nature by simulating her actions in dramatic guise, we must not be surprised if we find that real, living, human beings enacted the part of the unfortunate Dumu-zi and like him died, under the supposition that thereby a plenteous harvest would result. From this savage Magical Rite evolved in course of time the high Mystery Drama, which taught of death and resurrection and Immortal Life beyond the grave. And this is the reason why the hero is always called " THE WIDOW'S SON."

But the later Babylonians had a Mystery drama of these events which is of considerable importance to us in this enquiry. Mr. Sidney Smith[2] bases his account of this ceremony[a] on the important Babylonian text published by Dr. Ebeling and Prof. Zimmern, and from them comes to the conclusion that Assur and Marduk are practically the same god, and that Assur may be the origin of Osiris, with whose name Ausur, Assur, is connected.

" Certain texts from Nineveh and Ashur describe cult ceremonies performed at the New Year Festival."[b]   The part of

---

1.   The Epic of Gilgamish. Brit. Mus. p. 55.
2.   Sidney Smith, " The Relation of Marduk, Ashur and Osiris." Journal of Egyptian Archæology. Vol. VIII. (April 1922).
(a)   For what follows I am indebted to the great kindness of Bro. Sidney Smith, of the Assyrian Dept. of the British Museum, who has given me considerable help, not only in this, but on many other points.
(b)   Lancelot was destined to be " crowned in the midst of the fire " on New Year's Day had he accepted the throne of the burning city. See chapter xiv.

Marduk was played by the King, that of Nabu was enacted by the High Priest, and the rest of the worshippers also took part in a dramatic ritual of death and resurrection. The ceremonies covered twelve days, just as did those connected with the Lord of Misrule at Yule-tide in England, and the number no doubt refers to the Signs of the Zodiac and the months of the year.

The opening days were taken up by a drama of the Creation and then the god Zu stole from Marduk " the tablet of destiny," whose possession was essential to the god who would rule the universe. It was a kind of Palladium and its form immediately suggests a " Word of Power " and its loss, the " Lost Word." This loss led to the downfall of Marduk, who was buried in the " Mountain " which represents the " Underworld."

" A message was sent out, asking for someone to bring Marduk out. Nabu came from Borsippa to save his father. A goddess (almost certainly Beltis, the spouse of Marduk) appealed to Sin and Shamash to bring Bel to life; then went to the gate of the grave seeking him, where he was guarded by two watchmen in a prison, without sun or light: the goddess descended into the grave to save him. While Marduk was thus imprisoned, apparently with the actual evil-doer, confusion fell upon Babylon. Further details of the ritual are not easy to work into a story, but it is clear that Nabu and Beltis were both active in their endeavours to aid Marduk. Finally, Anshar sent Enurta out to capture Zu and he captured him; and then the gods bored through the door of the prison and brought Marduk out. It should be noted that the Colophon of the tablet shows that it was intended only for the eyes of those initiated into these religious mysteries."

In connection with this story it should be remembered that Nabu is the Mason god and had as his emblem the square. Mr. Smith points out the numerous points of similarity between this myth and that of Osiris. Beltis is Isis, Enurta and Zu are Horus and Set, while Nabu is similar to Thoth. In Assyria Ashur was the hero of the fight with Tiamat, as Marduk was in Babylon, and there is little doubt that Marduk is but the Babylonian name for Ashur; it is significant that Marduk is also called Asari. In bas-reliefs Ashur is always closely associated with a tree, over which a winged disk hovers. The tree seems to be similar to the Tat pillar of Egypt and the disk to the similar disk at Boghaz-Keui.

Mr. Smith considers that this tree is a cedar, whose connection with Tammuz is one of the best established facts we have concerning that Deity. The original Dying god in Babylonia was Tammuz, and it would therefore seem as if in the course of their policy of exalting Marduk, the god of their city, the Babylonian Priests identified Tammuz with him. It is clear that there, as in Judea, the priests were tending to replace polytheism by monotheism. The process was only half completed when the Persians captured the city and cut short an interesting religious development, but the tendency is unmistakeable. It took the form of identifying the various gods of the Pantheon in turn with Marduk, and though probably this was a more or less secret cult of the priests it is none the less significant.

So also is the fact that the king himself had to enact the part of the dying god, for it shows that, like the kings of Syria, he too was a divine king, the repository of the spirit of the vegetation god, which god was later identified with the god of light, a process which occurred elsewhere. In the substitution of a dramatic representation of death for the grim reality we have an example of the process which has taken place in many cults, and perhaps in Masonry itself. For all that the Babylonians also had an actual annual slaying of a substitute king, as we shall see later.

CHAPTER IV

ASTARTE AND ADONIS IN SYRIA AND CYPRUS

The legend of Adonis is best known to us from the Greek version, the word Adonis being merely a Hellenised form of his title, Adonai. The Greeks, a refined and civilised race, undoubtedly modified both the legend and the Rites connected therewith, omitting many of the more repulsive features.

According to the Greeks, Aphrodite loved the child Adonis as an infant and hid him in a chest which she placed in charge of Persephone, the Queen of the Underworld. But as soon as Persephone saw the lovely babe she refused to restore it to Aphrodite, although the Goddess descended into the Underworld itself in a desperate effort to recover the child. At length Zeus intervened and decided that Adonis must remain with Aphrodite for half the year, but during the rest of it he must dwell with Persephone. At last Adonis was slain, either by a boar, or, according to other accounts, by Ares, the God of War, who disguised himself as a wild boar in order to compass the death of his rival in Aphrodite's affections.[1]

There exists an interesting representation of the contest between Aphrodite and Persephone on an Etruscan mirror[2] wherein we see the two Goddesses on either side of Zeus, who is sternly admonishing Persephone. Aphrodite, in bitter grief, buries her face in her mantle, while her opponent holds a *branch* in one hand and with the other points at a closed chest, which probably contains the infant Adonis.

The confiding of the infant Adonis to Persephone no doubt symbolises the planting of the seed in Autumn; the period spent with Aphrodite represents Spring and early Summer when the corn is growing; while the actual death represents the harvesting of the grain, at which time the great lamentation took place. In this connection readers should note that, in the curious legend I have quoted on page 180, Hiram descended into the fiery Underworld, re-ascended to earth, completed his work and then was slain.

The branch in the hand of Persephone represents the plant into which the soul of the Vegetation God has been transferred, and brings to mind the branch mentioned in Ezekiel 8. 17, and also the sprig of acacia. (See chapter 21). The fact that there were two descents into the Underworld, at seed time and at harvest,

---

1. Frazer, " Adonis, Attis, Osiris," 3rd ed., Vol. 1. p. 11.
2. W. W. Graf Baudissin. " Adonis and Esman " (Leipsic, 1911), pp. 152 sq. and plate.

30

no doubt explains a problem which has puzzled many scholars, for whereas in some places the lamentation for Tammuz seems to have been in late Spring or early Summer, in others it appears to have occurred in Autumn.

In Palestine the barley-harvest was in March—April and the wheat harvest in May—June, and a festival of Lamentation during any part of that period would represent the slaying of the adult God. A similar festival in Autumn or early Winter would represent the depositing of the infant God in the hands of the Goddess of the Underworld, thereby symbolising the planting of the seed. Further, although the fact is not made clear in the Greek legend, originally Tammuz was the son as well as the mate of the Great Mother, for the corn is brought forth by her, is planted next season in her womb, and perishes in order that she may bear more " Corn " children.

In Syria the greatest centre of the Adonis Cult was at Byblos, whose Semetic name was Gebal. It was situated on the sea coast, but there were also several other important shrines to which we shall refer in due course. Byblos was said to have been founded by El, a name also used by the Jews for God. The great sanctuary of Astarte is described by Lucian[1] who tells us that a great cone, representing Astarte, rose in the midst of a fine courtyard which was surrounded by cloisters. The river which ran close by was called Adonis,[2] and descended thence from its source near the other great shrine on Mount Lebanon, namely, Aphaca.

This was the kingdom of the semi-mythical Cinyras[3] and up to the close of its existence it was ruled by Kings who may have been assisted by a kind of Senate[4]. It was from the name of the town, Gebal, that the words Giblim and Giblites, originated.[5] The names of these Kings, e.g. Adom-Melech, and Yehar-baal seem to indicate that they claim to be of divine descent, a custom almost universal among the Semitic races throughout the whole of this area.[6] We certainly know that the Kings of the neighbouring city of Tyre claimed to be the off-spring of Baal[7] and Gods, even during their life on earth.[8]

One of these Kings of Tyre called himself Abi-Melech, which

---

1. Lucian, " De dea Syria." 6.
    The shrine is also shown on numerous coins of the city, see T. L. Donaldson, " Architectura Numismatica," p. 105 sq.
2. Lucian. " De dea Syria " 6.
3. Eustathius. " Commentary on Dionysius-Periegetes," 912 (Geographia Graeci Minores. Ed. C. Muller, 11. 376).
4. Ezekiel, 27. 9.
5. I Kings, 5. 18.
6. Frazer, " Adonis, Attis, Osiris." 3rd ed. Vol. 1. p. 15.
7. Servius's Note on Virgil, " Aeneid." 1. 729 sq. Silius Italicus, " Punica."
    1. 28.
8. Ezekiel, 28. 2, and 9.

means " Father of the King " or " Father of Moloch," and is a title which implies that its bearer was the father of a God.[1]   From this we see that the title of Hiram Abiff, i.e., " Father of the Exaltation of Life," etc., becomes perfectly intelligible.   If one Tyrian King called himself " The Father of Moloch " why should not another call himself " The Father of the Exaltation of Life," or use the even more significant title of " The Father of Him Who Destroys," a title peculiarly suitable to Moloch, to whom victims were burnt alive ?

Frazer[2] points out that it was a regular Semitic custom to call a man the Father of " So and So," when that " So and So " was a King, for the King was considered a God-King.   A similar custom prevailed in Egypt where the Kings were literally worshipped as Divine.[3]   There the wife if the King was called " The Wife of the God," or " The Mother of the God," as the case might be, and the title " Father of the God " was borne not only by the King's real father, but also by his father-in-law.[4] Names such as Abi-Baal (Father of Baal) and Abi-Jah (Father of Jehovah) imply that a man was, in some strange way, father of the God, and such a custom becomes intelligible only when we realise that the God was supposed to transfer his Divine Soul from one generation of Kings to the next.   It seems, moreover, as if a King at the birth of his heir was supposed automatically to lose his Divine Soul, which henceforth dwelt in his son.

In some places a man regularly assumed the name of his son[5] and so a Divine King in later life might often be called " Father of So and So."[6]   In this Semitic custom we have an explanation of the curious fact that Adoniram's Father, Abda, called himself " The Father of the Beloved," " The Beloved " being a title of Adonis, thereby incidentally implying that Adoniram, the man, had within him the Divine Soul of Adonis.   In like manner the Phoenician architect similarly called himself " The Father of Him that Destroys," and the title " He that Destroys " was that by which Hiram, the reigning king of Tyre, was known.   This fact suggests that he likewise had passed on to his son the Divine Soul of the God, namely that God whom the Tyrian Kings claimed to be.

Josephus informs us that the father of King Hiram was called " Abi-Baal " which means, of course, " The Father of the God," and implies that he, at any rate, survived the period at which his son became the recipient of the Divine Soul.[7]   It would thus

---

1.   Frazer, Ibid. p. 16.
2.   Frazer, " Adonis, Attis, Osiris," 3rd ed. Vol. 1. p. 51.
3.   Frazer. Ibid. p. 52, also " The Magic Art and the Evolution of Kings,"
        Vol. 1. p. 418 sq.
4.   Frazer, " Adonis, Attis, Osiris." p. 52.
5.   Frazer, " Taboo and the Perils of the Soul," p. 331 sq.
6.   Frazer, " Adonis, Attis, Osiris," p. 51.
7.   Josephus, " Against Apion," c. 1. sect. 17.

appear as if Abi-Baal and Hiram Abiff were the same persons.
Certainly their titles imply precisely the same thing and connect
up with the same King of Tyre, Hiram.

If then, it was originally the custom for the King of Tyre,
like other divine Kings, to be sacrificed when his body grew old,
in order that the divine soul might pass into another and younger
body, we can easily understand that in the course of years such a
sacrifice might be mitigated. When the King grew old he would
abdicate, and would possibly pretend to die, and his son would
thereupon inherit the Divine Soul and with it the Kingdom.
Henceforth the older man would have lost his former divine title
and assume that of " The Father of the God," or " The Father of
Him That Destroys." My readers must definitely realise one
important fact. During this period, and long after it, Syria literally swarmed with Priest-Kings who were believed to be the
incarnations of their God. We have occasion to refer to several
of these later, but there is one feature common to practically
all of them. The man who assumed the doubtful privilege of
representing the incarnate God and being his Priest-King lost his
personal name and in its place took the name and title of the
God. For example, the High Priest of Cybele was called Attis
and also Papa, meaning " Father," the latter being a title of
Attis.

Although, however, the old savage custom of killing the King
as soon as he grew old may, by the time of Solomon, have been
mitigated, as we have indicated, yet at times of emergency and on
occasions of great solemnity we find that nations constantly hark
back to their savage and original customs. At such a moment a
royal victim would be required: sometimes, no doubt, a royal son
or cousin might serve, but if the old King was still alive he would
be the most obvious sacrifice. According to popular beliefs he
ought to have died when his son ascended the throne: he had lived
for several years beyond his allotted span, therefore he was the
man to represent the real king and die in his place. Perhaps the
completion of the great temple at Jerusalem was regarded by the
less civilised Phoenician workmen, as just such an occasion as
required that the old King should die and, with his blood, consecrate the temple.

Reverting to the Kings of Byblos and Tyre, we find that some
at any rate, were not only Kings but also Priests of Astarte.[1] We
learn in the same passage that the Father of Hiram called himself
Abibalus, i.e., Abi-Baal, which means the Father of Baal, and
that there was a line of Priest-Kings of Astarte who included one
called Pygmalion, a name whose significance will become clearer
when we turn to Cyprus. According to Josephus it was the sister
of Pygmalion, Dido, who built Carthage.

---

1. Josephus. " Against Apion," Bk. 1. 18, quoting Menander the Ephesan.

From the above we see that the Kings of Tyre were Priest-Kings and that King Hiram himself had a father who used the title of " Father of the God, Baal " and that this man appears to correspond with Hiram Abiff.

In these circumstances it seems desirable to decide exactly who the Baal of Tyre was. He was Melcarth (Moloch), whom the Greeks identified with Hercules, and this fact is borne out by Josephus[1] who tells us that King Hiram built and consecrated " The Temples of Hercules and Astarte." He also tells us that Baal was the God of the Phoenicians.[2] The Phoenicians, however, usually called him Melcarth, which means " The Divine King," while the alternative title Baal merely means " God." This Phoenician Baal was a God of Fertility, more especially of Corn and Wine, although he also had under his protection the animals. Indeed, these are the characteristics of the chief God of all the non-Jewish Semites, while the Greek Hercules was merely this male Semitic Deity imported into Greece and Hellenised. We shall learn a good deal about him from their literature when we come to the chapter on the Dying God in Asia Minor. Robertson Smith admirably summarizes the attributes of this great Semitic Deity in the words:—" the Baal was conceived as the male principle of reproduction, the husband of the land he fertilised."[3] Frazer considers that these Semitic Kings personated their God and had to marry the Goddess of the Earth, Astarte.[4] In short, we may say that Baal and Tammuz were really the same Deity, although, perhaps, viewed from a slightly different angle.

The last King of Byblos was called Cinyras.[5] He was slain by Pompey and the founder of the line was also Cinyras, the reputed father of Adonis, who is said to have built a shrine[6] on Mount Lebanon, which was almost certainly Aphaca, now a small village called Afka. The whole district was sacred to Adonis (Tammuz) and at Ghineh near by is depicted the following sculpture. Astarte is seated in a position of utter grief while Adonis with spear in hand awaits the attack of a bear (not, be it noted, a boar).[7] As the Goddess herself was originally a Bear Goddess, we see that Adonis was really destroyed by Astarte in her primitive and bestial form, despite the " crocodile tears " she sheds.

The significant fact, however, is that every year Adonis was supposed to be slain, the river ran red with his blood, and the scarlet anemones sprang from his freshly shed blood amid the

1.   Josephus, " Against Apion," Bk. 1. 18.
2.   Josephus, " Antiquities," Bk. 19. Ch. 6. para. 6.
3   W. Robertson Smith, " Religion of the Semites." pp 107 sq.
4.   Frazer, " Adonis, Attis, Osiris." 3rd ed. Vol. 1. p. 27.
5.   Strabo. XVI. 1. 18. p. 755.
6.   Lucian, " De dea Syria." 9.
7.   E. Renan, " Mission de Phenice." pp. 292 sq.

cedars of Lebanon. At this period of the year, Lucian tells us, the Syrian maidens wept for Adonis, slain.[1] Thus we see that the worship of Tammuz was not only inseparably interwoven with the lives of the people of Palestine, but the very King who helped Solomon to build his temple was himself a representative and a descendant of the Dying God; not merely a devoted worshipper of Him, or of his Divine Mistress, but in some strange way an earthly incarnation of a God Who every year was slain in order that the earth might be fertilised.

At Heirapolis (the modern Membij) Lucian[2] further informs us that there were two large phalli, thirty fathoms high, which stood at the door of the temple of Astarte, and that twice every year a man (probably one of the castrated Galli or Priests) climbed to the summit from the inside, where he was supposed to hold converse with the Gods, to ensure the prosperity and fertility of the land.[3] In reality he dramatically represented the process of fertilisation which produced the New Priest-King.

Here then we see not only the true nature of the two pillars in the porch of King Solomon's temple, but also the reason why they were made hollow. The explanation, that this was to enable them to serve as archives, was no doubt invented after the original object had been forgotten.

Let us now pass to Cyprus which, colonised by Phoenicians, was the other great centre of the worship of Adonis and Astarte, from whence these Rites spread to Greece.

There were several shrines to Adonis in Cyprus, as, for example, at Amathus, where the Rites of Adonis were so similar to those of Osiris that some of the Ancients considered he *was* Osiris.[4] The most famous shrine, however, was at Paphos, the modern Kuklia, and we can form a very good idea of its appearance from the coins of the time of the Cæsars,[5] and also from certain votive gold medals[6] found in the tombs at Mycenæ, which must be some 1200 years earlier than the coins, and show that but little change had taken place in the general plan and design,[7] in all the centuries which had elapsed between that period and the beginning of the Christian era.

1. Lucian, " De dea Syria." 8.
2. Ibid.
3. N. M. Penzer, " The Ocean of Story." Vol. I, p. 275.
4. Stephanus Byzantius s.v. Amathus.
5. G. F. Hill, " Catalogue of the Greek Coins of Cyprus " (London 1904). pp. 127—134, also plates.
   Geo. Macdonald. " Catalogue of Greek Coins in the Hunterian Collection " (Glasgow 1899—1905) ii 566.
6. G. Perrot et Ch. Chipiez, " Histoire de 'lArt dans l'Antiquité," vi. (Paris 1894) pp. 336 sq. 652—654.
   Journal of Hellenic Studies. ix (1888). p. 213 sq.
   P. Gardner, " New Chapters in Greek History." p. 181.
7. For existing remains see " Excavations in Cyprus " 1887-88. " Journal of Hellenic Studies." ix. (1888). pp. 193 sq.

As the date of these models is some two hundred years earlier than the traditional date of the building of King Solomon's temple, and the work was undoubtedly Phoenician, the details of the shrine at Paphos may explain certain peculiar features of the temple at Jerusalem built by Phoenician workmen.

On coins and models alike we find a fascade, on top of which are two doves. The fascade is divided into three parts, or chapels, the central part having a tall superstructure. This central part contains a cone, on either side of which is a lofty pillar " each terminating in a pair of ball-topped pinnacles, with a star and crescent appearing between the tops of the columns."[1] In each of the side chapels a similar pillar appears. Perched on various parts of the building are doves, the well known emblem of Astarte.

The cone symbolised the Goddess herself and is perhaps a crude representation of the female symbol, just as the pillars present the Phallus. Their duplication may be merely for the purpose of symmetry, but this is unlikely, and it is more probable that originally they symbolised the Dying God (a) as the father, and (b) as the son, for it must be remembered that Tammuz, who died when he mated with the Goddess, was reborn as her son, destined in due course to suffer the same fate as his father, who was, indeed, himself.

Such phalli, flanking Pagodas, are still found in Buddhist countries, particularly in Burma and Siam. In Bangkok there is a phallus of enormous height, which each year is repainted, the lower part in some dark colour, such as brown, and the top red, the result being unpleasantly realistic.

The two great pillars of red wood set up outside the gates of the Burmese exhibit at Wembley in 1924 were of course, also Phalli, though in Burma this fact seems to have been forgotten.

If we compare this shrine with the account of Solomon's temple we shall recognise several important features therein. The dome, to which reference is made in a certain masonic tradition, corresponds with the cone or superstructure at Paphos. The two pillars with their globes also become intelligible, and even the ornate chapiters with their detailed carving, conveying the idea of fertility, are nothing more than the remains of the prepuce (the rest being removed in circumcision) artistically disguised.

The three parts of the building correspond with the general design of the Eastern fascade of the temple, and though we have no mention of the dove, we know that up to the time of the Romans doves were on sale in the Temple for the purpose of burnt offerings. There seems, therefore, no doubt, that in its main outline King Solomon's temple corresponded with the temples of Astarte.

There is one fact whose significance we must not overlook

---

1. Frazer, " Adonis, Attis, Osiris." 3rd ed. Vol. 1. p. 33.

there is no mention in the Bible of the " globes." No doubt in reality these were domes, not true globes, and the fact that they indicated a phallic significance was not overlooked by the Hebrew revisers who deleted all reference to them. Nevertheless, the masonic tradition has retained them, and therein is undoubtedly correct. This fact is but one of many small pieces of evidence which show that the masonic tradition has come down from a time previous to the revision of the Bible by the Hebrew champions of Monotheism, and thus indicates the genuine antiquity of the masonic ceremonies.

The evidence in support of the view that the cone is an emblem of the Great Mother is abundant. It was under this symbol that she was worshipped at Byblos,[1] at Perga, in Pamphylia,[2] in Malta, a Phoenician settlement,[3] and at Sinai.[4] The sacred stone of Cybele, which was brought by the Romans to the " Eternal City " during the second Punic War, when they established the savage Rites of the Great Mother at the Vatican, was a small, black, jagged piece of rock which formed the face of the statue, but it is not certain whether it was conical in shape or not.[5] It was, however, black, not white, and in this connection we should remember that in the Song of Solomon the female Lover, who undoubtedly represents Astarte, says, " I am black, but comely."[6]

Probably the black stone of the Kaaba at Mecca originally represented the same Goddess. At Paphos it was customary to anoint this cone, and, as showing how old customs survive long after the religion which begot them has apparently been replaced by another, it is interesting to know that this custom is still maintained at Paphos to-day. D. G. Hogarth[7] tells us that " in honour of the maid of Bethlehem, the peasants of Kuklia (Paphos) anointed lately, and probably still anoint each year, the great corner stones of the ruined temple of the Paphian Goddess. As Aphrodite (Astarte) was supplicated once with cryptic Rites, so is Mary entreated still by Moslems, as well as Christians, with incantations and passings through perforated stones, to remove the curse of barrenness from Cypriote women, or increase the manhood of Cypriote men."

Passing through a hole in a stone or tree is found as a Rite of re-birth all over the world, and such Rites are often resorted to in

1. See Chapter 4, page 31.
2. B. V. Head, " Historia Numorum." (Oxford 1887). p. 58.
    P. Gardner, " Types of Greek Coins." (Camb. 1883) pl. xv. No. 3.
3. G. Perrot et Ch. Chipiez, " Histoire de l'Art dans l'Antiquité." iii. 273. 298 sq. 304 sq.
4. W. M. Flinders Petri, " Researches in Sinai." (London 1906) p. 135 sq.
5. Frazer, " Adonis, Attis, Osiris." 3rd ed. Vol. 1. p. 35.
6. Song of Solomon. 1. 5.
7. D. G. Hogarth, " A Wandering Scholar in the Levant." (London 1896). pp. 179 sq.

the hope that as a result thereof the blight of disease, and especially
of barrenness, will be removed.   If this old ceremony of anointing
the stone still survives to-day may not other Rites of Adonis have
likewise survived ?   Indeed, so strong is the hold that the ancient
Goddess has on the Cypriote peasantry that they still use her
name and worship the Virgin Mary under the title of " Panaghia
Aphroditessa."[1]

So much for the great shrine at Paphos, but what of the
Kings of that City ?   According to legend a Syrian named
Sandacus went to Cilicia and married the daughter of the King of
that country, in time becoming King.   Now Sandacus is clearly
the same as Sandan, a North Syrian God who corresponds very
closely to Melcarth of Tyre, and therefore to one aspect of Adonis.
This Sandacus had a son, Cinyras, who went to Cyprus and
married the daughter of Pygmalion, the King of that Country;[2]
he then founded Paphos and became the father of Adonis.

We have already mentioned that Sandacus has the same name
as Sandan, a variation of Melcarth, who, like that God, was burnt,
so we will now turn to consider Cinyras.   His name is identical
with the mythical founder of Byblos, who, like his Cypriote namesake, was the father of Adonis.   In short, all three were in turn
the human embodiments of Tammuz.

But Pygmalion, the father of the wife of Cinyras, and therefore Grandfather of Adonis, was himself a human incarnation of
Tammuz.   This Pygmalion, we are told, fell in love with the
statue of Aphrodite and took it to bed.[3]   Ovid, later, when relat-
ing the story changed the King into a sculptor and the image into
a statue of a beautiful woman, but the above was the original
version of the story and indicates that the Phoenician King[(a)]
had to go through the ceremony of marrying a statue of Astarte to
symbolise his marriage to the Goddess.   A somewhat similar
custom still prevails in India, except that it is a girl who marries
the statue of a God and henceforth is a temple prostitute.

Now Cinyras is said to have been a lover of Aphrodite[4] and
begot his son incestuously with his daughter Myrrha at a Harvest
Festival to the Goddess.[5]   It should be noted that in the Syrian
stories of the birth of Adonis sometimes other kings are mentioned as the father, but usually the mother is described as their
daughter.   Such incestuous acts are probably a latter day

1.   G. Perrot et Ch. Chipiez, " Histoire de l'Art dans l'Antiquité." III. 628.
2.   Apollodorus, " Bibliotheca."   III. 14. 3. (R. Wagner's ed.)
3.   Arnobius, " Adversus Nationes."   I. 22.
     Clement of Alexandria, " Protrept."   IV. 57. p. 51, ed. Potter.
4.   Clement of Alexandria, " Protrept," II. 33. p. 29, ed. Potter.
5.   Ovid, " Metam."   X. 298 sq.
     Hyginus, " Fab." 58. 64.
     Plutarch, " Parallela." 22.
(a)   Porphyry also says Pygmalion was a Phoenician in " De abstinentia."
     IV. 15.

description of a former royal custom, whose object was to keep the crown in the royal male line at a time when succession went by the female. They are parallel to the custom of the Egyptian Pharoahs, who married their own sisters, although the whole question of exogamy with its totemic prohibitions is involved, which cannot be discussed here.[1]

The four kings thus consist of three who were lovers of Aphrodite, each in their turn, while Sandacus also corresponds to Adonis. Thus it would appear as if we had a succession of Syrian Priest-Kings who considered themselves incarnations of the lover of the Great Mother, Astarte, and no doubt annually went through the ceremony of being married to her.

Sandacus seems to correspond with Sandan or Melcarth, and therefore it is desirable to indicate the relationship between Melcarth and Tammuz. Melcarth was the Baal, or Lord of Fertility, who annually mated with the Great Mother, and in consequence died, but was reincarnated in his son. As the living Divine King of the City he was worshipped under the title of Melcarth, but when he assumed his aspect of the Dying God he was bewailed as Tammuz or Adonis. In short, he was at once the husband and the son of Astarte.

There seems to be evidence, moreover, that all the sons of the human representatives of this Divinity were considered as like him, Divine, and it was no doubt this fact which enabled the custom of slaying them, and yet not destroying the whole royal house, to be maintained. It seems certain, moreover, that the annual marriage of these kings consisted of a more or less temporary union with the sacred women, or sacred prostitutes as they are often called, who were always attached to the temples of Astarte. In Palestine, these women were called Kedehsoth (Kadosh), a word which, strictly speaking, means " Sacred Women." In such circumstances the supply of Divine men, the offspring of such unions, would be fairly numerous, and the women themselves seem to have been regarded as human representatives of the Great Mother. Perhaps the Kedeshim, or " Sacred Men," whom Josiah[2] turned out of the temple of Jehovah were the superfluous Divine Men, the offspring of the sacred women.[a] This seems the more probable as in some areas, such as the Caucasus, it was one of these sacred men who was annually slain.[3]

For all that, each year there must have been one man who, for

---

1. See Frazer, " Folklore of the Old Testament."
2. II Kings. 23. 7.
3. Strabo. XI. 4. 7.
(a) The words used by the English translators may or may not correctly describe their conduct, but it is not an accurate translation of the word Kedeshim, which means " Sacred Men." In this passage the " Sacred Women " are said to weave garments for the Asherim, or wooden pillars which stood in the Sanctuaries.

the time being, peculiarly represented Tammuz, and in order to invest him with this doubtful privilege certain Rites were performed at the time of the death of his predecessor. What these Rites were we shall discover when we come to consider similar processes of transferring the Divine Soul in other lands, but among them no doubt was that of sniffing at a bough which grew out of the grave, the stepping over the grave or corpse, and so forth. The father of the man thus chosen to represent Tammuz might be proud to call himself " The Father of So and So."

To return to Adonis in Cyprus. We find that he was said to have reigned there[1] just as he did at Byblos, and his descendants regularly used the name Adonis. Nor was this title Adon, restricted to the reigning King, but was borne by all his sons.[2] Now just as there was a Cypriote Cinyras and a similarly named King at Byblos, so there was not only a Pygmalion in Cyprus but at least two of that name who reigned in Tyre. The one who is mentioned by Josephus[3] was the father of Dido, foundress of Carthage who, according to legend, burnt herself on the funeral pyre when Aeneas refused to stay with her. Death by fire seems to have been a popular method among the Phoenicians, for Hamilcar also burnt himself to death after his defeat.[4]

Since, according to all the legends, Adonis died a violent death, we must enquire whether a like fate befell Cinyras. There are three accounts and according to two of them he did, whereas the third makes him live to be 160 years old. Perhaps in the latter story we have an indication that the name Cinyras was regularly used by a series of monarchs, just as Augustus was among the Cæsars, and in connection therewith we must not forget that there is a Jewish tradition that Hiram of Tyre lived for over 400 years, namely, down to the destruction of the Temple.

The other two versions are no doubt nearer the truth, one is that he ventured to challenge Apollo to a trial of skill in music, was defeated and then slain by the God for his presumption in daring to challenge him.[5]

This story is almost identical with that told of Marsyas, who also was a Lover of Astarte[6] and was slain and flayed by Apollo, who then hung his skin on a tree.[7] Similar gruesome rites occur

---

1. Probius on Virgil. Ecl. X. 18.
2. Frazer. " Adonis, Attis, Osiris " p 49.
3. Josephus, " Against Apion." 1. 18.
   Ovid. " Fasti." III. 574.
   Virgil, " Aeneid." I. 346 sq.
4. Herodotus, VII. 167.
5. Scholiast and Eustathius on Homer. " Iliad " XI. 28.
   W. H. Engel, " Kypros " II. 109-116.
   Stoll, S. V. " Kinyras," in W. H. Roscher's " Lexikon der griech und
      röm Mythologie." II. 1191.
6. Diodorus Siculus. III. 58 sq.
7. Apollodorus, " Bibliotheca." 1. 4. 2. Hyginus " Fab." 165. Lucian.
      " Tragodopodagra." 315 sq.

in other parts of the world, notably in Mexico, and we cannot avoid the conclusion that the legend describes a former practice of slaying the human representative of the Divine Lover, and hanging him, or his skin, on a tree as part of the Fertility Rites. Even in the time of the Empire, the figure of a man was hung on a tree as part of the ceremonies of Cybele, and this no doubt was a substitute for the real man.

The other story relates that when he discovered that he had committed incest he slew himself.[1] This version suggests that the old king was sacrificed when a son had been born to him into whom the Divine Soul passed at birth, or at any rate could pass as soon as necessary.

We may take it, however, that these early Cypriote Kings who represented the Dying God sooner or later had to enact their part in deadly earnest, although in later years the civilising influence of Greek thought no doubt mitigated the horror of the Rite by substituting a dramatic representation of the death, or by the use of an image instead of a real man.

Thus far we have learnt that throughout Syria, Phoenicia and Cyprus, the Semitic races worshipped Astarte and a God, who, as the Lover of Astarte, was called Tammuz or Adonis, but who when viewed apart from her was usually called Melcarth, or Baal. We find that the Semitic Kings represented this God and like him had annually to marry the Goddess, or rather some representative of her. Like their Divine namesake they were also apparently slain, although whether this occurred after a stated period, when a son was born to them, or when they grew old is not quite clear.

We have seen that any one of the King's sons might inherit his Divinity, and therefore suffer the same fate as Adonis. For these reasons it will be of interest to discover the nature of the death they had to die.

It is clear that the important thing was that the God-man *should* die, and the exact method probably varied from place to place, and from one period to another. In some of the more savage districts, such as the Caucasus, the victim was stabbed in the side with a spear, and there seem to be traces of his being fastened to a tree before he was stabbed, according to the old legends, and in the Philippines this method survived almost to the present day. Sometimes the whole of the male member was cut off and the man bled to death, and in other places he was burnt. We may suspect a tendency in latter years to mitigate the cruelty of the death involved, by knocking the victim on the head before throwing him into the fire. Of these various methods fire seems to have been the most popular among the Semites, and we will therefore dispose of the first two as quickly as possible.

---

1. Hyginus, " Fab." 242.

Among the Albanians in the Caucasus there was a great sanctuary to the Moon, ruled by a High Priest, to which were attached a number of " Sacred Men." Sooner or later the Divine Spirit was supposed to descend into one of them and he wandered about through the forests prophesying. He was then seized and brought back to the Temple, where he was kept in semi-royal state for a year, like the God-King in Mexico. At the end of that period he was sacrificed to the Moon by having a spear thrust into his side. The worshippers drew omens from the position in which the body fell and afterwards stood on it as an act of purification.[1]

In this spear we may perhaps see the famous spear of Marduk, and, as its descendant, the spear of the Holy Graal legends which continually dropped blood.

We have already seen that Marsyas was slain, and his skin hung on a tree, and a similar fate seems to have befallen Cinyras, another lover of Astarte. These show that this was a method employed to kill the human representative of Tammuz. Among the Norse, men were sacrificed to Odin in Upsala by being hung on a tree, but sometimes the victims were hung and then stabbed with a spear.[2] Indeed, Odin himself is said to have " Hung himself " on a tree, and in the poem called " Havamal " he says:—

> " I know that I hung on the windy tree
> For nine whole nights
> Wounded with the spear, dedicated to Odin,
> Myself to myself."[3]

It has been suggested that the old English custom of hanging and then disembowelling criminals arose from the fact that criminals were formerly sacrificed to Odin in order to propitiate the God, Who would be incensed by their crimes. In any case the last line of the above verse is most significant, for it is the God-man the victim, speaking to the God. In like manner every human representative of Tammuz might have spoken.

A modern example of this ghastly Rite survived until quite recently among the Bagobos of Mindanao, one of the Philippine Islands. Each December when Orion appeared at 7 p.m., the people sacrificed a slave as a preliminary to sowing. This custom is thus precisely similar to the ideas underlying the slaying of Tammuz, who nominally died by mating with Astarte, or, in other words, represents the corn which is planted in the womb of Mother Earth.

The poor wretch was led to a big tree in the forest, tied with his back to the tree and his arms fastened high above his head. As he thus hung by his arms a spear was thrust through his side

---

1. Strabo. XI. 4. 7.
2. H. M. Chadwick, " The Cult of Odin " (London 1899). pp. 3-20.
   K. Simrock, " Die Edda." (Stuttgart, 1882). p. 382.
3. Havamal. 139 sq. (K. Simrock, " Die Edda." p. 55).

just beneath the arm-pit. Then the body was severed in twain at the waist line, and the upper half left hanging so that the fertilising blood might drain down into the soil.[1]

We cannot help suspecting that the cutting in two of the body replaced an older process, which, as indicated in the story of Attis, consisted in cutting off the male organ and leaving the man to bleed slowly to death. Doubtless as the original idea became forgotten more and more stress was laid on the fertilising quality of the blood, and hence it seemed desirable to obtain as large a diffusion as possible.

The custom of sacrificing animals by hanging and then stabbing them was widespread in Asia Minor, and at Heirapolis itself the victims were hung on a tree before they were burnt.[2] We thus see that there is abundant evidence to show that in many areas the human representatives of Adonis perished by being fastened to a tree and stabbed, and a tree in fact is constantly associated with the sacrifice, no matter whether the victim is stabbed or, as at Heirapolis, burnt.

Let us now turn to the method of cutting off the male member and then letting the victim bleed to death. The slow cruelty of this method seems quite early to have led to its mitigation, and the Rite developed in two directions. Either the victim lost his virile organ but the bleeding was stopped, or else a more expeditious method of causing his death was adopted, usually that of stabbing.

The story of Attis shows, however, what was the original method. Attis was the son and also the lover of Cybele,[3] and was conceived by his mother, although a virgin, because she put a pomegranate seed, or alternatively an almond, into her bosom. Undoubtedly he is the same God as Adonis,[4] and one form of the legend says that he too was slain by a boar,[5] but the other form declares that he cut off his male member under a pine tree and bled to death.[6] Servius, however, significantly says that the wound was not self inflicted.[7] It was because of this story that his Priests, the Galli, similarly mutilated themselves, but without the same fatal results.

---

1. Fay-Cooper Cole, " The Wild Tribes of Davao District Mindanao." (Chicago, 1913), pp. 114 sq. (Field Museum of Natural History, Publication, 170).
2. Lucian, " De dea Syria." 49.
3. Scholiast on Lucian " Jupiter Tragoedus." 8. p. 60. Ed. H. Rabe. (Leipsic 1906) (Vol. IV. p. 173. ed. c. Jacobitz).
   Hippolytus, " Refutatio ominum hæresium." V. 9. pp. 168, 170 Ed. Duncker and Schneidewin.
4. Diodorus Siculus III. 59. 7.
   H. Hepding, " Attis, seine Mythen und sein Kult." (Giessen 1903).
5. Hermesianax in Pausanias VII. 17.
6. Pausanias. VIII. 17.
7. Servius on Virgil, " Aen." IX. 115.

In his Rites, which were celebrated by the Romans at the shrine of Cybele at the Vatican, a figure of the God was hung on a tree on March 23rd in each year, but as we shall have to consider this primitive and barbarous form of the Fertility Rite in some detail later, here we need only emphasise the manner of his death, which unquestionably represents the way in which his human representatives died. It should also be noted that Set similarly cut off the male member of Osiris, which was swallowed by a fish, and in the Egyptian Story of the Two Brothers, the younger brother when falsely accused of having seduced his elder brother's wife cut off his male organ and flung it into the River Nile, where it was also swallowed by a fish.[1] Undoubtedly in " The Story of the Two Brothers " we have a distorted tradition of the old Fertility Rites, even the transmigration of the soul into a tree and its ultimate re-birth into human form being included.

The most usual method, however, seems to have included burning, though often we find that the victim was killed before being placed on the funeral pyre. It is this form of death which seems peculiarly associated with Melcarth or Moloch, for not only were victims burnt in his honour but the God himself, or at least his image, was annually burnt. If, therefore, the God himself was burnt we must not be surprised if we find traces of the same fate being meted out to his earthly representatives, even when they were Kings, although in latter years this ceremony was mitigated by permitting the King merely to walk through the fire.

Melcarth of Tyre was adopted by the Greeks under the name of Hercules. According to their fables when he felt the pain of the poisoned cloak eating into his flesh (which cloak, be it noted, was sent to him by his *wife* and donned by him when about to offer a sacrifice), he climbed on to a pyre and persuaded his friend to set fire to it. His soul then ascended in a cloud while the thunder crashed over head.[2] Although the version given by Sophocles states that the scene of his transference took place on Mount Oeta another account places it at Tyre, which is certainly in a sense more correct.[3] An annual festival held in January at Tyre commemorated this event, and was called, " The Awakening of Hercules."[4] We thus see that not only was there a dramatic representation of the *death* of the God but also of his *resurrection*.

1.   G. Maspero, " Popular Stories of Ancient Egypt." (London, 1915). p. 9.
2.   Sophocles, " Trachiniae." 1119 sq.
      Apollodorus, " Bibliotheca." II. 7. 7.
      Diodorus Siculus. IV. 38.
      Hyginus, " Fab." 36.
3.   S. Clementis Romani, " Recognitiones." X. 24. p. 233, ed. E. G. Gersdorf (Migne's Patrologia Graecia. I. 1434).
4.   Josephus, " Antiq. Jud." VIII. 5. 3. " Against Apion." 1. 18., also 2 Maccabees. IV. 18. 20, where, however, it is said to be held once in four years and was probably the same feast on a more splendid scale.

As is often the case, we must turn to Greek sources for a connected account of the life of this essentially Semitic God. Hercules,[1] though fathered by Zeus, had a human mother, and soon became famous for his enormous strength. Even when a tiny baby he strangled two huge snakes, an incident which no doubt points to his association with serpent worship, which is usually connected with Gods of Fertility. All the legends indicate that, coupled with superhuman strength, he possessed a peculiar and almost demoniacal temper, which at times turned into homicidal madness. He was closely associated with the lion, whose skin he wore, which together with his other peculiarities show that he, like other forms of the Deity in Syria, was originally a Lion God, and of a savage and blood-thirsty nature.

The chief incidents in his life, known to most of my readers, are the " Twelve Labours." The majority of these obviously refer to the passage of the sun through the signs of the Zodiac, more particularly in relation to the work and difficulties which the peasant farmer had to face during the various months of the year. Thus his slaying of the Erymantian Boar is but an allegory of the efforts needed from most farmers to destroy wild boars, which in primitive times did enormous damage to the growing crops. In similar manner his capture of the hind Cerunitis indicates another type of animal which prayed on the farmer's crops.

A careful study of the " Labours " shows that originally there were only ten, corresponding to the ancient year of ten,[2] not twelve, months. My readers are doubtless aware that in Mediterranean countries in ancient days the year originally consisted of only ten months, and it was the Roman King Numa who reformed the calendar and added two new ones, which henceforth bore the names of January and February. To this day the last month of the year is called December, which means the tenth, and not the twelfth. The change was due to the growth of more precise knowledge of the course of the sun and of astronomy and has left its traces in the legends of Hercules.

Tradition relates that the hard taskmaster of Hercules, Eurystheus, by a legal quibble refused to accept two of the original series, although he had only claimed ten labours, and insisted on two more as substitutes for those whose accomplishment he considered technically not complete.

Now these last two Labours, which are called the eleventh and twelfth, are of quite a different type from the others, and appear to be part of the traditional history of what befell Hercules after his death on the pyre. They were transferred to

---

1. See E. M. Berens, " The Myths and Legends of Ancient Greece and Rome." p. 234 sq.
2. See " Calendar," Encycl. Brit. 11th ed. Vol. 4. p. 989.

his mortal life in order to make two more Labours, corresponding with the new months, whose acceptance gradually spread Westward.

These two Labours really depict the journey of the dead hero through the Underworld, and on to the Isles of the Blest. The latter was a kind of earthly Paradise to which the souls of the heroes went, but it must not be confounded with Mount Olympus, the High Heavens, where only the Gods dwelt. Hercules was ultimately admitted into Olympus because of his divine soul, but according to Lucian his human soul remained with the other shades in the Isles of the Blest.[1]

This careful distinction between the divine and human souls of these God-men is important to us, as it explains how it was that the Divine Soul of the dying representative of Adonis *could* be transferred to a living successor.

The two episodes have not only been transferred to this world but have been transposed, a fact which still further disguises their true meaning. Taking therefore the Twelfth Labour first, we find Hercules was sent to carry off Cerberus from the Underworld. He was not content to do this only, but tried " to rescue the souls which were in bondage." Most great religions tell of some beneficent being who thus descended into the Underworld to aid those who were in anguish. The Christian Church specifically says it was Christ, while the Chinese Buddhists say that the Blessed Kwan Yin in like manner rescued those who were in Hell.

In the case of Hercules we seem to have a dim remembrance, therefore, of the descent of Melcarth, that is Tammuz, into the Underworld and of the alleviation which he brought to sufferers therein. Another interesting detail is that Hercules is said to have taken the precaution of being first initiated into the Eleusinian Mysteries, from whose priests he obtained the information necessary to enable him to enter in safety the awful regions of the dead.

He was then led by Hermes, the Conductor of the Dead, into the Underworld, and at the gates of Hades Hercules released Theseus from the torment he was in, and later Æsculapius. The King of the Underworld, 'Aides, tried to bar his path, but Hercules wounded him so sore that he was only too glad to grant his request, and so Hercules carried off Cerberus in triumph.

The eleventh Labour, which should have *followed* the above, was to fetch the golden apples from the Garden of the Hesperides. These represent the Isles of the Blest, and during this adventure, he was nearly offered up as a human sacrifice in Egypt. Ultimately, he obtained the apples through the help of the giant Atlas, but when they were laid on the altar of Pallas-Athene

---

1. Lucian, " Vera Historia."

significantly enough she wafted them back to the Isles of the Hesperides in the West.

The death of Hercules occurred in this manner. Hercules had married Deianeira after divorcing his first wife, but his wayward fancy caused him to look favourably on a third lady, Iole, or at any rate so Deianeira believed. When therefore he sent a message asking her to send him his sacrificial robes she poured on to the garments liquid from a phial, which she believed to be a love potion. It was, however, a deadly poison, and as soon as Hercules put on the robe the flames of the sacrificial fire caused the poison to penetrate into his flesh.

Unable to bear the agony, he climbed a funeral pyre which, at his earnest request, was fired by his friend Philoctetes. As the flames rushed upward a great cloud descended, the lightnings flamed across the sky, and, amid the roar of thunder, Pallas-Athene bore the demi-god to Heaven in her chariot. Here, as a token of reconciliation, his life-long enemy Hera bestowed on him the hand of her daughter Hebe, the Goddess of Eternal Youth.

In this Greek legend we have undoubtedly the main outline of the supposed career of Melcarth, save only that the descent into the Underworld, corresponding to the initiation Rite of being swallowed by a monster, should come after the burning. Then should come the journey to the Hesperides, and only thereafter the Ascent into Heaven. Unless, indeed, we prefer to regard the incidents of the Underworld and of the Hesperides as appertaining to the Human soul of the representatives of Melcarth, while the Divine soul ascended direct to Heaven from the funeral pyre.[a]

From the preceding summary of the life of Hercules we see that much therein is in striking analogy with Tammuz, and although the Greeks distinguished him from Adonis, this was, I suggest, because they failed to recognise that Melcarth and Tammuz were but different aspects of the same Semitic Deity. That Melcarth and Hercules are identical no scholars deny, and we can even trace the evolution of the Greek artistic conception of Hercules from certain sculptures of Melcarth which have been found in Cyprus.

At Gades, the modern Cadiz, in Spain, the Phoenicians annually burnt a gigantic figure of Melcarth, and there is abundant evidence to show that the custom was widespread.[1] In like manner at Tarsus, in Cilicia, Sandan, the Fertility God of that area, was annually burnt and by the Greeks he was identified with Hercules. Now as Sandan was the father of Cinyras of Cyprus, and grandfather of the ill-fated Adonis, it is extremely important

---

1. Frazer, Ibid. p. 113.   Pausanias. X. 4. 5.
(a) For a detailed description of the ancient beliefs concerning the " Geography " of the Underworld, of the Isles of the Blest, and the City of the Gods, see Ward, " The Hung Society," vol. 2.

to find that he was the same as Melcarth and that his statue was regularly burnt, for thereby we complete the tale of the fatal history of these early Priest-Kings, or God-men, the lovers of the Destroying Goddess, Astarte, who was alike the Great Mother and the Semitic Goddess of War.

At Tarsus the god Sudan was burnt in effigy[1] and the coins of the city show that the pyre rested on an altar with a figure of Sandan in the midst. An eagle perches on the top of the pyre and doubtless represents the soul of the god about to ascend to Heaven.[2] This latter detail is important and should be compared with the eagle which is being released by the Babylonian Deity on the seal depicting the descent of Tammuz, or Shamash, into the Underworld. Probably it was a real eagle which was released at the psychological moment, for this was certainly the procedure at the funeral of a Roman Emperor. At death, or sometimes before death, the Roman Emperors were Deified, and therefore when one died an effigy was solemnly cremated upright on a pyre, and at the same moment an eagle was let loose from the top of the pyre to symbolise the ascent of the Divine Soul of the Emperor to the abode of the Gods.

The chief symbol of Sandan was the axe, especially a double headed axe, which in general appearance looks very much like a gavel. We shall find this symbol elsewhere associated with the Syrian god of fertility, but before wandering further North let us retrace our steps towards Syria proper.

We thus see that the Syrians burnt their god annually. The exact reason for the custom is still a matter of question, but the most generally accepted view is that thereby they purified the god, by destroying his earthly body, or its substitute, so that his spirit might ascend pure and unsullied to the heavens, and thence re-incarnate in a new body.

The burning of an effigy is merely a substitute for the burning of a man, such substitutions taking place when civilisation had advanced sufficiently to make human sacrifices abhorrent to the majority. Moreover the custom is more reasonable if the figure represents the god-man himself. In brief, the king of the country represented the god of fertility and, like Tammuz, had annually to marry the Goddess, who was usually represented by one of her sacred women, although perhaps at a later date here

---

1.   Dio Chrysostom, " Or." XXXIII. Vol. 2. p. 16. ed. L. Dindorf. (Leipsic 1857).
     K. O. Muller, " Sandon und Sardanapal." Kunstarchæologische Werke III. 6 sq.
     Raoul-Rochette, " Sur l'Hercule Assyrien et Phénicien," " Memoires de l'Academie des Inscriptions, etc." XVII. Second pt. (Paris, 1848.) p. 178 sq.
2.   G. F. Hill, " Catalogue of the Greek Coins of Lycaonia, Isauria and Cilicia." (London 1900). p. 180 sq. Plates XXXIII. 2, 3. XXXIV, 10. XXXVII, 9.

also a statue was substituted. At such times there was a considerable amount of promiscuous intercourse among the worshippers, intended as sympathetic magic which would increase the fertility of the whole country.

As Tammuz was slain his human embodiment had also to be slain, and so the life of these Divine Kings would tend to be a short one. In practice, however, an annual slaying of the king had obvious disadvantages, not for the man, for primitive communities have but little regard for the feelings of the individual, but for the whole community. To meet this difficulty a tendancy grew up to appoint a substitute King for each year, dress him in the royal robes, crown him with the King's crown and treat him royally. At the end of his year of office this King was slain and another took his place.

Operative masons will at once perceive the similarity to their drama. Such substitute kings survived until quite recent times in Europe, although no longer subject to the fear of real death since this part resolved itself into play acting. Unquestionably the Lord of Misrule, who in England presided over the Christmas revels for twelve days, is the lineal descendant of the King Saturn, who was made king in mockery and killed in deadly earnest at the Saturnalia held by the Roman legionaries.

These substitutes for the king were probably of royal or semi-royal descent, children of his concubines or of the sacred women, but though for a time they might thus save their father there came a time when the real king himself had originally to follow the same cruel path. This was when his bodily strength, and especially his capacity to beget offspring, began to wane, and I shall give examples of the survival of this custom in some parts of the world to-day at a later stage in the book.

A familiar example to all students is the Priest-King at Nemi. Any man who could tear a bough of mistletoe from the oak tree which he guarded at Nemi could attack the Priest-king with impunity and if he succeeded in slaying him he became Priest-king in his stead, till he too went forth by the same road. To this day a similar custom exists among the " Devil Worshippers " of Kurdistan. The last chief was in open durbar murdered by his brother, who at once assumed the throne and was acknowledged as lawful ruler by the community.[1]

Thus there was an annual slaying of a substitute king and an occasional slaying of the real king. In the course of time both tragedies were modified, the former by a dramatic representation or by the substitution of a statue, as at Tarsus, the latter by allowing the king to walk *through* the fire instead of being burnt in it. No doubt once this substitution had become accepted there would be places where the king would do without any substitute

---

1. Dr. Wigram so informs me ; he was in the neighbourhood at the time.

and merely walk through the fire each year, as was the case at
Tyre, or else enact the whole drama, as occurred at Babylon.

That the Kings of Tyre did have to walk through the fire, we
learn from Ezekiel, and also that they claimed to be Gods.[1]

Such " walking the fires " still occur in India, Fiji and elsewhere, and while some of them seem to have evolved from a
different idea, namely from a desire to test the candidate's faith,
purity, etc., the conclusive evidence we possess that the Phoenicians burnt their god annually, and that their Kings claimed to be
divine, leaves no doubt that the fire walk of the king of Tyre was a
substitute for death by fire.

We have abundant evidence also that human victims were
regularly, at one time, sacrificed to Astarte. Even the Greeks
were guilty of this appalling custom. For example, men and
women were sacrificed to the Tauric Artemis, being first slain by
the sword and then burnt. Iphigenia had to do this horrible
work and her brother Orestes carried off the statue of the goddess
to Greece where, according to the legends, he established the
same terrible custom.[2]

No doubt the ashes of such victims were then scattered to the
four cardinal points of heaven so that they might fertilise the soil.
In India the dead are " burnt in honour of Shiva," whose title is
" He that Destroys." Their ashes are then scattered over the
waters of the Ganges, not in order that no remnant of so vile a
wretch may remain, but as a symbolic sacrifice to Mother Ganges.
In the Christian burial service the same idea survives, for the
Priest scatters a handful of earth on the coffin with the significant
words, " *Ashes to ashes, dust to dust.*"

As a result of our investigations we are compelled to believe
that originally the victims were hung on a tree, castrated and
allowed to bleed to death in order that their blood might fertilise
the soil. Then the corpse was burnt and the ashes scattered
over the field. Later, as in the example quoted from the Philippines, the body would be severed in twain and then subsequently
burnt. In connection therewith we must not forget what we have
already learnt, namely, that criminals often inherit as their
punishment the mode of sacrificing a victim, because in order to
expiate their offence against the angry god they were sacrificed to
him. If the penalty of hanging and drawing, i.e., disembowelling,
a culprit originated in the custom of sacrificing a victim to Odin
in that manner, similar cruel penalties no doubt can be traced
back to the same idea.

In India Vishnu is said to have taken on the form of a *lion*
in order to overthrow a terrible ogre, whom he slew by disembowelling him,[3] and in this lion incarnation he is often shown

---

1.   Ezekiel. 27. 14, 16.
2.   See Chapter VI. p. 90.
3.   Ward, " Freemasonry and the Ancient Gods." Illus. op. p. 244.

making a certain peculiar sign, namely, pointing with both hands to his stomach as if about to tear it open. The sign therefore shows that it was *Vishnu* who was originally disembowelled, and no doubt he, like Odin, sacrificed himself to himself. Vishnu indeed has many of the characteristics of Hiram Abiff, and probably he originally represented a god of vegetation, although as the Solar Cult evolved he came to represent the sun at its meridian. Nevertheless, he is still closely associated with the element of water, and also with corn. The Chinese likewise use this sign, and call it the sign of earth, a fact of obvious significance.

If you sever a hanging body at the waist the bowels will gush out, and it would seem that Judas Iscariot must have been similarly cut in half, otherwise how could he by hanging himself cause his bowels to gush forth. It would therefore appear as if at one period in the evolution of the Fertility Rites the representative of Tammuz was hung on a tree, his body severed at twain, his bowels torn out, and the body finally burnt to ashes at the centre of the Court of the Temple, on the Altar of sacrifice. That a more merciful death than that of being slowly burnt was granted to the victims offered to Astarte, we know from ancient records.

At Salamis, in Cyprus, despite the humanising influence of Greece, human sacrifices continued to be made up to the time of the Emperor Hadrian. They were offered in the " Month of Aphrodite " to Diomede, but he shared the sanctuary with Agraulus, said to be the daughter of Cecrops, but who no doubt really represented the ubiquitous Astarte, and originally the sacrifices were offered to her.

The man who was sacrificed doubtless represented Tammuz, disguised as Diomede at a later date, to whom ultimately the sacrifice was transferred. The manner of the man's death was as follows:—He was led or dragged by youths (perhaps with a halter round his neck) around the altar three times. He was then stabbed in the throat with a spear, and his body was afterwards burnt on a pyre.[1] The stabbing in the neck corresponds to the custom of cutting the throat of a ram for sacrifice, and perhaps the victim's three symbolic journeys were for the purpose of proving to the worshippers that he was a victim properly prepared.

We also know that when offering human sacrifices the Priests in Mexico cut open the breast of the victim and tore the heart therefrom,[2] and among the Romans, who had substituted animal for human sacrifices, the heart and the entrails were examined and from them the omens taken.

---

1. Porphyry, " De Abstinentia," ii. 54 sq.
   Lactantius, " Divin. Inst. 1. 2.
2. Prescott, " Conquest of Mexico." Ch. 3. ed. J. Foster (London 1885).
   Sahagun, " Hist. de Nueva-España," lib. 2.

Although the ordinary method of sacrificing included burning the body, there is good reason for believing that among the maritime races of the Mediterranean the body was thrown into the sea, as an offering to the Sea God, for Melcarth was also God of the Sea, and as such was worshipped by the Greeks under the name of Melicertes, and depicted riding on a dolphin. In confirmation of this view the evidence of Pausanias is important, for he says that when Cleon of Magnesia returned to Gades, from which he had been turned out while the Phoenicians were celebrating the burning of Hercules (Moloch), he found on the seashore the smouldering remains of a huge man of the sea.[1] Moreover, in Alexandria, after the period of mourning for Adonis was ended, the worshippers flung the figure of Adonis, or sometimes the head only, into the sea.[2] In like manner in India Maharam ends with the throwing of the replicas of the tombs into a lake. The object of such practices is to fertilise the sea, or lake, and make it produce large quantities of fish, which to many races is quite as important a source of food as is corn.

Some races, however, leave the victim to the birds of the air or the ravening beasts of the field as prey, in order that the animal life may multiply. Such races are usually at the nomadic and semi-hunting stage of civilisation. Even to-day in Tibet, when a man dies they literally cut him up and distribute his body among the vultures, wild dogs, etc., which gather round, well knowing what they will receive. The explanation now given is that the dead man thereby performs a meritorious deed in feeding his humbler brethren. Probably the Towers of Silence, whereon the Parsees leave their dead to be eaten by the vultures, likewise originated from similar rites.

Among the Mexicans the victim, whose heart had been torn out, was subsequently eaten by the human worshippers.[3] As a method of punishment the tearing out of the heart is world-wide, the culprit being left to rot on the gallows or to be devoured by wild beasts and birds. In mediæval England after being hanged a traitor was cut down whilst still alive: his heart and bowels were then torn out, the former being flung in his face. The body was afterwards divided by being quartered and the head struck off. The five portions which thus resulted were fixed in some conspicuous place, ostensibly as a warning to others; undoubtedly the original intention was that his remains should feed the fowls of the air, and, as we have already pointed out, the methods of punishing a criminal were originally the way in which victims were sacrificed to some God.

While we have definite traces of the practice of throwing the corpse into the sea, or alternatively of burning it, we cannot in

1. Pausanias. X. 4. 5.
2. Theocritus. XV.
3. Prescott, " The Conquest of Mexico." Ch. 3.

ASTARTE AND ADONIS IN SYRIA AND CYPRUS 53

Syria prove that the third method, viz., throwing it to the beasts, was also in vogue. In view, however, of the widespread nature of this practice elsewhere, we cannot help suspecting that it was also practised in the more remote and mountainous areas, such as Lebanon, where hunting would be the main source of food. Perhaps the savage custom, which grew up quite late in Roman history, of throwing men to the lions was adopted from some Asiatic religious rite. Indeed, the numerous stories we have which avowedly come from Asia, such as Daniel in the lions' den, compel us to believe that such a custom did survive there, for Melcarth was a Lion God. It is to the latter fact that we owe the name of the lion's grip, by which he, in the form of Tammuz, raised the souls of the victims from corruption to incorruption. All the above facts will prove of interest to masons.

Let us now see what we can learn concerning the Adonis Rites during the opening years of the Christian era, for thereby we may be able to gather a few more details as to what was taking place in Judea about the time Solomon was building his temple. At a later point in the book we shall see what the Bible itself tells us of the Jewish form of the Adonis Rite, which survived long after the days of Solomon, indeed, not only up to the conquest of Jerusalem by the Babylonians but even up to the time of Christ.

If we turn to the second century A.D. we find much more detailed information available concerning the cult of Adonis, but we must bear in mind that by the time of Lucian, our chief authority, the civilising influence of Greece had undoubtedly mitigated to some extent the primitive and savage nature of the Cult. Nevertheless, there still survived cruel customs which show that in an earlier period even more terrible scenes had been enacted.

Lucian tells us[1] that at Heirapolis, which has already been described, there were eunuch priests similar to those of Cybele and of Diana of Ephesus. The mourning for Tammuz occurred in the Spring, and the priests, worked up to a state of frenzy by the wild music of flutes and drums, slashed themselves so that the blood ran down, in order that it might fertilise the soil. At such times those desirous of entering the priesthood tore off all their clothing and, seizing one of the swords which stood ready, castrated themselves. Then, holding the bleeding fragments in their hands, they ran through the streets and flung them into the houses, whose owners had thereupon to supply each of them with a complete outfit of female clothing, which henceforward they always had to wear. It will be found that the method employed to dispose of the fragments differs from that used by the worshippers of Cybele at Rome.[2] No doubt it was considered that by thus giving to a

1. Lucian, " De dea Syria." 49-51.
2. See p. 69.

particular household the emblem of fertility the novice conferred on them the promise of a fertile and prosperous year. We are not specifically told how the householders disposed of the ghastly trophies, but from the analogous rites of Cybele we may justly assume that they buried them in their gardens as an offering to the Great Mother.

Repulsive as such scenes were, they were not restricted to Syria, and are not yet extinct in some parts of the world. The ancient Egyptian priests, according to Eustathius, similarly sacrificed their male member to their Gods,[1] and the curious story of " The Two Brothers," to which we referred earlier in the chapter, also describes a similar sacrifice. In this story the younger brother was approached by the wife of his elder brother with an improper proposal. He refused to do as she wished and so when her husband came home she told him that the younger brother had forced her. The elder brother thereupon went after his younger brother intending to kill him, but the latter escaped to the opposite side of the Nile, and then cutting off his male member flung it into the river. He next told his brother the truth and added that he was going to place his heart, or soul, in a certain acacia tree. When the acacia tree was afterwards cut down a chip flew into the mouth of the wife of his brother, and she conceived. In this manner the younger brother was reborn as her son.[2]

In this story we undoubtedly have a popular and distorted version of the myth of the fertility god and the great Mother, Isis, in its more primitive form, and unrefined by the priests. The similarity to the Osiris legend is emphasised in many points: for example, the male member of Osiris was swallowed by a fish, and in like manner the male member of the younger brother was also swallowed by a fish. In this story we thus have not only the self-castration of the hero but also the transference of his soul to an acacia tree, and finally, his rebirth in the womb of the Great Mother, for it is she that the wicked and treacherous wife represents.

But this custom of sacrificing the male organ to the Great Mother was still in existence in Africa up to the 20th century. Among the Ekoi of South Nigeria, at the annual festival which was celebrated with a view to producing a bountiful harvest, men were similarly castrated and allowed to die from loss of blood.[3][a]

---

1. Eustathius (on Homer, " Iliad." XIX. 254. p. 1183.)
2. G. Maspero " Popular Stories of Ancient Egypt " (London 1915). p. 9 sq.
3. P. Amaury Talbot, " In the Shadow of the Bush " (London 1912). pp. 74 sq.
(a) There appears to be evidence that women were also sacrificed in a similar way. No doubt in honour of an Ekoi Persephone or Corn Maiden.

One case is quoted by Mr. Talbot[1] in which a man, at the season of the Yam planting, cut off his male member. In the Congo youths are castrated to fit them to become priests of the prevailing phallic cult, and in some villages these youths perform a curious mad dance at the New Year Moon. During this a white cock, whose wings have been clipped, is thrown into the air and when it falls to the ground the eunuchs pluck it alive. Formerly a human being was thrown into the air and then torn to pieces,[2] thus irresistibly reminding us of the death of Orpheus, torn to pieces by the Bacchanals. The similarity between these black priests and the Galli of Syria is obvious. Moreover, the circumcision of initiates, which is an almost universal feature of primitive initiation rites, is only a modification of the same sacrifice. The connection of this practice with that of the Operative Masons, who used to fasten the loop of a running noose attached to a cord round the whole virile member, is obvious and will be considered in detail in the next chapter.

Although the Greeks modified the rites of Adonis, we must not forget that their own legends indicate quite clearly that at one time human sacrifices were offered even in Greece, and the modification of the Adonis cult must therefore be fairly late.

To the wailing of flutes the God was lamented, mostly by the women, who mourned over an image which was made to look like a corpse. This " Corpse " was then carried in solemn procession as if for burial, but instead of being placed in the earth was thrown into the sea or, if more convenient, into a stream or pool.[3] The resurrection of the god was celebrated soon after, sometimes on the next day.[4] The close association between his marriage with the Great Goddess and his death is well brought out in the account extant of what occurred at Alexandria, in Egypt, where his cult survived into the 5th century A.D. At this city figures of Adonis and Aphrodite were placed on two couches surrounded by cakes, fruit, and plants in pots, while they were overshadowed by bowers made of greenery. The marriage of the pair was cele-

---

1. Letter from Mr. Talbot quoted by Frazer, " Adonis, Attis, Osiris," p. 270, note 2.
2. A. H. Johnston, " The Races of the Congo." Journal of the Anthrop. Inst. XIII. (1884) p. 473.
3. Eustanthius on Homer " Od." XI. 590.
   Zenobius, " Centur." 1. 49.
   Plutarch, " Alcibiades." 18 and " Nicias." 13.
   Athenæus IV. 76.
   Polux. IV.
4. Lucian, " De dea Syria," 6.
   Origen, " Selecta in Ezechielem " (Migne's Patrologia Græca XIII. 800).
   Jerome, " Commentar. in Ezechielem." VIII. 13, 14. (Migme's Patrologia Latina. XXV. 82. 83).
   Cyril of Alexandria, " In Isaiam." lib. ii. tomus. III (Migne's Patrologia Græca. LXX. 441).

brated on one day and on the next the corpse of Adonis was borne
by a weeping crowd, who flung it into the sea. According to some
versions it was only the head which was thrown into the sea,
perhaps the rest of the body did not exist and consisted only
of clothes draped over a few sticks. The worshippers, however,
consoled themselves with the belief that Adonis would soon
rise from the dead.[1]

At Byblos, in like manner, the people wailed for Adonis, but
the next day he was supposed to rise from the dead and ascend to
Heaven in the presence of the worshippers,[2] amid their rejoic-
ing. How this was simulated we do not know, but probably
it was by the setting free of an eagle. This Phoenician festival
took place in the spring, when the waters of the river Adonis
turned red, an event which occurred in February or March.[3]

One legend connected with the death of Adonis is that
Aphrodite, when she saw him wounded by the boar, rushed to
his aid and accidentally trod on a spray of white roses, whose
thorns tore her feet, the blood from which dyed the roses red.
In this pretty story we have, of course, a reference to the white
rose of virginity being changed into the red rose of the married
woman.

In Greece, however, the festival was held about midsummer,[4]
the difference in time probably being explained by the fact that in
Phoenicia Adonis was peculiarly identified with the barley, and
the barley harvest in that country falls in March.   In Greece, on
the other hand, the wheat harvest occurs in June, and it is with
this that Adonis is associated.

At Antioch the festival coincided with the rising of Venus,
the star of Astarte, in the East at dawn, that is when Venus
became " that bright morning star whose coming brings peace and
salvation " to the human race, by proclaiming that Adonis has
arisen from the grave. We know this fact because Ammianus
tells us that the Emperor Julian entered Antioch at this period
and that as he approached the city the lamentations changed into
rejoicings, which he seems to have taken as meant for himself,
thus arrogating to himself the praises of Adonis.[5]

As Adonis represents the god of vegetation it is not surprising
to find that according to some accounts he was born from the
trunk of a myrrh tree, whose bark split to enable him to come
forth. He is said to have lain within it for ten months, and the
number corresponds with the ten days which is often said to

1. Theocritus. XV.
2. Lucian, Ibid. 6.
    F. C. Novers, " Die Phoenizier." I. 243 sq.
3. H. Maundrell, in Bohn's " Early Travels in Palestine." ed. Th. Wright
    (London 1848), pp. 411 sq., also Renan, " Mission de Phenice,"
    p. 283.
4. Frazer, " Adonis, Attis, Osiris." p. 227, quoting Plutarch.
5. Ammianus Marcellenus. XXII. 9. 15.

elapse during the journey of a soul through the Underworld. For example, Dante took ten days to pass through Hell, Purgatory and Heaven, and the same number of days is required in the ritual of the Hung Society for the Hung Heroes to perform their mystical journey to the Holy city. Therefore ten, instead of nine, months indicates that he was journeying through the Underworld, and in the festival of Maharam the fasting for Hussain and Hussan, is for ten days likewise. The use of myrrh both for incense and for embalming also means that he was reborn after death, while the fact that he was reborn from a tree not only indicates his special connection with vegetation but also that his soul passed into a tree, and thus explains the important part a branch played in the Jewish ceremonies, and in masonry to-day. The Jews sniffed this branch because in it was the soul of Adonis, which was thus transferred to the man who sniffed it.

In many areas the cult of the vegetation god is blended with a kind of All-Hallows E'en, and the souls of the human dead are propitiated at the same time as the slain god is lamented. It is thus easy to understand how men might draw the conclusion that as the vegetation god was slain and rose again, being present in every plant and animal, so likewise the dead did not perish utterly. Like him they passed into the plants which grew from their graves, there awaited an opportunity of entering once more into the womb of some woman, and in this manner returned to human life.

This belief is well brought out in the story given in Virgil of how Aeneas discovered that Polydorus had been murdered[1] when he plucked the branch of a shrub, but as we shall give the story in full in chapter XXI, it need not detain us here. All we need note is that it shows that the souls of the dead were supposed to pass into the trees. One interesting custom connected with these beliefs was that the women used to plant seeds in pots and tend them for eight days. These they called "gardens of Adonis," and they were charms to promote the growth of vegetation in Spring. At the end of the eight days they were thrown into the sea or river with the figure of Adonis. Similar ceremonies still exist in various parts of the world, especially in India,[2] but for us their chief interest lies in the fact that they survived in Europe and have been transferred to St. John in Summer. In Sardinia,[3] for example, these gardens are still made, and even to-day their destruction is accompanied by the notes of the flute, whose age-long association with Tammuz has previously been

---

1. Virgil, " Aen." 3. 19 sq.
2. Mrs. J. C. Murray-Aynsley, " Secular and Religious Dances." (Folklore Journal V. 1887). pp. 253 sq.
   Baboo Ishuree Dass, " Domestic Manners and Customs of the Hindoos of Northern India." (Benares 1860) pp. 111 sq.
3. Tenant, " Sardinia and its Resources." (London 1885) p. 187.

shown. Similar customs are observed in Sicily, and it is worth noting that one of the favourite plants is Basil,[1] which explains the origin of Coleridge's Poem on the " Pot of Basil."

Other ceremonial actions associated with Adonis and the cult of vegetation have also been transferred to St. John. For example, the midsummer fires, ceremonial bathing on St. John's Day, and the like.[2] We thus begin to see why Freemasonry is also closely associated with the two St. Johns.

A custom which still survives in Scotland brings out this point admirably. At Melrose on Midsummer's Eve the local masonic lodges gather amid the ruins of Melrose Abbey and go in procession bearing torches in their hands. When they reach the chancel they turn down these torches and beat them out on the ground. Here we have a dim remembrance of a custom which is specifically recorded of the Eleusinian mysteries, wherein a torch was " turned down " to imply the death and descent of Persephone into the Underworld, and another was pointed upward to remind the initiates of her resurrection.

It is, however, well to remember that the cult of the vegetation god was, and is, far more widely spread than was the cult of the individual god Adonis, although this fact does not affect the other arguments I shall set forth to show that Freemasonry is a descendant of the Adonis cult.

To return to Palestine, Jerome has a pregnant passage in which he says that Bethlehem had a grove sacred to Adonis, where the women wept for Tammuz even at the time of the birth of Christ.[3] Moreover, Bethlehem means, " The House of Bread,"[4] a name peculiarly appropriate to a place sacred to Tammuz, the corn god. The evidence of Jerome that the Tammuz cult survived even up to this day in the very heart of Palestine is important to us, as it shows that the local population had not even then lost their devotion to the old cult, despite the apparent triumph of monotheism, and suggests that the Essenes, whose secret rites we shall consider later, must have known of Adonis.

At Antioch, as we have seen, the festival of Adonis took place when Venus rose as a morning star, and at Aphaca, in Lebanon, it commenced when a certain meteor fell each Spring, which meteor was identified with Astarte.[5]

---

1. G. Pitre, " Usi e Costumi, Credenze e Presuidizi del Popolo Siciliano. (Palermo 1889) ii. 271-278.
2. Frazer, " Adonis, Attis, Osiris," pp. 246-249.
3. Jerome, " Epist." LVIII. 3. (Migne's Patrologia Latina XXII. 581).
4. G. A. Smith, s.v. " Bethlehem," Encycl. Biblica. 1. 560.
   Frazer, " Adonis, Attis, Osiris." p. 257.
5. Zosimus, " Hist." I. 58.
   Sozomenus, " Hist. Eccles." II. 5. (Migne's Patrologia Græca LXVII. 948).

Thus we find that the cult of Adonis not only dealt with death and resurrection, but its hero was murdered and the annual celebration started when a certain bright star appeared in the East at dawn. Further, we have seen that certain fragments of this cult still survive as popular customs in Europe to this day. This being so there is nothing impossible in a reformed version of it taking refuge in Freemasonry.

CHAPTER V

THE DYING GOD IN ASIA MINOR

A god of fertility corresponding with Tammuz is found throughout Asia Minor associated with the Great Mother. The most famous forms of these Deities are Cybele and Attis, who are essentially the same as Adonis and Astarte. It is convenient, however, to distinguish the two cults, because while that of Adonis, under the humanising influence of the Greeks, tended more and more to lose its primitive savage aspect, the Attis cult, which was adopted by the Romans, retained almost to the end primitive features which, though extremely repulsive to us, are of value to science as indicating the original meaning of many "fertility customs," which in their refined form are almost unintelligible.

In Asia Minor we also find intermediate forms of the cult, half way between the primitive Attis cult and the Hellenised Adonis Rites, and hints, in the form of ancient rock sculptures, of days when the " Fertility Cult " was even more barbarous than it was in the form in which it survived under the name of Attis-Cybele.

One feature which strikes us forcibly when studying these ancient rock sculptures of a long forgotten race is that they are usually found at the head of a rocky ravine, near to a fall of water, amid the most beautiful scenery. The sites correspond in a remarkable manner with those associated with Adonis in Syria, especially with that of Aphaca. The one at Boghaz-Keui may be taken as characteristic of the others, and practically constitutes a Lodge room, whose walls are the precipitous sides of the ravine and whose roof is the vault of Heaven. Indeed, we are again and again reminded of an old Masonic saying that Lodges were formerly held under the vault of Heaven, on the highest hill or in the lowest valley, where never dog barked nor cock crew; that is to say, far away from human habitation.

When we turn to the great Hittite sculptures at Boghaz-Keui, although we can feel sure that he is the fertility god, we do not know by what local name he was called. Boghaz-Keui means " The Village in the Defile," and stands at the mouth of a gorge on the banks of a small tributary of the Halys. It is in north west Cappadocia, and immediately behind it rises the fortifications of a once mighty city, whose very name has perished.[a] These walls, fourteen feet thick, are broken at intervals by gates, that in the south being flanked by two huge

(a) Frazer considers it was Pteria which Croesus, King of Lydia, captured during his wars with Cyrus. See " Herodotus I. 76, and Frazer, " Adonis, Attis, Osiris." I. p. 128.

60

stone lions. It is strange how again and again we find the lion associated with the dying god. As we shall see later, this was because he was a lion god, begotten of a lion goddess, and it is not the least remarkable feature of the masonic ceremonies that a certain method of clasping hands is termed the " lion's grip."

It is, however, the sanctuary which is about a mile and a half away which chiefly interests us. " Here among the grey limestone cliffs there is a spacious natural chamber or hall of roughly oblong shape, roofed only by the sky, and enclosed on three sides by high rocks. One of the short sides is open and through it you look out on the broken slopes beyond . . . . The length of the chamber is about 100 feet, its breadth varies from 25 to 50 feet. A nearly level sward forms the floor. On the right hand side, as you face inwards, a narrow opening in the rock leads into another but much smaller chamber, or rather corridor, which would seem to have been the inner sanctuary or Holy of Holies." [1]

On the walls of the larger chamber two processions are sculptured in relief. On the left wall are men and on the right women. The processions meet at the short end opposite the gap, and each is headed by an appropriate group. A bearded Hittite god is carried at the head of the men's procession, his feet resting on the heads of two men; he carries in his right hand a mace and in his left a curious symbol, a kind of trident, on which rests an oval with a cross bar. Behind him is a similar figure, representing either a High Priest or another god, but his feet rest on what are either two mountain tops or else fir cones. The objects in question remind us of the similar mountains or fir cones between which Shamash, or Tammuz, is sinking, as depicted on the Babylonian seal. In his right hand he holds a mace like the other Deity, but in his left he holds aloft a sword. Is he the executioner ?

The female procession is led by a goddess who stands on a *lioness*, and in her right hand she holds out her symbol to touch that of the male deity. Her symbol seems to consist of a short branch, with four side twigs cut off and surmounted by an oval with a cross bar. No doubt this symbol corresponds with the systrum of Isis, and represents the vesica piscis crossed by the phallus.

Beneath the outstretched arms of the god and goddess appear the forequarters of two goats, a fact which suggests that the popular association of the goat with modern Freemasonry may have some solid tradition behind it. The animals wear on their heads the conical Hittite cap, which suggests that, like the bull in the Orphic Rites, they may have been dressed up to represent men. We cannot, however, say definitely, that this was so, for the rest of their bodies are covered by those of the deities.

---

1.   Frazer, " Adonis, Attis, Osiris."   I. p. 129.

Just behind the goddess, and constituting the only male in the procession of women, is a smaller male figure, standing, like her, on a lioness or panther. Now the panther or lion was constantly associated with Bacchus, the Asiatic fertility god adopted by the Greeks, and there is even a legend that on one occasion he transformed himself into a lion in order to destroy some men who had carried him off captive in a ship.[1] On this occasion he was also supported by a mysterious bear, and as this was one of the early forms of Astarte we see that Bacchus represents Tammuz, and may even be the direct Hellenistic form of this Hittite divinity.

In this sculpture the youthful priest, or god, holds a *double-headed axe* in his left hand, which reminds us of the symbol of Sandan and of the masonic gavel. In his right he holds a rod, which ends in an " Armless doll, with the symbol of the cross-barred oval instead of a head,"[2] which, of course, indicates his close connection with the two fertility deities. He is undoubtedly the son and lover of Astarte, while the bearded deity represents Moloch, or the god in his aspect of the former lover.

Behind the young man are two goddesses, both standing on the same double-headed eagle, an emblem which at once calls to mind the double-headed eagle of the 30th degree, or Knights Kadosh. As the kadosh, or sacred men and women, were peculiarly associated with the worship of Astarte and Adonis, we cannot lightly brush aside this interesting detail. Neither can we forget that at the burning of Sandan, or Hercules, in Asia Minor an eagle was released from the top of the pyre to symbolise the ascent of the divine soul to Heaven.[a]

In the inner sanctuary there is a procession of twelve men, who may symbolise the twelve signs of the zodiac, and three other figures, making *fifteen* in all. It is the three other figures, however, to which we must direct our attention. The first is a colossal sculpture of a God with a man's head, the body being composed of four lions, while the legs from the knees downward form a huge dagger. The face is beardless and reminds us of the young god standing on the lioness in the outer hall.

This being is the son and lover of Astarte, depicted in his ancient animal form, a form which was doubtless shown only to the priests and initiates. While to the outside world he was represented in human shape, here in the inner sanctuary the terrible truth was revealed that Tammuz was half beast and half man. The dagger formed by his legs reminds us that in some initiation rites a dagger plays an important part at the admission of a novice.

---

1.   E. H. Berens, " The Myths and Legends of Ancient Greece and Rome."   p. 127.
2.   Frazer, " Adonis, Attis, Osiris."   I. p. 131.
(a)   The same feature is depicted on the Babylonian seal.

The other two figures seem to constitute a commentary on the larger figure, and are sculptured in a special recess. The larger clearly represents the son of Astarte in a similar form to that in which he appears in the outer chamber. With his right hand, in which he holds the symbol of the armless doll, he points towards the colossal sculpture, and his left is placed lovingly round the neck of a smaller male figure as if comforting or protecting him.

The smaller figure in Frazer's opinion is a priest-king.[1] His left hand holds a crozier and the wrist of his right is clasped by the left hand of the god. In the upper corner of the design is a winged disc resting on two Ionic columns. In this latter symbol we perceive a similarity to the pillars which stood outside the doors of the Temple of Jerusalem, between which the twenty-five elders looked out towards the East, watching for the sun to rise, the symbol of the resurrection of Tammuz.

Frazer considers that the bearded deity is distinct from Tammuz and represents the thunder god, although he admits that formerly he considered him to be the same. I venture to think, however, that his original view was correct, and the points which seem to tell against this view are explicable in the following way. In my opinion the bearded god represents Moloch, and Moloch himself was simply Tammuz in Heaven. Tammuz, on the other hand, represented the god incarnate, in the flesh and on earth. We might almost say that Moloch was God the Father, and Tammuz, God the Son, but that in essence they were the same. Therefore the bearded god represents the Father coming to greet His Son at the moment when the latter is about to lose his relationship of son to the Goddess by becoming her spouse, and so by the subsequent death of his body ascend into heaven, where he will be one with the Father.

If this view is correct it explains the burning of Moloch, or Sandan, a bearded deity. It also explains the presence of the same deity at the wedding of the son Tammuz, who is mystically the same as himself. On the other hand, if the bearded deity is an entirely different god, why is he depicted as present at the nuptials of Astarte with her own son, and why is he bearing the same symbol as that son ? To me this sculpture clearly indicates the difference between, and also the essential oneness of, Moloch and Tammuz, neither are we obliged to deny to this bearded deity the attributes of the thunder god. In the Greek legends Hercules, though a lion god and a fertility god, ascends to heaven in a clap of thunder. As thunder is usually associated with heavy rain, and rain is naturally associated with the fertility god, there is no unsurmountable difficulty in connecting the risen Tammuz, who dwells in Heaven, with the thunder, without losing sight of the

---

1. Frazer, " Adonis, Attis, Osiris." I. p. 131.

fact that both aspects are essentially the same. Tammuz incarnate on earth is doomed to die in order that men may live,
and when he ascends to heaven amid the roar of thunder becomes
Moloch and sends down the rain. Thus the two male figures in
the outer chamber are the same deity, and yet represent the Past
and the Present, the Father and the Son, the Eternal and the
Mortal aspects of the same Being.

The goddess is unquestionably the Great Mother, and her
head-dress, which is very similar to the turreted crown of Cybele,
suggests that the Hittite form was similar to Cybele.[1] Her lions
also support this view, for Cybele was usually depicted in a car
drawn by lions. The lion was likewise closely associated with
the Syrian Astarte, particularly in her form of Atargaetis at
Hierapolis-Bambyce,[2] where also she wore a turreted crown.
Furthermore, in Babylonia the Great Mother was depicted with
lions standing on her knees,[3] and by the Greeks was identified
with Rhea.

The beardless youth on the lion is Tammuz in his aspect of
Son and lover of the Great Mother,[4(a)] and his " blood relationship " is shown by the fact that, like the mother, he stands on a
lion and bears the emblem of the bearded god. This scene
represents the marriage of Tammuz and Astarte, but that in the
Holy of Holies points to the impending tragedy which follows the
marriage. Tammuz is pointing out to his priest his true form,
i.e., the lion monster. As Frazer adopts this view it appears as
if he has forgotten the strength of his objection to their being two
representations of the same god in the same scene! Tammuz is
preparing his priest to play his part in some religious ceremony.
What was the Rite which required all the courage of the priest-
king and all the help he could obtain from his god ? Frazer gives
it in words which can never, I think, be bettered. " He seems to
be leading his minister onward, comforting him with the assurance
that no harm can come near him while the divine arm is around
him and the divine hand clasps his. Whither is he leading him ?
Perhaps to death. The deep shadows of the rocks which fall
on the two figures in the gloomy chasm may be an emblem
of darker shadows soon to fall on the priest. Yet still he grasps
his pastoral staff and goes forward, as though he said; —' Yea,

1. Lucretius. II. 600 sq.
    Catullus. LXIII. 76 sq.
2. Lucian, " De dea Syria." 31.
3. Diodorus Siculus. II. 9. 5.
4. Frazer, " Adonis, Attis, Osiris." I. p. 137.
    Sir W. M. Ramsay, " Journal of the Royal Asiatic Society." N.S. XV.
        (1883) pp. 118-120.
    Prof. J. Garstang, " The Land of the Hittites " p. 235.
    G. Perrot et Ch. Chipiez, " Historie de l'Art dans l'Antiquité." IV. 651.
(a) Prof. Perrot considers that the youth and the bearded god are the same,
     and so supports the view I adopt.

though I walk through the valley of the shadow of death, I will fear no evil; for thou art with me; thy rod and thy staff they comfort me'."[1]

We know that in many parts of the Near East there were lines of priest-kings who represented the god Tammuz and who on assuming office lost their personal names in his. Thus, at Pessinus, in Phrygia, the priest of Cybele was called Attis; so was her high priest at Rome; the priests of Sabazus were called Saboi; the worshippers of Bacchus, Bacchoi. Such priest-kings, moreover, wore the regalia of the gods they served.[2]

There can, therefore, be little doubt that in this great Lodge room, roofed with the canopy of Heaven, at stated intervals the terrible scene of the slaying of the man-god was enacted in grim earnest. We can picture that great rock-guarded temple thronged with worshippers worked up to a mad Bacchic frenzy, such as that which, according to the Greeks, led the Mother and Sister of *King* Pentheus of Thebes to tear him limb from limb.[3] In that case we are specifically told that the mob consisted solely of women, and perhaps therein we may see that these Bacchantes represented the sacred women of Astarte, who were supposed to be inspired directly by her. If so, here again we have evidence that originally the death of Tammuz was due to the Great Mother herself.

Let us try and picture the scene:—the great towering rock wall, the level sward, crowded with frenzied worshippers, and from between the monster guarded gates of the inner sanctuary there comes forth a solitary human figure. He is clad in the royal robes of the Divine King. In his right hand is his pastoral staff and in his left he raises aloft the symbol of his high office.

The conch shells blow up, the flutes wail and the notes of the tum-tums roll and reverberate from wall to wall of the canon. Women, with hair streaming wildly behind them, dance to the clash of cymbals, while from a thousand throats peal the words of an age-old litany. Faster and faster beat the drums, wilder and wilder whirl the dancers, as the crowd closes round that small, lone figure. Now is he lost to sight, mercifully lost to sight, so far as we are concerned, and we can only guess what is happening. Was he dead before they tore him limb from limb ? And did we really see three men, more humane than the rest, armed with heavy wooden hammers, strike him down ? We cannot say, for the dust of three thousand years covers worshippers and sacrifice alike with its all-obliterating pall.

Like a mirage the scene vanishes, and we are alone on the grassy level sward. The sun shines brightly from an azure sky,

1. Frazer, " Adonis, Attis, Osiris,"   I. p. 139.
2. Ibid, p. 141.
3. E. M. Berens, " Myths and Legends of Ancient Greece and Rome,"
       p. 127.

and a bird trills its song of praise to the King of Kings, while slowly overhead, so high above us that it seems but a tiny speck, an eagle floats by, and brings to mind another eagle which was once released from the top of a pyre whereon a god was burnt. And as we meditate on the strange scene which has risen before our eyes we recollect that the sculptures on this strange temple were carven by men who lived, and died, long years before King Solomon raised his temple at Jerusalem.

Let us now turn away from Boghaz-keui and consider Cybele and Attis, who are, indeed, merely Astarte and Adonis under another name, but whose rites retained their more primitive and savage form almost to the end, and thus form an historical link with the scene depicted at the former place.

This cult took its rise in Phrygia, and Attis was the name given to the god of vegetation whose death and resurrection were annually celebrated each Spring.[1] Even the ancients often identified him with Adonis,[2] and therein they were correct. He was a shepherd who was loved by Cybele, the Great Mother, and according to some accounts he was her son.[3] In any case his Mother was called Nama, which merely means, " mother," and thus indicates that she was the Great Mother. She was said to be a virgin and conceived because she placed a pomegranate, or alternatively an almond, in her bosom. We have already seen that primitive races believe that the soul of the dead enter a tree or plant, and if the flower or fruit of such a tree falls on a woman she will conceive, even if she be a virgin.

The pomegranate has been regarded as the symbol of plenty, or, rather, of fertility, among most ancient nations of the Near East, and it will be remembered that rows of pomegranates adorned the chapiters of the two pillars of King Solomon's temple. It also seems to be the fruit which the goddess is dropping into the grave into which Shamash or Tammuz is descending. Furthermore, the pomegranate played an important part in the myth of the kindred cult at Eleusis, for it was because Persephone had swallowed a few seeds of a pomegranate that she had to remain for part of each year in the Underworld with 'Aides. We thus see that this fruit typifies the seed of any kind of vegetation which is buried in order that mother earth may bring forth the harvest.

1. Diodorus Siculus. III. 59. 7.
   Firmicus Maternus, " De errore profanarum religionum." 3 and 22.
   H. Hepding, " Attis, seine Mythen und sein Kult."
   Hippolytus, " Refutatio omnium hæresium." V. 9.   p. 168. ed. L.
       Duncker & E. G. Schneidewin (Gottingen, 1859).
2. Socrates, " Historia Eccles." III. 23. 51 sq.
3. Scholiast on Lucian, " Jupiter Tragoedus." 8. p. 60. ed. H. Rabe
       (Leipsic 1906).
   Hippolytus, Ibid. V. 9. p. 168.

The almond tree plays an important part in the Phrygian myths of the creation, for according to Pausanias it was the father of all things,[1] and so typifies the " First seed." The name Attis deserves attention, for he was also called " Papa," " Father," which shows that he was father as well as son, and in a sense father of all life. This title " Papa " was used also by his high priest and seems to be the origin of the title of the Pope, for the great centre of the Attis-Cybele cult at Rome was on the Vatican. Thus his mother's name was " Mother," and his own " Father," and he was the Father, the Son and the Lover.

There are two versions of his death, one being that he was slain by a boar.[2] This is undoubtedly late, and was probably adopted from the Greek form of the Adonis cult. No doubt the boar was supposed to be the slayer of the corn god because of the great damage done by wild pigs to the crops of primitive races. The other story is allegorically nearer the truth, though no doubt in its present form it was invented to explain the custom of the Galli, or priests of Cybele, who castrated themselves. As the priests, however, did not regularly die from the wound, we can see that this custom was in itself a modified survival of the custom of sacrificing a man by castrating him and then allowing him to bleed to death, as already suggested.

This version of his death is that he castrated himself under a pine tree and bled to death,[3] and from his blood sprang up the violets. This latter detail explains a curious superstition still current in some parts of England, namely, that you must not give violets to a friend, for if you do you will be parted from him or her. How this fragment of the Attis cult reached England we will not now discuss, but the meaning is clear enough. If Attis by his death was separated from his beloved, the flowers which sprang from his blood as a result would naturally lead to separation. This is the regular line of argument followed in sympathetic magic. Servius,[4] however, says that the wound from which he died was *not* self-inflicted, although otherwise his version is that he was castrated. The original story was, in my opinion, that the Great Mother in her ecstasy tore from him the male member, as does the Queen Bee. Hence the name " King Bee " which was given to the chief Galli at Ephesus, himself a Eunuch, was particularly appropriate. After his death Attis was transformed into a pine tree.[5] In this detail we see the old belief that the souls of the dead migrated into plants which grew

---

1. Pausanias. VII. 17.
2. Pausanias, Ibid.
3. Arnobius, " Adversus Nationes." V. 5 sq.
4. Servius upon Virgil, " Aen." IX. 115.
   Franz Cummout, " Les Religions Orientales dans le Paganisme Romain."
        (Paris 1909). pp. 77, 113, 335.
5. Ovid, " Metam " X. 103 sq.

from their grave, which belief explains the important part which a branch played in the Jewish cult at Tammuz, and the Sprig of Acacia in another legend.

The cult of Cybele was brought to Rome in April, B.C. 204 from Pessinus in Phrygia, and a small black stone, her emblem, was installed in a temple on the Palatine.[1] This stone was used to form the face of the idol,[2] the rest of the figure being made of precious metals. It is significant that like the Queen of Sheba and the " Lady " in the Song of Solomon, Cybele, was thus represented as black and to this day in India, Kali, who undoubtedly represents the savage aspects of the Great Mother, is likewise painted black and is even called the " Black Goddess." No doubt the colour chosen is intended to represent the colour of the earth, and later of the Underworld.

One of the objects aimed at by those who introduced the worship of Cybele is shown by the statement of Pliny, that the harvest which followed her arrival was the most abundant Rome had ever had.[3]

The Rites as celebrated in Rome during the time of the Emperors were as follows:—On March 22nd a pine tree was cut down and brought into the shrine of Cybele by a special guild of " Tree-Bearers." The stem was wrapped with woollen bands as if it were a corpse[a] and decorated with wreaths of violets, the sacred flower of Attis, while to the middle of the trunk an image of Attis was fastened.[4] This completed the ceremonies of the first day. On March 23rd the festival was formally proclaimed by trumpets,[5] which were ceremonially purified.

March 24th was well named the " Day of Blood." It began by the High Priest drawing blood from his arms and offering it as a sacrifice to Attis, whose name the High Priest always bore. The worshippers worked themselves up into a state of frenzy, stirred by the wild music and still wilder dancing of the priests, who gashed themselves with knives till the blood flowed, and poured it out on the sacred tree and on the altar.[6]

But the most ghastly scenes were when those who were about to enter the Priesthood, seizing the swords which stood ever ready,

1.   Livy XXIX. chs. 10, 11, and 14.
     Ovid, " Fasti." IV. 259 sq.
     Herodian. II. 11.
2.   Arnobius, " Adversus Nationes." VII. 49.
3.   Pliny, " Nat. Hist." XVIII. 16.
4.   Julian, " Orat." V. 168. p. 218. ed. F. C. Hertlein (Leipsic 1875).
     Arnobius, " Adversus Nationes." V. chs. 7, 16, 39.
     Firmicus Maternus, " De errore." 27.
     Joannes Lydus, " De mensibus." IV. 41.
     H. Hepding, " Attis." pp. 147 sq.
5.   Julian. Ibid. 168.
6.   Trebillius Pollio, " Claudius." 4.
     Tertullian, " Apologeticus." 25.
(a) Compare with the "wrapping" of the tree trunk by Isis at Byblos; see p.91

castrated themselves and hurled the bleeding fragments against the image of Cybele. These emblems of fertility were afterwards buried either in Mother earth or else in subterranean chambers sacred to Cybele.[1] In this last detail we have conclusive evidence of the underlying belief that the Great Mother needed the male organ of her lovers to fertilise herself, and, through her, all nature, and that it was therefore she herself who annually slew her mate, whether he was called " Attis," Adonis, or by some other name. Indeed, the legend of the begetting of Attis bears out this view, for we are told that his mother conceived because she placed in her bosom a pomegranate which sprung from the severed genitals of a semi-human monster called Agdestis, who was, of course, the double of Attis, just as Melcarth was of Tammuz.[2]

Similar scenes occurred at Hierapolis and also at Ephesus, and a like sacrifice until recently was still required in Nigeria, the Congo, and elsewhere. Is not the peculiar method of leading in a candidate formerly adopted in an Operative Lodge a modification of the same ceremony ? Up to a few years ago—and still according to the ritual—the candidates were first stripped and bathed. They then had a white cloak, open in front, placed over their shoulders and various ropes were attached to them. One of these, having a running noose, was fastened round their genitals and by this and the other ropes they were led round the room. The explanation usually given for this was to prove to the members that they were perfect in all their parts, but obviously this is not adequate, for a mere ocular demonstration would have been sufficient. The tightened string, however, is a symbolic way of suggesting the castrations once performed by the Galli.

This latter is undoubtedly a very old custom and cannot be disassociated from the almost universal custom of circumcision, which in all primitive rites is an essential part of the initiation of a boy into manhood. So far as the Operative Lodges are concerned, those which still exist have in recent years omitted the stripping and now place the rope round the waist. Thus 100 years hence, if no written rituals survive, probably an entirely new and false explanation of the custom of encircling the waist of a novice with a noose will have arisen.

I know several men still living who had to submit to this custom, and forty years ago a similar ceremony existed in some of the Welsh Speculative Lodges.[3]

1. Minucius Felix, " Octavius." 22, 24.
   Schol. on Lucian, " Jupiter Tragoedus." 8.
   Servius on Virgil, " Aen." IX. 115.
   Arnobius, Ibid. V. 14.
   H. Hepding, " Attis." pp. 163 sq.
   Frazer, " Adonis, Attis, Osiris." 3rd edit. Vol. I. p. 268 sq.
2. Arnobius, " Adversus Nationes." V. 5 sq.
3. A. Heiron, " Ancient Freemasonry and the Old Dundee Lodge, No. 18."
   p. 153.

The true object of the custom and its real origin may be seen if we consider the kindred rite of circumcision. As now done among the Jews, the end of the prepuce is pulled forward and a metal clip is fastened near the base of the penis, all beyond the metal clip is then cut off. The clip thus not only prevents the accidental cutting of the penis itself, but acts as a temporary ligature and reduces the loss of blood. In like manner a cord tightly drawn round the whole male member would prevent the cut damaging the stomach, and at the same time serve as a ligature. Probably this was the original purpose of the noose and in time the placing of it round the member would be accepted as a substitute for the actual sacrifice.

While on the subject of circumcision it should be noted that in most primitive initiation rites the cutting is more painful and drastic than among the Jews of to-day, and often involved subincision as well. The remains of the severed part of the prepuce are usually carefully buried by the boys in the ground as a sacrifice, no doubt, to the Great Mother, just as the Galli in Rome buried their severed members. It is most significant also that the sign of G. and D. is made by a boy in British East Africa to show that he is ready for the cutting to begin,[1] and in the Yao Rites in Nyasaland one of their " Tracing Boards " depicts the Great Mother in her animal form with two little figures making the same sign to her.[2] During the Yao Rites the boys are, of course, circumcised and in addition a grave is dug in the form of a man making this sign, and plays an important part in the ceremony.

The above facts all show that in theory every male had to sacrifice his virility to the Great Mother to enable her to bring forth abundantly, and though many men may have avoided paying the price by offering a substitute, a few, the most religious, felt that they must sacrifice themselves, or if necessary be sacrificed, for the good of the community.

We thus see that the " Day of Blood " held in honour of Cybele was well named. It was during this day that the ordinary worshippers wailed for Attis, and the figure of the God was afterwards taken down from the tree on which it had hung and was buried.[3] During the whole period of mourning the worshippers fasted, just as the worshippers fast throughout the whole of Maharan, in India. The reasons given in the case of the worshippers of Cybele was that Cybele had fasted while she mourned

1. Ward, " Fremasonry and the Ancient Gods." Illus. op. p. 106.
2. Major Sanderson in a private letter to me, and also a photograph of the " Tracing Board " illus. op. p. 178.
3. Diodorus Siculus, III. 59.
   Scholiast on Nicander, " Alixipharmaca." 8.
   Arnobius, " Adversus Nationes." V. 16.
   Servius on " Aen." IX. 115.

for Attis.[1] The real reason no doubt was because they felt it would be hypocrisy to grind up the corn, the flesh of Attis, at the very time when they were supposed to be mourning his death.

There still exists an account by an Arab writer of the Tammuz festival as celebrated among the heathen Syrians in the 10th century A.D. at Harran, the reputed birth place of Jonah. He says:—" Tammuz (June—July). In the middle of this month is the festival of El-Bugât, that is ' Of the Weeping Women,' and this is the Tâ-uz festival, which is celebrated in honour of the God Tâ-uz. The women bewail him because his Lord slew him so cruelly, ground his bones in a mill, and then scattered them to the winds. The women (during this festival) eat nothing which has been ground in a mill but limit their diet to steeped wheat, sweet vetches, dates, raisins and the like."[2]

This account is of interest to us for several reasons. Firstly, it shows that although Mahomedanism had been established in Syria for 300 years it had not, even by the 10th century, completely swept away the worship of Tammuz, for of course Tâ-uz is merely a contraction of his name. Secondly, it shows that the god of all vegetation had grown to be regarded as the God of Corn only, no doubt because by that date it was the chief form of vegetable food the worshippers needed. Thirdly, the fasting is clearly due to the fact that the people felt it would be hypocrisy to pretend to weep for the Corn God at the very moment when they were grinding him under their grind stones. Fourthly, it shows why in Ecclesiastes specific mention is made of the fact that " the sound of the grinders is low,"[3] but we shall deal with this point in chapter 8, and so it need not detain us here. Enough has, however, been written to indicate the true origin of the fasting by the worshippers of Cybele during this period.

But that night sorrow was changed into joy, for a light appeared and on the tomb being opened it was found to be empty, and the priests declared that the God had risen from the dead and that they in like manner would ultimately triumph over the grave.[4] This light was thus the star which brought salvation to the multitude, and was no doubt connected with Venus as a morning star, just as it was at Ephesus.[5]

---

1. Arnobius, Ibid.
2. D. Chwolsohn, " Die Ssabier und der Ssabismus." (St. Petersburg, 1856). Vol. II. 27.
   Id., " Ueber Tammuz und die Menschenverehrung bei den alten Babyloniern." (St. Petersburg, 1860), p. 38.
   Frazer, " Adonis, Attis, Osiris." 3rd ed. Vol. I., p. 230 quoting the above.
3. See chap. VIII. p. 117.
4. Firmicus Maternus, " De errore profan. relig." 22.
   Fr. Cumont, " Les Religions Orientales dans le Paganisme Romain." (Paris 1909), pp. 89 sq.
5. See chapter IV. p. 56.

Although Cybele had her public festivals, she had also her secret initiation rites, similar to those of the Ndembo in the Congo, and these Rites also have a definite relation to Freemasonry. In considering them we must remember that Cybele and Astarte, Attis and Tammuz, are in essence the same. What slight variations we can detect are due to the fact that the Roman rites remained nearer the original barbaric form than did those of Adonis.

These secret ceremonies aimed at bringing the worshippers into closer communion with the Goddess than was possible at the public festivals. The initiate was baptised in the blood of a bull. He stood in a pit over which was a grating, and the bull was speared to death over this head. The blood thus poured down upon the novice, who came forth with his clothes literally dyed scarlet, and was considered to have washed away his sins in the blood of a bull[a] and to have been reborn.[1] For some time thereafter the initiate pretended to be a baby and was fed on milk.[2] Herein he resembled those who have been reborn in the Ndembo Society of the Congo, who pretend they cannot even talk the language of their fellows.[3]

This ceremony took place at the Spring Equinox,[4] that is at the same period as witnessed the death and resurrection of Attis, and as the bull was sacred to the god there is little doubt that at one time it was a man, and not a bull, who supplied the blood for the baptism. The favourite spot for this ceremony was at the shrine of Cybele on the Vatican, at the very place where St. Peter's stands to-day.[5] A very significant fact is that the testicles played a very important part in the ceremony,[6] which immediately brings to mind what befell the bull slain by Enkidu in the Babylonian story.

In addition to the bath of blood, which among the Jewish Essenes was no doubt represented by their baptism of water,

---

(a)   The origin of the Taurobolium is still a matter of dispute, but it was certainly during the Imperial period part of the Rites of Cybele. Some scholars hold that it also formed part of the Mithraic ceremonies, and a similar grating was found in a Mithraic Temple at Rome.

1.   Prudentius, " Peristephan." X. 1006-1050.
      Firmicus Maternus, " De errore." 28. 8.
      " Corpus Inscriptionum Latinarum." VI. No. 510.
      H. Dessau, " Inscriptiones Latinæ Selectæ." Vol. II. par. 1, pp. 140-142. Nos. 4118-4159.
      J. Toutain, " Les Cultes Paiens dans l'Empire Romain." II. 84 sq.
2.   Sallustius philosophus, " De diis et mundo." IV. " Fragmenta Philosophorum Græcorum," ed. F. G. A. Mullach, III. 33.
3.   J. H. Weeks, " Among the Primitive Ba-Kongo." p. 156 sq.
4.   Sallustius, as above.
5.   Frazer, " Adonis, Attis, Osiris." I. p. 275.
      " Corpus Inscriptionum Latinarum." VI. No. 497-504.
      H. Hepding, " Attis." pp. 83, 86-88, 176.
6.   " Corpus Inscriptionum Latinarum." XIII. No. 1751.
      H. Dessau. Ibid. Nos. 4127, 4129, 4131, 4140.
      H. Hepding, " Attis." p. 191.

there was also a sacramental meal. Of what exactly it consisted is not quite clear, but almost certainly its chief constituents were bread and wine. The Essenes likewise had a communal meal which was probably sacramental. What other ceremonies took place in the inner sanctuaries we can only surmise, but that they included a dramatic representation of the death and resurrection of the god, in which the initiate represented Attis, we may consider certain.

Some of the titles of Attis are of peculiar interest to us. We know that Abib means, " Ears of corn," and that a certain password means the same, and so we cannot fail to be impressed by the fact that one of the titles of Attis was the " Green Ear of Corn,"[1] and ancient writers did not hesitate to identify him with the corn. Ears of corn and pomegranates adorned his statues,[2] etc., bringing to mind the rows of pomegranates carved on the two pillars outside the temple of Solomon.

In a certain higher degree a cock appears as an emblem, and therefore the fact that a cock whose tail feathers are made to look like ears of corn stands on an urn[3] which once contained the ashes of a high priest of Attis is certainly significant. This is the more so as that particular degree is connected with the Templars, who quite independently seem to have carried on some of the old rites of Tammuz.

Attis means " father,"[4] and another of his titles was " Papas," or " Father,"[5] which was the title also used by his high priest, and was apparently later adopted by the Popes, who not only took over the site of the Temple of Cybele on the Vatican whereon to build St. Peters, but also seem to have adopted many of the customs connected with his worship. Thus the castrated priests of Attis are represented to-day by the Eunuch choir of St. Peters, and some vestige of the old custom of mutilation survives in the rule which demands that the Pope's manhood should be tested by touch in the Porphry Chair, although he is not deprived of it.

Other customs connected with the Papacy are of especial interest to Freemasons, and since the Pope can hardly have adopted them in recent years from an Order which he has officially excommunicated, it seems as if he and they must have inherited them from the same original source, namely, Tammuz or Attis. For example, when at Christmas 1924 the Pope proclaimed a year of Jubilee he did so by giving three distinct knocks with a gavel

---

1. Hippolytus, " Refutatio omnium hæresium." V. 8 & 9.
   Firmicus Maternus, " De errore." 3.
   Sallustius philosophus, " De diis et mundo " etc. III. 33.
2. W. Helbig, " Fuhrer durch die offentlichen Sammlungen klassischer Altertumer in Rom." (Leipsic 1899) I. 481. No. 721.
3. Frazer, " Adonis, Attis, Osiris." I. 279.
4. Ibid. 280.
5. Diodorus Siculus, III. 58. 4.
   Hippolytus. Ibid. 1. 9.

on the outer side of a bricked up door in St. Peters. At these knocks the brick work, which had been previously loosened, fell down and the door was thus opened. Throughout the year of Jubilee Pilgrims must enter St. Peters by this door.

It should be noted that at the Consecration of a Church the Bishop knocks thrice on the door before he is admitted by an official on guard.

When the Pope has died, a high official, armed with a small ivory hammer or gavel, goes up to the dead man and lightly taps him: once on each temple, and once on the centre of the forehead. After each knock he calls on him to arise, and only when the third summons has been made in vain does he officially proclaim the sad news that the Pope is dead and therefore a successor must be elected. We can hardly doubt that in this ceremony we have a custom which replaces one in which the high priest of Attis was knocked on the head, and killed, in order that a new high priest might take his place and serve as the vehicle for the divine soul of Attis.

Even the claim of the Pope to be a King as well as a Bishop may take its rise from the time when the high priests of Attis, like those of Adonis in Syria, were Priest-Kings. This is perfectly possible notwithstanding the fact that political considerations at a later date may have helped to bolster up the claim.

The above are not the only facts which show that when Christianity overthrew the rival cult of Attis at Rome it took over many of its customs, just as it also absorbed and Christian- ised customs appertaining to Adonis, Mithra and other heathen systems. In doing so she doubtless purified them of many of their grosser features and, transferring them to Christ and His saints, often gave them a loftier meaning. Since we can trace these old rites in the modern church it will not be surprising to find that a similar process took place with regard to the inner mysteries of Attis and Adonis.

Two facts stand out very clearly in the case of Attis and are of great importance to us when deciding who Hiram Abiff really was. Firstly, his priests lost their personal names and were known by his titles, and secondly, they represented him on the Day of Blood. Thus, like him, they were castrated, but though they bled on that day as he did, yet they did not in Imperial times have to bleed to death. That, in the more barbarous times, in Phrygia they were actually slain is, however, the opinion of Sir W. M. Ramsey, who writes that the Phrygians, " enacted the story of his birth and life and death; the Earth, the Mother, is fertilised only by an act of violence by her own child; the repre- sentative of the god was probably slain each year by a cruel death, just as the god himself died." [1]

---

1. Article " Phrygia."   Encycl. Brit. 11th ed. (1911) XXI. p. 544.

Furthermore, the fact that Solomon would allow no iron tools to be used on the Temple site, where Hiram Abiff was working, is analogous to a rule laid down by Croesus, King of Lydia, that iron weapons must not be brought near his son who was named Atys.[1] Atys ultimately was killed while hunting a boar, and the story is recognised by scholars as being merely a variation of that legend which thus accounts for the death of Attis.[2] It seems therefore as if iron tools might not be brought into the presence of the human representative of the vegetation god, no doubt because with iron axes men cut the trees of Lebanon and with iron sickles reaped the corn. To parade the cause of the future death of vegetation before its incarnate god would obviously be an insult and naturally arouse his wrath.

In conclusion it must be remembered that at Antioch and Ephesus[a] Cybele blended with Astarte and there we find Eunuch priests, some of whom are known as King-bees, which suggests that the survival of the Bee in Freemasonry may be due to the fact that it reminded men of the sacrifice the male insect makes in order that the Queen may be fertilised, the present theory that it is an emblem of industry being merely a later explanation put forward at a time when the original meaning had become lost. At any rate, we can say quite definitely that as the emblem of Astarte of Ephesus it could hardly represent industry, for she was essentially a wanton. Neither can it be said that the Galli or King Bees[b] were remarkable for their industry and toil; classical writers, indeed, usually describe them as lazy, idle vagrants who lived by their wits on the alms collected from the superstitious and ignorant.

---

1. Herodotus, 1. 34-45.
2. Stein on Herodotus. 1. 43. ed. Meyer, S. V. " Atys " in Pauly-Wissowa's " Real-Encyclopädie der classischen-Altertumswissenschaft. II. 2. col. 2262.
   Frazer, " Adonis." I. p. 287.
(a) Of special interest to some of my readers is the fact that when Ephesus was beseiged by Croesus in the 6th century B.C. the city dedicated itself to Artemis by stretching a rope from the city to the Sanctuary : whereupon Croesus withdrew. Herein we see that the city enacted the part of a victim offered for sacrifice with a halter round its neck, or of an initiate similarly dedicating himself to the Goddess. (see Article " Ephesus," Encycl. Brit. 11th ed. (1911) IX. p. 672.)
(b) According to the article in Encycl. Brit. on " Artemis." 11th ed. II. p. 665, one group of these priests were called Essenes, which suggests that the Jewish sect of the same name may have originated from a similar order of priests attached to a local form of Astarte.

CHAPTER VI

THE DYING GOD IN OTHER LANDS

Legends of a Dying God are found all round the world and it is impossible to devote the same amount of space to them as we have given to Adonis and Attis. To the anthropologist they are of great interest, since they show how universal is the belief in such a god and how widespread are the ceremonies associated with his worship which have survived even up to the present day.

We, however, are investigating the diffusion of one specific cult in order to ascertain whether it has survived in the form of modern Freemasonry. Therefore these other cults are chiefly of interest to us in so far as it seems possible that they, and not Adonis, may be the origin of Hiram Abiff, or if they may have helped to strengthen and keep alive the tradition of a dying god originally derived from elsewhere. We can therefore dismiss fairly rapidly the legends of the Dying God in Teutonic and Celtic lands, devoting most of our space to Greece and Egypt. We will commence with our national Dying God, Baldur.

Baldur has several analogies with Adonis. He was the son of Odin who was also apparently slain,[1] for the latter specifically says that he hung for nine days on a windy tree. Moreover, Odin descended into Hell before the death of Baldur, in order, so the legend runs, to ascertain what was the fate overshadowing Baldur. In this comparatively late version of the myth we have an attempt to rationalise the story of the death and resurrection of the older god. Thus Odin corresponds to Melcarth, and Baldur to Tammuz.

In this legend there is no hint of an early resurrection of the god. At the most there is merely a dim and distant hope that after the destruction of the world at Ragnarok a better world shall arise, over which Baldur and his wife, Nanna, shall reign as King and Queen in the place of Odin and Frigga. The myth thus varies in a very important point from that of Tammuz, but there is reason for suspecting that the story as we now have it is late, and does not truly represent the original cult.

The ceremonies connected with Baldur took place at Yule-tide, or Christmas, at which time the Yule log was,[2] and in many European countries still is, lighted with much ceremony. That it represented the god of vegetation is shown by the custom in many countries of sprinkling corn on it, or near it. Moreover, in the middle ages a man was chosen who was called the " Lord of

---

1. See chapter IV. p. 42.
2. Frazer, " Baldur the Beautiful." Ed. 2. Vol. 1. p. 246 sq.

Misrule." He reigned for twelve days, during which time a kind of Saturnalia prevailed. On Twelfth Night his reign ended, and incidentally the children were well whipped to remind them that law and order had been restored in the world.[a] Kissing under the mistletoe is also associated with the death of the god of Law and Order, and is a mild substitute for a much more primitive licence which is still encouraged at similar fertility festivals in more savage countries.

From these old Yule-tide customs, now almost extinct in England, we can see that Baldur was supposed to rise again after twelve days in the Underworld. The twelve days, no doubt, each represent a month of the year. The disappearance of this feature from the myth may be due to the fact that it comes down to us via Christian writers, who might hesitate to suggest that Baldur, like Christ, rose from the dead.

In the Edda we also find vague fragments of the myth of another god who died, Odur, whose name may be merely a variant of the name of Odin. He was married to Freyja, who is undoubtedly an earth goddess, and left her because she went to the realm of the dwarfs and obtained from them a wonderful necklace. She sought Odur with bitter tears but he never returned. This legend, fragmentary as it is, yet resembles the Astarte and Tammuz cult more closely than does the myth of Baldur, but in the Edda it is a dim memory and nothing more.

The old Celtic legends have come down to us in such a fragmentary and late form that from them we can glean but little. We know that the Gauls and Britons regarded the mistletoe as sacred and cut a sprig from an oak every year with much ceremony. We also know that periodically they burnt huge wicker figures of giants or gods, which they filled with human and animal victims.[1]

This custom reminds us at once of the burning of Melcarth and suggests that the Celts likewise had a dying god who was sacrificed in order that the fertility of the soil might be maintained. Moreover, these " Giants " survived in many parts of France,[2] and even in Britain, well into the 19th century, for Gog and Magog at the Guildhall undoubtedly belong to this illustrious ancestry.

In some of the Welsh stories, however, though we cannot

(a) Compare, however, with the scourging of the " Criminal " King of Babylon. Perhaps the children were whipped instead of the Lord of Misrule, just as Edward VI. had a " whipping boy."
1. Cæsar, " Bell. Gall." VI. 15.
Strabo, IV. 4. 5. pp. 197 sq.
Diodorus Siculus. V. 32.
W. Mannhardt, " Baumkultus." pp. 525 sq.
2. Madame Clement, " Histoire des fêtes civiles et religieuses de departement du Nord." (Cambrai 1836).
3. F. W. Fairholt, " Gog and Magog, the Giants in the Guildhall, their real and legendary History." (London, 1859) pp. 78-87.

78 WHO WAS HIRAM ABIFF ?

definitely identify a dying god, we find traces of certain things which were peculiarly associated with the Tammuz cult, and, what is more, there is a definite tradition that they came originally from Syria. Since we know that the Phoenicians visited Cornwall for tin, it is quite possible that these details are imported direct from the Tammuz cult, and as they have had a profound influence on the Graal Legends we cannot entirely ignore them here, although in a later chapter we shall consider them in more detail.

In the original Tammuz cult among the Jews a cauldron plays an important part, and is referred to by both Jeremiah and Ezekiel, who, however, give us few details concerning it. Now in the Mabinogion,[1] in the story of Branwen, the daughter of Llyr, we learn of this mysterious cauldron, and as therein we are told what was its function we will devote a short time to discovering all we can about it.

We there learn that Bendigeid Vran said to Matholwch, " I will give unto thee a cauldron, the property of which is, that if one of thy men be slain to-day, and be cast therein, to-morrow he will be as well as ever he was at the best, except that he will not regain his speech." We learn further that originally this cauldron belonged to a gigantic man of Ireland who with his wife had been befriended by Matholwch, but ultimately became such a nuisance to the community in Ireland that the people determined to get rid of them. So they persuaded the giant, his wife and children to enter a house made of iron, and when they were therein, piled fuel around it and set this on fire. When the house was white hot the giant and his wife broke through and excaped to Britain, where they were kindly received by the British, but the children perished. The refugees gave their cauldron to Bendigeid Vran, who by his gift thus restored it to Ireland.

Later he had cause to regret his generosity, for the Irish treated his sister Branwen very badly, and to avenge her he crossed the sea with a vast host. As soon as he had landed the Irish broke down the Bridges across the river Linon and believed themselves safe because there was " a loadstone at the bottom of the river that neither ship nor vessel could pass." When Bendigeid Vran, who was of gigantic size, came to the river, he laid himself down across it and formed the bridge for the army saying, " He who will be a chief, let him be a bridge," which saying became a proverb.

In the battle which ultimately ensued the British found themselves at a great disadvantage, for every evening the Irish threw their dead into this magic cauldron and next morning the dead arose as fit as before they were slain, save that they could not

1. Lady Charlotte Guest, " The Mabinogion." (Everyman ed.) pp. 37-38 44, also note, " The Cauldron." p. 295.

speak. Seeing that his side was likely to be defeated, another British chief, pretending to be dead, threw himself among the slain Irish and was in mistake thrown into the Cauldron. " And he stretched himself out in the cauldron, so that he rent the cauldron into four pieces and burst his own heart also."

The legend of how this cauldron came to Ireland is also instructive. The Tuatha de Danaan were a race of magicians who came from Syria, and in their war with the Syrians used their magic cauldron to revive their own slain. But the Syrians adopted the policy of driving a stake of mountain ash through the bodies of all they slew and " if they had been animated by demons they instantly turned into worms." The Tuatha therefore had to leave Syria and wandered westward to Ireland, still bearing with them their magic cauldron.

This cauldron also had the property of bestowing fertility on the land to which it came, and in the course of years became converted in the Graal Legends into the Chalice, which nevertheless still retained many of the cauldron's magical properties. The Graal story clearly indicates a semi-magical initiation rite of death and resurrection, such as is found in other parts of the world, and its connection with the old fertility cult is vouched for not only by the mention of a similar cauldron in the Jewish rites of Tammuz,[1] but by the fact that for its companions it has the severed head, which in some versions talks,[2] the spear which drips blood, and a magic sword.[3] The spear is similar to the spear of Marduk and the spear with which the human representative of Tammuz was slain. The head reminds us of the head of Tammuz, which was thrown into the sea at Alexandria, and the sword, the magic sword of Solomon.

We shall consider these " hallows " later, in connection with the Graal and the Templars, all we now need note is that their presence in the Celtic legends points to a connection with the fertility cult, just as the branch of mistletoe cut by the Druids is a near relative to the branch used in the Jewish fertility rites, and to the sprig of Acacia.

The incident of the Demi-god Bendigeid Vran making a bridge for his people, reminds us of the mythical bridge which links earth and the city of the gods, and suggests that he sacrificed himself to save his people. Although the true meaning of the incident had become forgotten in the days when the Mabinogion were committed to writing, the fact that he subsequently died and yet his severed head continued to talk strengthens this belief.

The importance of the Celtic traditions, fragmentary though they be, rests in the fact that they undoubtedly form the basis of the Graal legends, which themselves seem to have been a survival

---

1.   See chapter VII.
2.   Mabinogion. p. 45.
3.   Ibid. " Peredur." pp. 185, 219.

of the fertility cult of Adonis.[1]   As the Graal was in some way
mixed up with the Templars and the latter are avowedly inter-
linked with Freemasonry it will be necessary for us to consider
this part of the question later.   Here we need merely add that the
Phoenicians did come to Britain and probably to Ireland, and
the local tradition concerning the source of the cauldron cannot be
ignored.   Finally, the Celts believed implicitly in reincarnation,
a doctrine which is the basis of the Adonis cult.   On this point
we not only have the evidence of Cæsar, but in the story of Taliesin
it forms the very basis of the tale.   Thus Taliesin says:
" I have been chief director of the work of the tower of Nimrod,
    I am a wonder whose origin is not known.
  I have been in Asia with Noah in the Ark."
He also tells us that when in his last incarnation, as Gwion, he
changed himself into a bird, but the woman who was pursuing
him changed into a hawk, so he landed on the ground and changed
into *an ear of wheat*.   The woman changed herself into a black
hen and swallowed him, but on resuming her human form found
she was pregnant.   In due course she gave birth to a baby who
was none other than Taliesin.[2]

In this story we have a close analogy with the transmigration
of the soul of the younger brother in the Egyptian story, and in
connection therewith cannot forget that Pythagoras, who was
supposed to be a " Masonic " worthy, definitely taught the
doctrine of the transmigration of souls.   It is also interesting to
see that Taliesin claimed to be the chief architect at the building
of the Tower of Babel, a building which is referred to in some of
the older masonic rituals, although it has practically vanished
from masonry to-day.

We will now leave the misty shores of Celtic Britain for the
clear air and more precise beliefs of ancient Greece, where we
shall find more than one story of a dying god, but shall have to
realise that they are not the originals of Hiram Abiff.   Their
value consists in the fact that they shed further light on the
underlying principles of the Tammuz cult and of Freemasonry.

GREECE

Greece was the medium through which many of the cults of
Asia passed into Europe, and in the process were refined and purified of much of their original savage nature.   For all that the
Greeks themselves still retained in their legends, and even in some
of their customs, traces of rites as savage as those we have met
with in Syria, and seem to have had a fertility cult of their own.
Nevertheless, their proximity to Asia and their settlements in
many parts of Asia Minor resulted in the importation of so many

1.   See J. Weston, " The Quest of the Holy Graal."
2.   Lady Charlotte Guest, " The Mabinogion." (Everyman ed.) pp. 263 sq.

avowedly Asiatic cults and deities that it is difficult to point definitely to any god or custom and say, " this is indigenous."

THE CONFLICTS OF THE GODS

The gods of Olympus are divided into three generations, that of the classical era being the third, and these were ruled over by Zeus.[1]   Uranus and Gæa were produced out of Chaos, the former representing the heavens and the latter earth, from whom were begotten a series of Deities which included the Giants and the Titans.   Of the latter the most important was Cronus.   As the Giants proved unruly and turbulent, Uranus cast them into Tartarus, but this enraged their mother Gæa, who entered into a conspiracy with Cronus.

Supported by the other Titans Cronus overthrew Uranus and castrated him,[2] and from the blood which thus poured down to earth sprang up a second brood of Earth Giants.   From the same source arose Aphrodite, only in her case she sprang from the mingling of his blood with the sea.[3]   The significance of this story is obvious when we remember that Aphrodite was merely another form of Astarte.   Uranus was thus dethroned and rendered impotent, but he cursed Cronus for his treachery and foretold that he in like manner would be overthrown by his son.

In this story there are obvious analogies with the Babylonian story of Tiamat, and although Uranus was not killed the fact that he was rendered impotent shows that the same principle underlies this legend as we find in the myth of Attis.   Neither can we overlook the fact that in reality the castration of Uranus is brought about by Gæa, the great Earth Mother.

Cronus now became supreme ruler of the gods and mated with Rhea, who likewise represents the Great Mother.   Though for " decency's sake " the Greeks made it appear as if she was the daughter of Gæa, in reality she is, of course, the same.   We thus have a son who becomes the lover of his mother, as occurs in the case of Attis.   Moreover, Rhea herself was avowedly none other than Cybele, and like her, wore a turreted crown and rode on a chariot drawn by lions.   Her original home was Crete, where she was worshipped with the same licentious rites as was Astarte. Just as the Great Mother in her form of Gæa caused the overthrow of Uranus, so in her form of Rhea she brought about the downfall of Cronus.

Cronus, mindful of the prophecy of his father, made it a rule to " swallow " each of his children as soon as they were born, and

1.   E. M. Berens, " Myths and Legends of Ancient Greece and Rome." pp. 11 sq.   I have utilised this book throughout most of this section because it is more accessible to the average reader than the original classical authorities, and have merely checked or supplemented the accounts from the original authorities such as Hesiod, Homer, etc.
2.   Hesiod, " Theogony." pp. 159 sq.   3.   Berens. Ibid. p. 59.

thus disposed of the first five, but when Zeus was born Rhea substituted a stone for the babe, which Cronus likewise swallowed. Zeus was then hidden in a cave in Crete, in the heart of Mount Ida. When grown to man's estate he managed to persuade Cronus to swallow an emetic, which caused him to vomit forth the other five children of Rhea.

In this incident we have a clear reference to the kindred initiation rites of Syria, wherein the candidates are supposed to be swallowed by a monster and later vomited forth. My readers will find that in like manner Solomon was supposed to have been swallowed by the Demon Asmodeus and then spued forth.[1]

Cronus, when he discovered the trick that had been played upon him proceeded to attack Zeus, who after a long and desperate struggle overthrew his father and castrated him,[2] as he had castrated Uranus.

Cronus, although in classical times regarded as the god of Time, seems originally to have been a corn god, a character retained by him among the Romans, where he was known as Saturn. He is usually depicted as a bearded man holding in his left hand ears of corn and in his right a sickle, while he drives a chariot drawn by serpents, a well recognised fertility emblem. In view of the barbarous custom which survived among the Roman legionaries on the Danube of electing a man as King Saturn who was soon afterwards slain,[3] it is evident that the castration of Cronus is similar to the tale told of Attis and had the same original significance.

HERACLES AND APHRODITE

Heracles, or as the Romans called him, Hercules, is merely the Phoenician Melcarth, and since we have already devoted considerable space to his myth all that is necessary here is to point out that he is one variant of the dying god.

In like manner Aphrodite is merely Astarte, but the Greeks, who had a mania for departmentalising the pantheon, sub-divided the great Fertility Goddess and created a number of goddesses, each of whom merely represented varying aspects of the same Semitic Deity. Demeter and Artemis are similar variations of Astarte, but for our purpose they are so important that we must deal with them separately and for the moment will concentrate attention on two other representatives of the dying god, of whom Dionysius is undoubtedly Asiatic, while Orpheus is also probably derived from the same source.

---

1. See chapter VIII.
2. Porphyry, " De antro nympharum." 16.
   Aristides. " Or." III. (Vol. I. p. 35. ed. G. Dindorf, Leipsic, 1892).
   Scholist on Apollonius Rhodius, " Argon." IV. 983.
   See also J. Weston, " The Quest of the Holy Graal." p. 70. Compare p.80.
3. J. G. Fraser, " The Scapegoat." p. 308, sq.

ORPHEUS[1]

Orpheus was supposed to be the son of Apollo and Calliope, the Muse of Epic poetry, and is said to have taught the Orphic Mysteries. When he played on the lyre the beasts and birds gathered around him and even the winds were still. These facts at once suggest that originally he was the god of wild life, or a fertility god.

He married Eurydice, but his half brother Aristæus tried to carry her off. Aristæus, was a rural deity and was supposed to have taught men how to catch bees and utilise honey. Here we have a distorted memory of the significance of the bee in the fertility cult. Eurydice fled across the fields and in her flight stepped on a snake which bit her. The snake, as my readers are already aware, is closely associated with the fertility cult, so much so that at one time it was usual to speak of the cult as tree and serpent worship, and in the Bible itself the serpent and the Tree of Knowledge in conjunction with a woman, according to Genesis, caused death to come into the world.

Whereas in the Syrian cult it was the male who perished, here, as in the story of Persephone, it was the female, and Orpheus, like Ishtar, set out for the Underworld hoping to recover his lost love. He literally played his way through the horrors of Hades and his music for the moment brought peace and relief to the sufferers even in Tartarus. The grim King 'Aides was touched by his devotion, and even more by his music, and agreed to release Eurydice on condition that Orpheus refrained from even looking at his wife until they had both reached the upper air. Orpheus therefore set out on his return journey followed by Eurydice, but as they were approaching the confines of Hades the sight of some of the souls in torment caused her to cry out and Orpheus looked back. At once she vanished and he knew that his labour was in vain.

Thus the Greek story, unlike the Syrian, fails of a happy ending, and henceforth tragedy is piled on tragedy. Though he returned to the upper world Orpheus refused to be comforted, and even his old companions, the Nymphs, could not alleviate his gloom. At length one day it chanced that he came across a band of Thracian women who were worked up to frenzy through the wild rites of Dionysius, a fertility festival, be it noted. He refused to join in their orgies and they turned on him and tore him to pieces. His mutilated fragments were buried by the Muses at the foot of Mount Olympus, but his head had been thrown into the river Hebrus.

In this last episode we return to the original Asiatic rites of Adonis. We have already learnt that the victim who represented

---

1. E. M. Berens, " The Myths and Legends of Ancient Greece and Rome." pp. 80 sq.

the fertility god was sometimes torn to pieces by the frenzied worshippers whilst still alive, and eaten raw. We know that at Alexandria, the head of the figure of Adonis was flung into the sea, and therefore may feel certain that Orpheus is either the vegetation god himself or one of his numerous human representatives who in primitive times literally suffered as he is said to have done. When considering this story my readers must not overlook two important details; firstly, Orpheus was divine, having a god for his father and a demi-goddess as his mother, and secondly, he taught the Orphic rites, but their exact nature is uncertain.

DIONYSIUS OR BACCHUS

Dionysius was the son of Zeus and Semele, and in view of the important part fire played in the Semitic fertility cult the first incident in his life is significant. His mother, Semele, was the daughter of Cadmus, king of *Phoenicia*, and was persuaded by Hera, who was jealous of her, to ask Zeus to appear to her in all his divine majesty. Having just previously promised to do whatever she asked, Zeus had to do so, and she was immediately consumed by the lightning which flamed about his head. He, however, succeeded in snatching Dionysius from the flames and placed him in charge of Hermes. The babe was thus born amid the flames and out of the ashes of his mother.

As Hermes was the Conductor of the Soul through the Underworld, we seem to have in this story a dim remembrance of the burning of the Phoenician god Melcarth, and his resurrection from the dead. Dionysius was subsequently brought up in a cave among wood nymphs, satyrs and shepherds. He discovered the possibility of making wine from the grape, and set forth on a kind of pilgrimage to teach the secret to the rest of the world. He travelled throughout Syria, Arabia, India and Egypt, planting the vine and gathering supporters. He then returned to Greece, where, however, his further progress was opposed by Lycurgus, king of Thrace, and Pentheus, king of Thebes.

Lycurgus went so far as to chase Dionysius into the sea, an incident which again reminds us that at Alexandria a figure of Adonis was similarly committed to the waves. Dionysius, however, escaped from peril, and Lycurgus, as a punishment, was stricken with madness and killed his own son. Pentheus also came to a tragic end, for he was literally torn to pieces by a mob of female devotees of Dionysius, led by the King's mother, Agade, and her two sisters, because they caught him spying on their rites. Thus Pentheus was slain by three female villains.

That Dionysius was not one to be insulted with impunity is shown by another story. Some Tyrrhenian pirates saw Dionysius standing on the Greek shore and promptly carried him off as a slave. The chains with which they had bound him, however, fell off, and the pilot, realising that the youth must be divine, begged the others to release him. This they refused to do, whereupon the masts sprouted and soon the whole ship was wreathed with vines and ivy,[a] plants sacred to the god, and sounds of strange music were heard. Then Dionysius changed into a lion, while a savage bear also appeared and tore the captain to pieces. The rest of the crew in panic flung themselves into the sea and were immediately transformed into Dolphins.

The god and the pilot then proceeded on their way and at Naxos Dionysius landed and married Ariadne. One of the last acts of Dionysius before he *ascended* to heaven was to *descend* into the Underworld and bring forth his mother Semele in triumph to Olympus, where she was made one of the Immortals under the name of Thyone.[1] Dionysius is depicted crowned with ivy or vine leaves, riding on a panther or a lion, and bearing in his hand the Thyrsus, the wand entwined with vine branches and surmounted by a fir cone.

From this legend we see that Dionysius was originally the Phoenician god of vegetation and the fir cone is particularly characteristic of these Semitic fertility gods. Although we have in this story no account of his death, the fact that he was chased into the sea, and that subsequently he descended into the Underworld and rescued therefrom someone in bondage, clearly shows his true character. His complete identification with the Syrian god is proved, not only by his transformation into a lion, but by the appearance of the bear. As we have already mentioned, Astarte in one of her forms was a Bear Goddess, and in this aspect is depicted at Aphaca about to destroy Adonis. Moreover, the incident of the ship undoubtedly refers to the solar barque, in which the souls of the dead journeyed through the Underworld and on their way often encountered fierce opposition from the powers of evil. Even the incident of his marriage with Ariadne, accompanied as it was by riotous jollifications, brings to mind the ceremonies with which the Great Mother was annually married to her lover.

Dionysius was also regarded as patron of the drama and the Dionysian Artificers were named after him. Associated with his name were certain secret rites of initiation connected with his public festival of " The Dionysia."

In these secret rites, a bull dressed up in human clothing was torn to pieces and eaten by the frenzied devotees, and there is little doubt that originally it was a man, the human representative of Dionysius, who thus perished. As the dismembered carcase of the bull was eaten raw by the worshippers there is no doubt that the sacramental feast, for such it was, was originally a cannibalistic meal. It seems probable that in early days these secret rites

(a) Lucian makes fun of this incident in his " Vera Historia."
1. E. M. Berens, " Myths and Legends of Ancient Greece and Rome." pp. 124 sq.

were restricted to women, but at a later date men also were
admitted. Like most fertility rites, at times they were of a
distinctly licentious character, and must be carefully distinguished
from the much more dignified ceremonies of Eleusis. In these
rites Dionysius, under the name of Iaccus, also played a part, but
his exact position therein is still a matter of dispute amongst
scholars. The incident of the death of Orpheus, already mentioned, and the slaying of Pentheus show that the Greeks in
early times were every bit as savage as the Semites.

In conclusion, it must be said that the cult of Dionysius probably helped to strengthen the cult of Adonis in Greece, and
so may have contributed to masonic traditions, if only to a
slight extent. It survived, however, up to 1908 in Thrace, in
a slightly modified form at Viza, and may even still exist.[1] This
fact shows how long old customs linger and how unreasonable
it is to argue that the masonic mysteries cannot possibly be the
survival of an old Mystery Rite.

DEMETER

Demeter has many similarities to the great mother, but, unlike Astarte, she is always represented as highly " respectable."
In the story of her search for Persephone there are several incidents
which remind us forcibly of the Egyptian Isis, e.g., her attempt
to make the son of King Celeus immortal. We cannot say
definitely which cult has borrowed from the other or whether
both have evolved independently.

There is, however, one marked feature which distinguishes
her and her Mysteries from both the Syrian and the Egyptian
cults. The victim is a woman, not a man. Thus Persephone
represents the " Corn-maiden " who still survives in agricultural
areas in Scandinavia and England. Moreover, the male organ
plays no important part in the rites whereas it was a dominant
feature in the Syrian cult. Furthermore, Demeter is not associated with the lion, and all these facts suggest that she is probably
the original Greek goddess of fertility, unlike Rhea or Aphrodite
who were undoubtedly imported from Asia.

THE LEGEND[2]

Demeter had a daughter by Zeus, named Persephone, who
plucked a flower by the sea shore, whereupon the earth opened
and 'Aides appeared and carried her off to the Underworld. Demeter set out to seek for her daughter, bearing in her hand two
torches, and for nine days sought in vain. On the tenth she met
Hecate, an ancient goddess of the Underworld, who was later
identified with Artemis. This Being told her that she had heard

1. R. M. Dawkins, Journal of Hellenic Studies, XXVI. (1906). pp. 191-206.
2. E. M. Berens, " Myths and Legends of Ancient Greece and Rome." pp.52.

Persephone's cries but knew not where she had gone. On her advice the distracted mother appealed to Helios, the Sun, who has seen all and told Demeter what had happened. The ten days which elapsed between the loss of Persephone and her mother's discovery forcibly remind us of similar legends in which the number ten plays an important part. For example, Odin hung for nine days on " the windy tree," and presumably descended therefrom on the tenth. Dante took ten days to pass through Hell, Purgatory and Heaven, while the Hung heroes according to the Triad ritual spent ten days in their journey towards the Mystic City of Willows.[1] Although there is no sprig of acacia in this story, a mysterious flower plays an important part, for it is by plucking that flower that Persephone causes the gates of the Underworld to open, an incident which is analogous to the English superstition that the gates of Fairyland open to those who have plucked the four-leaved clover, and to the similar story told in Ireland of the four-leaved shamrock.[a] Incidentally the Fairyland of the English folk tales undoubtedly represents the pre-Christian Underworld, for in some of the old ballads we learn that those who partake of food in Fairyland cannot return to earth, which reminds us of what occurred in the case of Persephone.

When Demeter found that Zeus had given 'Aides leave to carry off Persephone she was furious, and, leaving her home on Olympus, refused food, disguised herself as an old woman and set out on a long and weary pilgrimage. As a result of her wrath the earth ceased to produce crops, and soon all mankind was likely to perish. At length she reached Eleusis and sat down under an olive tree near to a well. The daughters of King Celeus came to draw water and, taking pity on the forlorn stranger, took her to their father's house where she was kindly received and appointed nurse to their infant brother, Triptolemus. The stranger still refused to eat anything for a long time, but at last she was persuaded to partake of a little barley meal mixed with mint and water. She took charge of the infant whom every evening she secretly laid in the fire in order to render him immortal, but one day his mother, the Queen Metaneira, spied on the stranger and on seeing what she was doing to her son, shrieked aloud. At this the goddess snatched the child from the flames, disclosed her true identity, and told the Queen that she had intended to render the little Prince immortal, but her curiosity had rendered this impossible. She then departed, but before doing so established her sacred rites at Eleusis.

Meanwhile Demeter continued to prevent the corn from growing, and at length the gods begged her to return to Olympus and allow it to grow once more. The goddess swore by the Styx

1. Ward and Stirling, " The Hung Society," Vol. I.
(a) Aeneas had to pluck a sprig of mistletoe before he could enter the Underworld. See Virgil, " Aen," VI.

that she would not comply with their request until Persephone was restored to her, and in consequence Zeus sent Hermes to 'Aides to demand the return of Demeter's daughter. This was conceded, but it was found that Persephone had eaten six seeds of a pomegranate and so 'Aides claimed that henceforth she was his. In witness of his assertion he produced Ascalaphus, whereupon the angry goddess hurled a rock at him which pinned him down in Tartarus until he was rescued by Hercules.

As a compromise Zeus arranged that Persephone should remain for six months in the Underworld, and for the remainder of the year should reside with her mother in Olympus. There-upon the vegetation once more decked the surface of the earth.

This legend is the basis of the Eleusinian mysteries, and all we need point out here is that since the chief character is a woman, Persephone, and not a man, these cannot be the origin of the masonic tradition. For all that there are two features to which special attention must be drawn. Firstly, the important part played by the pomegranate, which brings to our mind its use on the pillars of Solomon and its appearance on the Babylonian seal. Secondly, the attempt to render Triptolemus immortal is similar to the story related of Isis, so much so as to suggest that one has been borrowed from the other. It is difficult to say, how-ever, which has done the borrowing, and as the Egyptian story places the incident at Byblos it is possible that both cults have borrowed from the cult of Adonis. The fact that Moloch was annually burnt in Syria, renders this highly probable, and the legends indicate that the underlying principle which caused that ceremony was that of burning away the human and perishable elements, and so renewing the youth of the god, thereby preserv-ing his immortality.

ARTEMIS

The Greeks gathered together under the name of Artemis a number of primitive goddesses of their own, and also various forms of the Semitic Great Mother. In consequence we have a number of tales which depict her in very different aspects. More-over, during the classical period they tended more and more to indentify Selene, the Moon, with Artemis, and even attached to her Hecate, an old, primitive goddess of the Underworld.

It is, therefore, best to consider her under four aspects, represented by four distinct sub-titles, viz., the Arcadian, the Brauronian, the Ephesian and the Selene, Artemis.

The Arcadian Artemis was the goddess of wild life, and was fabled to be the child of Zeus and Leto, and a twin sister of Apollo. In this aspect she is a huntress and a chaste virgin, and has little in common with Astarte. Nevertheless, some of her legends point to a fairly savage origin. The fact that the bear was one of the animals sacred to her and the story of her setting her dogs on Actæon, whereby he was torn to pieces, suggest analogies with the manner in which Orpheus and Pentheus met their deaths. That she presided over child-birth also suggests that artemis, even among the Greeks, was originally a fertility goddess. Moreover, she was a Harvest Goddess and was supposed to slay the Aloidæ, or Corn Spirits.[1] At Orchomenus a wooden image of her stood in a large *cedar*, a tree whose close association with Astarte and Adonis we have already noted. Many of her titles also indicate her position as a tree goddess, i.e., " The Nut-tree goddess," while her title of " The Suspended," clearly refers to the custom of hanging her image on a tree at certain festivals to denote that she was a tree spirit.[2] As the goddess of wild animals she was especially a bear goddess, and the legend of Kallisto, who was changed into a bear by Zeus, and in that form slain by Artemis, is merely a legend of the goddess in her primitive and totem form of a bear[1].

When we turn to Artemis Brauronia, the primitive aspects of the goddess are even more in evidence. One of the ceremonies connected with this goddess was avowedly intended to propitiate her, as the bear goddess, for killing bears, and for this purpose a number of girls danced a " Bear dance," clad in bear skins.

Furthermore, in her honour, Spartan boys were flogged till the blood poured down in front of her altar at Limmæum in Laconia, and we are told that often the unfortunate lads died under the lash. This custom is undoubtedly similar to that of the priests of Cybele, who gashed themselves till the blood ran down on her altar in order that the earth might be fertilised. Nor can we overlook the fact that in Homer she is the goddess of death, therein having another feature in common with Astarte, who was not only the Great Mother but also the Goddess of War and Destruction, being therein very similar to the Indian Goddess, Kali, the wife of Shiva.

The story of Iphigenia provides us with many important details as to the nature of the worship offered to the Brauronian or, as she is sometimes called, the Taurice Artemis. When the Greek fleet was ready to sail it could not depart because of contrary winds, and it was found that Artemis was angry with Agamemnon and would only be appeased if he sacrificed to her his daughter Iphigenia. The King therefore sent for her, telling his Queen Clytemnestra that Achilles wished to marry her. When the unfortunate girl arrived, despite her appeals for mercy, she was bound to the altar, but just as the sacrificial knife was about to descend she vanished, and in her place a deer appeared which was offered in her stead. Artemis, meanwhile, had wafted

---

1. See " Artemis in Encycl. Brit." 11th ed. (1910 pp. 663 sq.)
2. Farnell, " Cults of the Greek States." II. p. 429.

away the Princess to Taurica, in the Crimea, where, however, she found she had only exchanged one awful fate for another.

Here she had to offer up any strangers who came to the country as a sacrifice to Artemis.   After many years two strangers were brought to her whom she recognised as Greeks, and on further investigation discovered they were her brother, Orestes, and his cousin, Pylades.   Orestes had come to Tauris in order to carry off the statue of the goddess to Attica, a task set him as an expiation for having slain his mother because she had killed his father and her husband Agamemnon.

Iphigenia and the two men succeeded in making their escape and carried off the sacred image to Greece, where the practice of offering human sacrifices to her continued in Sparta, till the time of Lycurgus, who substituted the flogging of boys, to which we have previously referred.[1]

At Ephesus, Artemis is simply Astarte, hardly Hellenised at all.   Here she seems to have been especially worshipped as the goddess of the Underworld, but she has all the usual attributes of Astarte, including her Eunuch priests.   The upper half of the statue was shaped like a woman, but with several rows of breasts, to indicate her fertile nature, while the lower half was a pillar, on which were sculptured rows of animals, reptiles, etc.   Her sacred animals were the lion, the bear, the bee, and the goat. As, however, we have already dealt with this goddess in her true Asiatic character she need not detain us now.

Selene Artemis represents the blending of the old Homeric Moon goddess, Selene, with Artemis.   In this character she wears on her head a crescent moon and has had transferred to her some of the legends of Selene such as that of Endymion.   We must, however, remember that the moon is supposed by primitive races to have a profound influence on the growth of crops, and in Asia the moon goddess soon became more or less identified with Astarte.

Aphrodite, although at first sight quite distinct from Artemis, is but Astarte purged of some of her more cruel and destructive characteristics.   In Greek hands this aspect of the great Semitic goddess retains her wanton character, but for the most part has lost her savage and bloodthirsty nature, which so far as it did survive was transferred to Artemis.   On the other hand there seems to be little doubt that, save as representing the planet Venus, she has no original in primitive Greece.

OSIRIS

According to Plutarch, Osiris was the son of the earth god Seb and the sky goddess Nut, and had two brothers, Horus, the

---

1.   E. M. Berens, " The Myths and Legends of Ancient Greece and Rome." p. 36.

elder, and Set, who afterwards murdered him; he had also two sisters Isis and Nephthys. Osiris married Isis and became King of Egypt, while Set married Nephthys.

Osiris[1] civilised the Egyptians, who had been cannibals, weaning them from this horrible habit by teaching them how to grow corn, which Isis discovered growing wild. But Set was jealous of the love and worship poured out by a grateful people and conspired with 72 others to murder him. He therefore made a chest and persuaded Osiris to get into it. As soon as he did so the conspirators nailed it down and flung it into the Nile.

When Isis discovered what had happened she cut her hair, donned mourning, and set forth to seek the body. The chest meanwhile floated away to Byblos, in Syria, the sacred city of Adonis. It stranded and an erica tree sprang up and, growing round the chest, completely enclosed it in its trunk. This tree the king of Byblos decided to cut down in order to use the trunk in his palace for a column, not knowing what it contained. Isis learned in some way what had happened, and set out for Byblos. When she reached that city she sat down and wept by a well, and while there certain female servants of the king came to the well to fetch water. They told the Queen of the mysterious stranger by the well, and she invited Isis to come to the palace and act as nurse to her son. The goddess tried to make the babe immortal by placing it in the fire at night, while she transformed herself into a swallow and fluttered round the column which held the body of her husband.[a]

The Queen, however, had been secretly watching her and now rushed in and snatched the child from the flames, thereby depriving him of the chance of becoming immortal. The goddess revealed herself in her true form and begged for the pillar, which request being granted, she cut it open and obtained therefrom the corpse. This done she threw herself upon it and embraced it, from which action she subsequently conceived.[2] As to the trunk of the tree, this she preserved carefully, and wrapping it in fine linen, anointed it and gave it to the King and Queen, who set it up in the local temple where, according to Plutarch, it still stood in his day.

---

1. General References. Plutarch, " Isis et Osiris." 12. 20.
   A. Wiedemann, " Religion of the Ancient Egyptians." (London, 1897). pp. 207 sq.
   G. Maspero, " Histoire ancienne des Peuples de l'Orient Classique." I. pp. 172 sq.
   E. A. Wallis Budge, " The Gods of the Egyptians." II. pp. 123 sq.
   Id. " Osiris and Egyptian Resurrection." I. pp. 1. sq.
   J. N. Breasted, " Development of Religion and Thought in Ancient Egypt."
2. " Pyramid Texts." See J. N. Breasted, " Development of Religion and Thought in Ancient Egypt." p. 28.
(a) The similarity of these details to those found in the story of Demeter is most suspicious, as also is the fact that the events are said to have occurred at the sacred city of Adonis, Byblos.

Isis then returned to Egypt by boat, bearing the body in its chest, and this she hid among the swamps of the delta, whither she went to bring forth her son Horus. After his birth she hid him carefully from Set who would, she knew, slay the child. One day while she was away from the chest visiting her son Horus at Buto, Set found it when out boar hunting, by the light of a full moon.[1] He recognised the body, and, tearing it into fourteen pieces, scattered it throughout the land; but Isis set forth once more on her weary quest and by degrees gathered together the fragments, except the genital organs, which had been eaten by a fish, and to replace it Isis made a wooden substitute. Then she and Nephthys lifted up their voices in a lamentation, which brings to mind that of the Syrians over Tammuz and of the Jews over their Kings.

" Come to thy house. Come to thy house, O god On . . . . I am thy sister, whom thou lovest, thou shalt not part from me . . . . I see thee not, yet doth my heart yearn after thee and my eyes desire thee.[a]   Come to her who loves thee . . . . come to thy sister, come to thy wife, . . . I call after thee and weep so that my cry is heard in Heaven, but thou hearest not my voice; Yet am I thy sister, whom thou didst love on earth; thou didst love none but me, my brother! My brother! "[2]

The lamentation of the two sisters caused Ra, the Sun God, to send to them Anubis, who, with the additional help of Thoth and Horus, assisted them to reconstruct the whole body. Thus there were five persons, reminding us of the five F.C.'s, who assisted at the raising of Osiris. So they raised him from the dead, and henceforth he reigned as the Lord of Truth and King of the Underworld. Because he had thus risen from the dead all Egyptians, trusting in him, believed that they too should rise again.

As the judge of the Underworld they had to appear before him, and in order to gain admission to his realm had to prove that they had lived a good moral life and were filled with Truth. Those who failed were cast into a place of torment,[3] or, according to some accounts, annihilated.[4]

In addition to the story of the raising of Osiris, we have accounts of the raising of two children by Isis. In the first we are told that while wandering amid the swamps of the Delta, Isis accompanied by seven scorpions, came to a cottage. The woman who owned the house was frightened of the scorpions and shut the door in the face of the goddess, whereupon one of the scorpions crept under the door, and stung the woman's child so that he died. When, however, Isis heard the wailing of the stricken mother, her

---

1. Plutarch, " Isis et Osiris."   8. 18.
2. E. A. Wallis Budge, " Osiris and the Egyptian Resurrection." II, 59 sq.
3. Maspero, " Popular Stories of Ancient Egypt." p. 149.
4. E. A. Wallis Budge, " The Book of the Dead," Vol. I. p. lxv.
(a) Compare also the Song of Solomon.

heart was touched, and, laying her hands on the dead child, she spake words of power which drove the poison out of his body and restored him to life.

The second story relates how one day she found her own son, Horus, who was still a child, stretched stiff and lifeless in the place where she had hidden him from Set, viz, in Buto. He had been stung by a scorpion. Thereupon she appealed to Ra, who stopped the solar barque in which he was travelling and sent Thoth to her aid. He taught her a powerful spell by which she re-animated the dead body of Horus.[1]

These two stories are of special interest as they indicate that Isis, who is, of course, the Great Mother, is largely, at any rate, the agent of the Resurrection. The death and resurrection of Horus, the son of the dead Osiris, no doubt represents the planting of the seed and its resurrection as the green corn, whereas the death of Isiris refers to the harvesting of the previous crop, its winnowing and subsequent scattering over the ploughed field. Therefore Osiris represents the Semitic Moloch, and Horus, Tammuz.

Turning back to the main legend the following points are important:—

(1). The begetting of a son by the corpse, which clearly refers to the corn slain at the harvest and gathered into bins, which, although thus " killed," is yet able to beget in the womb of mother earth a son, corn.

(2). The loss of the Phallus, shows that originally in Egypt as among the Semites, the god was deprived of his male member by the goddess, though later the incident was remembered in connection with her in her animal form, which is here a fish, whereas her human aspect is acquitted of responsibility. Among the Yaos the Great Mother is still represented as a Marine monster.

(3). The wooden Phallus is a remnant of the earlier conception of Isiris as a tree god, an aspect which was never entirely obliterated in Egypt.

(4). The erica, or tamarisk tree, which grew round the corpse, and the subsequent veneration of the trunk also point to this aspect of Osiris as a tree god.

(5). The connection of Byblos[(a)] with the myth indicates a much closer connection between Osiris and Adonis than most people suspect, and suggests that in part the myth of Osiris was derived from the Semites, although no doubt there was an indigenous fertility cult in Egypt.

---

1. A. Wiedemann, " Religion of the Ancient Egyptians." (London, 1897). pp. 213 sq.
     E. A. Wallis Budge, " The Gods of the Egyptians." I. 487 sq., and II. 206-211.
     Id. " Osiris and the Egyptian Resurrection." (London, 1911). I. 92-96 : II. 84, 274-276.
(a)   Some scholars consider Byblos is not the city in Syria but the Delta. Plutarch, however, clearly indicates the former.

(6). The similarity of certain of the events at Byblos with those associated with Demeter at Eleusis suggests that these two widely separated areas had drawn these incidents from a common centre at Byblos, which is half-way between the two countries by the land route. Moreover, as the Phoenicians were great sea-farers, it is more likely that they carried to Egypt and Greece portions of their cult than that Greece at such an early period borrowed direct from Egypt, or vice versa. When in conjunction with these facts we have the tradition that Isis went to Byblos, we feel that there can be little doubt on this point.

Thus the death of Osiris seems to have symbolised the harvesting and the planting of the grain, but quite early in the history of Egypt the god gathered about him many of the attributes of the moon and even of the sun. Furthermore, many competent scholars[1] consider that in part we have the records of a real man, one of the first Kings of Egypt, and in support of this view Frazer[2] quotes numerous examples of real kings who were subsequently worshipped as gods by their grateful subjects. There even exist in India Temples to an Englishman, Nicholson, who died in the Mutiny.

Among the Shilluks of the White Nile the spirits of their dead kings are regularly worshipped, and until the country passed under British rule the Kings were regularly slain as soon as they began to lose their virility, because it was thought that if they continued to rule the cattle and crops would decline.

The founder of the line, Nyakang, was a real man, and it is his spirit which is transferred from each king to his successor by means of certain ceremonies.[3] As we shall have to deal with this subject in a later chapter it need not detain us now, but the fact, combined with the worship of a real man, suggests that Osiris may likewise have been a great Priest-King of a primitive vegetation cult.

It is clear that at quite an early date the Egyptian religious system was drastically reformed, and the old semi-magical fertility cult was spiritualised to a large extent. The lofty and inspiring doctrines of the resurrection and of happiness of the dead earned by a good moral life on earth must owe their origin to some great teacher. All faiths of permanent value owe their origin to a human founder, and although around these founders gather the myths and legends of the older cults, this must not blind us to the fact that for such a system to start there must have been someone to teach it. The doctrines of the Egyptian faith are so

1.   See E. A. Wallis Budge in " Osiris and the Egyptian Resurrection."
2.   Frazer, " Adonis, Attis, Osiris." II. 158 sq.
3.   C. G. Seligman, " The Cult of Nyakang and the Divine Kings of the Shilluks. (Khartum, 1911). pp. 216-232.
Diedricht Westermann, " The Shilluk People, their Language and Folklore." (Berlin, 1912). pp. XXXIX sq.

clear and explicit from the very first moment that we find any records of them, that we cannot help feeling that some man, probably a Priest-King of the ancient cult, was the prophet who transformed the old faith. It is possible that Osiris represents not only a great reformer but the last of the Priest-Kings of Egypt to be slain. Slain by the conservative and reactionary followers of the old cult, who regarded his reforms as a breach of the ancient landmarks. If so it may well be that, like a Greater than he, Osiris's death assured the victory of the cause for which he had struggled. While the time for definitely deciding this problem is not yet ripe, it should be borne in mind, for a like explanation may account for the survival among us of the name of Hiram Abiff.

The dismemberment of Osiris not only represents the scattering of the corn over the land, but the old savage custom of tearing the corn god's human representative limb from limb, of which we have seen examples in Greece. Even still in modern Europe the figure of " death " is similarly treated,[1] and in some savage parts of the world men are still sacrificed in this manner in order to increase the fertility of the soil.[2] Moreover, Plutarch informs us, quoting Manetho, that the Egyptians sacrificed red headed men[(a)] and scattered their ashes in a winnowing fan at the grave of Osiris.[3]

Furthermore, not only was Osiris dismembered, but, according to one account, so was his enemy Set,[4] which event was annually commemorated. A like Ceremony also prevailed in Chios in honour of Dionysius.[5] Let us, however, turn from these grim details and consider another important aspect of the worship of Osiris. In Babylon we know that the Kings enacted the part of the dying god, and the same occurred in Egypt at the Sed Festival, which was held once every thirty years. It dates back to the very dawn of Egyptian history and was for the purpose of " renewing " the King's strength.[6]

The ceremony consisted of a dramatic representation of the King's death and re-birth, wherein he enacted the part of Osiris. In the monuments he is depicted clothed like the mummified

1.   Frazer, " The Dying God " p. 250.
2.   Frazer, " Spirits of the Corn and of the Wild." I. 236 sq.
3.   Plutarch, " Isis et Osiris." 73. 33. Compare Diodorus Siculus I. 88.
       5, also E. A. Wallis Budge, " Osiris and the Egyptian Resurrection."
       I. 197 sq.
4.   Scholiast in " Cæsaris Germanici Aratea," in F. Eyssenhardt's ed. of
       Martianus Capella. p. 408. (Leipsic, 1866).
5.   Porphry, " De Abstinentia." II. 55.
6.   A. Moret, " Du caractere religieux de la royaulte Pharaonique." (Paris,
       1902). pp. 235-273.
       Miss M. A. Murrey, " The Osireion at Abydos." pp. 32-34.
       W. M. Flinders Petrie, " Researches in Sinai." pp. 176-185.
(a)   Probably because therein they resembled the colour of the corn.

Osiris, and it is only by the fact that his name is graven beneath the figure that we can be sure that it is a human king and not the god himself. During the ceremony the Queen stood near him and discharged arrows towards the four quarters, while the King similarly threw rings. Finally, an image of the King was buried in the tomb.[1]

Flinders Petrie considers that originally the King was actually slain and his place taken by his successor, who inherited his divine soul, but that, as manners became milder, " this fierce custom became changed, as in other lands, by appointing a deputy king to die in his stead; which idea survived in the Coptic Abu Nerus. . . . After the death of the deputy, the real king renewed his life and reigned."

M. Moret,[2] in his important work on the subject, says that the Sed festival " consisted essentially in a representation of the ritual death of the king followed by his rebirth. . . . How was this fiction carried out ? . . . By the sacrifice of human or animal victims. On behalf of the king a priest lay down in the skin of the animal victim; he assumed the position characteristic of an embryo in its mother's womb: When he came forth from the skin he was deemed to be reborn; and Pharoah, for whom this rite was celebrated, was himself reborn. . . . Perhaps the fictitious death of the King may be regarded as a mitigation of the primitive murder of the divine king, as transition from a barbarous reality to symbolism."

As we shall see later, the Egyptians had, in addition to the external rites, certain secret mysteries, which in the time of the Cæsars spread throughout the Roman Empire under the name of the Cult of Isis. Perhaps in the earliest representations of the Sed Festival, which dates from 5,500 B.C., we have the origin out of which these inner mystery rites evolved.

This was not, however, the only case in which the Egyptian King and Queen played an important part in ceremonies which commemorated the myth of Osiris. Firmicus tells us that each year a pine tree was cut down, a large hole made in the trunk, and in this was placed an image of Osiris. A year later the image was solemnly burnt,[3] a fate similar to that which befell the figure of Attis, fastened on a pine tree.[4] We know from the Egyptian monuments that one of the great festivals was that connected with the setting up of a pillar or pillars, Tat and Tattu. This pillar, according to the monument, had four crossed bars at the top, and was sometimes made to look like a human figure by having a

---

1. J. Capart, " Bulletin critique des religions de l'Egypte " in " Revue de l'Histoire des Religions. LIII. (1906). pp. 332 sq.
2. Frazer, " Adonis, Attis, Osiris," 3rd ed. Vol. 2. p. 155 sq. quoting A Moret " Mysteres Egyptiens " (Paris, 1913). pp. 187-190.
3. Firmicus Maternus, " De errore profan. relig." 27.
4. See Frazer, " Adonis, Attis, Osiris." Vol. 1. pp. 267-277.

face carved on it, the lower part being clothed in robes, whilst on the top were placed the symbols of Osiris. To complete the transformation arms were added, holding the shepherd's crook and the flail sceptre of Osiris.

This form makes it clear that Osiris was the god of vegetation and of fertility generally. The tree trunk with the four cross-pieces would represent a tree with the leaves and most of the branches cut off. The flail reminds us of the corn which was threshed with it, and the crook indicates the god's connection with flocks and herds. It is therefore, quite natural that the Egyptians should call the Tat the backbone of Osiris, in his aspect of a tree god, and the fanciful explanation of the four cross-pieces as representing the earth put forward by some writers may be quickly dismissed. If the Egyptians had wished to represent the pillar as surmounted by an emblem of the earth they would have depicted it as a square. Neither can we consider the Tat as the origin of the pillars outside King Solomon's temple, which are clearly, from their shape and ornamentation, Phallic. The most that we can admit is that at a late period these two emblems may have become confused together in the minds of the populace.

Prof. P. E. Newberry in a private letter to Sir J. G. Frazer quoted by him,[1] sets forth an interesting theory suggesting that Osiris was originally a god of the cedar, imported into Egypt from Lebanon, and that the Tat is simply a lopped cedar tree. He considers that the flail sceptre is really a tool used for extracting incense, and in support of this view points out that the peasants of Crete still use a flail to extract the ladanum gum from shrubs.

As Mr. Sidney Smith on quite independent grounds also considers that Osiris may be a Semitic vegetation god, these points are important. It may well be that to the Semites we owe not only the origin of monotheism but also that of the dying god, and that, far from the Adonis cult being a debtor to Egypt, the latter merely took over and spiritualized Tammuz himself. Scholars are more and more coming to the conclusion that the dominant race in Egypt were Semitic invaders, and this being so, it is not improbable that they should bring with them their local gods.

The reformed and spiritualised form of the cult of Osiris may be due to the rise of a great King and teacher on the banks of the Nile, whose personality stamped the cult with those peculiar features which henceforth distinguished it from the original cult whence it was derived.

Before returning to Judea, let us just glance at a certain strange divinity who, well known among the Greeks and Romans, was by them associated with the Jews.

---

1. Frazer, " Adonis, Attis, Osiris." Vol. II. p. 109. Note 1.

SABAZIUS

This deity was a Prygian or Thracian god, usually identified with Dionysius in Greece and occasionally with Zeus. His worship was closely associated with Attis, whom he no doubt was, under another name. From the statement in Val. Max. 1.3.2, it has been thought that he was in early days the same as the Jewish Sabaoth. As Plutarch[1] declares that the Jews worshipped Dionysius and that their Sabbath was so named after Sabazius, there does seem to be evidence to support the view that even in the days of the Cæsars the old fertility cult had not lost all its open supporters among the Jews.

We know that in 139 B.C. the first Jews who tried to settle at Rome were expelled under the terms of a law which forbad the teaching of the cult of " Jupiter Sabazius," and thus there seems no doubt that the worship of Sabazius, or Tammuz, was generally considered to be common among the Jews.

By the second century A.D., however, this cult had gained a firm foothold in Rome, for numerous votive tablets inscribed with his name have been found there. Gradually, he became completely merged in Attis,[2] and his chief interest to us in this book is because the above facts show that the cult of Tammuz under the name of Sabazius was, among the Romans, associated not merely with the Syrians but actually with the Jews themselves.

---

1. Plutarch, " Synus." IV. 6.
2. See Article, " Sabazius " Encycl. Brit. 11th ed. (1911). Vol. XXIII. p. 958.
   J. E. Harrison, " Prologomena in Greek Religion." (1908) p. 414.

CHAPTER VII

THE ADONIS RITES OF JUDAH

The vision of Ezekiel in c.B.C. 594[1] gives a clear picture of the secret rites of Tammuz. He starts as follows:—

He " brought me . . . to the door of the inner gate that looks towards the north where was the image of Jealousy which provoketh to jealousy."

What was the " Image of Jealousy " opposite the north gate —the symbolic place of darkness ? It was Ashtoreth, that is to say, Astarte, the Great Mother, the Lover of Tammuz. In II Kings[2] we read that the good king Josiah broke down and defiled the high places " which Solomon the King of Israel had builded for Ashtoreth," and also for Chemosh and Milcom. So that there should be no doubt of the situation of the shrine of Ashtoreth, we are carefully told that it was on the right-hand side. As the temple had its Sanctuary in the west it follows that the right-hand side was on the North. The exact spot on which the shrine of Astarte stood was the Mount of Olives.

Jeremiah,[3] about B.C. 600, gives us the following significant details concerning one of the ceremonies performed in honour of Astarte, whom he calls " The Queen of Heaven," which was one of her later titles.

" Seest thou not what they do in the cities of Judah and in the streets of Jerusalem ? The children gather wood and the fathers kindle the fire, and the women kneed dough *to make cakes* and to pour out drink offerings unto other Gods."

Here we should note the use of bread and wine for a sacramental feast, while we know from similar observances elsewhere, which survived in Europe up to the 19th century, that these cakes were in the shape of the male organ.[4]

Moreover, Jeremiah complains that even the remnant who fled to Egypt after the fall of Jerusalem would not abandon this custom, and to his protests gave an answer which explains exactly the purpose of these obscene emblems, and of similar incidents connected with the worship of the great Fertility Goddess, who by then had largely absorbed the attributes of the Moon, just as her son and lover has partly absorbed those of the Sun.

They " answered " Jeremiah saying,[5] " The Word that thou

---

1. Ezekiel 8. 3. sq.
2. II. Kings, 23. 13.
3. Jeremiah 8. 17 sq.
4. N. M. Penzer, " Ocean of Story," Vol. II. p. 13. Note 3.
5. Jeremiah 44. 16 sq.

hast spoken unto us in the name of the Lord we will not hearken unto thee, but will certainly do whatsoever thing goeth out of our own mouth, to burn incense unto the Queen of Heaven and to pour out drink offerings unto her, as we have done, we and our fathers, our kings and our princes, in the cities of Judah and in the streets of Jerusalem; for then had we plenty of bread, and were well, and saw no evil.   But since we left off to burn incense to the Queen of Heaven and to pour out drink offerings unto her, we have wanted all and have been consumed by the sword and by the famine.

"And when we burned incense to the Queen of Heaven and poured out drink offerings unto her, did we make her cakes to worship her and pour out drink offerings to her without our men (husbands)[a]."

From this answer we learn that the worshippers believed that unless they offered the Goddess these Phallic cakes they would receive from her no harvest.   The reason is clear: the corn God represents the seed which is buried in the womb of the earth. The male organ of the drone bee is literally plucked out by the Queen bee and remains embedded in her for the rest of her life; it is in this way that she is fertilised, but at the cost of the life of the drone.   In like manner Attis and Tammuz die that the earth may be fertile, hence the reason why the Priests of Cybele and of Artemis at Ephesus had to castrate themselves and offer up their male organs to the Goddess.

Therefore the Jewish women, like other worshippers of the Great Goddess, offered as substitutes for the male organs of their husbands, models made out of the "Flesh" of the slain corn God, and poured out wine to symbolise the blood which naturally flowed when the human male organ was cut off, as in the case of the Priests of Cybele.

In order to make themselves one with God, the worshippers ate the bread and drank some of the wine.   Similar rites were performed all over the world to the Goddess of Fertility, and here we have clear evidence of their survival among the Jews up to B.C. 587.

We learn further that naturally these offerings of cakes were made only by the women and at the shrine of Astarte at the north gate.   No doubt it was at this time that the women wept for Tammuz slain, whose sad fate they thus commemorated while hoping thereby to gain an abundant harvest.

We also see why fire played an important part in these old rites.   The children gathered the sticks; at one time they formed the fuel for the sacrifice of burning!   The men lighted the fire; they had begotten the children, and hence the symbolism of the

---

(a)   It was the women alone who carried the obscene emblems in the procession of Isis in Egypt.   Frazer.   "Adonis" Vol. 2. p. 112.

act! It was the women, however, who made the cakes, for from them come forth men, as does corn from the Earth.

But what were the men doing while the women were busy at the north gate ? We shall find that some of them were at the *centre* in a hidden vault, namely the tomb itself, while others stood watching the east so that they might proclaim the resurrection of the slain God; that the corn would come forth from the womb of Mother Earth; that a new son of the Goddess would be born, destined like his father to wed the Goddess and thereby lose his life. Thus Astarte was every year a widow, and her son posthumous.

But though the women had their duties outside the closely barred door of the hidden mysteries, they were evidently not admitted therein. This was the men's house and therefore we will return to Ezekiel and see what he says on the subject, having thus decided whom the " Figure of Jealousy " represented and what was taking place before it.

Ezekiel dismisses most of what is taking place before Astarte with the words, see " . . . . the great abominations which the House of Israel committeth here,"[1] and then turns to something which seemed to him even worse, " And He brought me to the door of the court; and when I looked, behold a hole in the wall.[2] Then said He unto me, Son of man dig now in the wall; And when I digged in the wall, behold a door. And He said unto me, Go in, and behold the wicked abominations which they do here. So I went in and saw; and behold every form of creeping thing and abominable beast, and all the idols of the House of Israel, portrayed upon the walls round about."[a]

We thus learn that this vault, which still exists, was close tiled by being filled in with wet plaster or mud during the ceremony. The creeping things, etc., would be the animals and beasts, such as the bee, the serpent, and the goat, sacred to Astarte, who with the other Gods were painted in frescoes round this chamber. We also notice that the prophet does not call these the Gods of the Canaanites but of " the house of Israel," a most significant fact. What was happening in this close shut chamber away from the light of day ?

" And there stood before them the seventy men of the Ancients of the house of Israel, and in the midst of them stood Jaazaniah, the son of Shaphan, with every man his censor in his hand, and a thick cloud of incense went up."

The first fact that strikes us is that there were seventy, plus a Master of Ceremonies, whose name is given. We are told these

---

1. Ezekiel 8. 6.   2. Ezekiel 8. 8.
(a) This actually exists to-day in the South-East corner of the " Rock " of the altar of sacrifice and leads into the vault. See later ref.
Dean Stanley. " Sinai and Palestine " also Dudley Wright. " Masonic Legends," p. 37 sq.

were the ancients of Israel, and as we know that the Sanhedrin at the time of the second temple consisted of 72 of the elders of Israel, we can hardly fail to recognise that these men are the Sanhedrin. This would explain the bitter indignation of the true prophet who thus saw the spiritual rulers of the people presiding at what, to him, were unholy rites. But there were only 71, where then was the missing member ? We may be sure he was there, but perhaps he could no longer speak, and was either simulating a corpse or, more probably, in grim earnest lying stiff and cold. He no doubt was the representative of Tammuz whom the women were bewailing above ground at the North gate.

This explanation is supported by the emphasis laid on the use of incense. There were apparently no statues in this rock hewn tomb, for otherwise assuredly Ezekiel would have mentioned them. He carefully says, however, that the figures were painted on the walls of the chamber, and incense is not offered to frescoes in religious ceremonies.

Let us refresh our memories as to what happened in Babylonia at the lamentation for Tammuz. " The dirges were seemingly chanted over an effigy of the dead God, which was washed with pure water, anointed with oil and clad in red robes, while the fumes of incense rose into the air, as if to stir his dormant senses by their pungent fragrance and waken him from his sleep of death." [1]

Thus we see that the stress laid on the use of incense is perfectly intelligible : there was no need for Ezekiel to go into details which were well known to every Jew, while if the figure was in truth a dead man his repugnance in referring to it is perfectly intelligible. The Babylonians who were more civilised at that epoch than the Jews may well have substituted an image for a man, just as the Greeks did later ; perhaps when all went well the Jews also had learnt to do the same, but in the hour of dread and danger, blood, and only human blood, could satisfy the Goddess.

The prophets of Jehovah, Jeremiah and Ezekiel, had proclaimed that He had doomed Judah to destruction. What then of the Great Mother. Perhaps she at least would hear them ? But in this hour of extremity no paltry substitutes would suffice. We may well believe that the frenzied worshippers of Astarte cried, " It is meet that one man should die for the whole people." And who but the High Priest of Tammuz could prove an acceptable sacrifice ?

But Exekiel leaves us in little doubt on the point, for in the next chapter but two he says:—" Moreover, the Spirit lifted me up and brought me unto the East gate of the Lord's house, which looketh eastwards, and behold at the door of the gate five and

---

1.   Frazer, " Adonis, Attis, Osiris." 3rd ed. Vol. I. p. 9.

twenty men, among whom I saw Jaazaniah, the son of Azur, and Pelatiah, the son of Benaiah, Princes of the people. Then said He unto me, Son of Man, these are the men that devise mischief and give wicked counsel in this city: which say, Let us build houses: this city is the cauldron and we be the flesh."[1]

The meaning of this phrase seems obscure, but we will follow it up in a moment. Meanwhile we obtain one of the keys to the problem, two verses further on, in the fiery denunciation of the Prophet.

" Ye have multiplied your slain in this city, ye have filled the streets thereof with slain. Therefore, thus saith the Lord God; Your slain whom ye have lain in the midst of it they are the flesh and this the cauldron. . . . Ye have feared the sword, and I will bring a sword upon you, saith the Lord God."

Here, from the burning and justifiable wrath of the prophet we learn that these twenty-five men, in order to avert the threatened attack by the Babylonians, had recently had a great " Day of Blood," no doubt like that of Cybele in Rome, but with fatal results. We learn also that Jaazaniah was one of the Princes of Israel, and have previously seen that the old Syrian Kings considered that they were incarnations of the God Tammuz. Thus there can, I fear, be little doubt as to whether it was a real or simulated corpse which lay in the rock hewn tomb while the voice of lamentation went up at the North gate.

The reference to the cauldron and the flesh must now be considered. Jeremiah when the Lord asked him " What seest thou ?"[2] answered, " And I said, I see a seething pot; and the face thereof is towards the North." It will be noticed that the face of the pot is towards the place where stood the shrine of Astarte: the place of darkness and of the Underworld, which is most significant. At first sight it might be thought that this pot was merely a parable, but it appears that it was really one of the chief causes of the wrath of Jehovah, since it stood for a Pagan Rite which He abominated. There is a widespread magical process of which we find many traces whereby if a man is slain, cut up and boiled in a pot, he will be restored to youth and life. According to Greek legends Medea took advantage of this superstition to encompass the death of her father-in-law, and the ancient British God of the Sea had a magic cauldron in which he placed the bodies of men who had been slain in battle and brought them back to life again.[3]

In the High History of the Holy Graal we have a very unpleasant story concerning such a cauldron. The Son of a King who followed the *Old Law* was slain by a Giant. Sir Gawain killed the Giant and brought back the boy's corpse, whereupon to

1. Ezekiel 11. 1 sq.
2. Jeremiah 1. 13.
3. Mabinogion pp. 37, 44. Everyman ed.

his amazement the father took the corpse, cut it up, boiled it in a cauldron and then distributed the pieces among his chief men.[1]

Many competent critics now consider that the Graal legends incorporate incidents from the old cult of Adonis,[2] a view with which I agree, and if so we at once see that this cauldron was used by the Jews to perform a ceremony intended to assist in the rejuvenation and resurrection of the slain Adonis, and for this reason it was placed with its face towards the North. Whether the worshippers, like the King and nobles in the Graal story, partook of the ghastly food, we cannot definitely say, but unfortunately this seems probable. We know that similar cannibalistic feasts take place among savage tribes; we know that the corn was spoken of as the body of the Dead God, and as such was sacramentally consumed by the worshippers; we know that the wine was likened to his blood, and that these substitutes were an amelioration of an older cannibalistic feast. Therefore, at a time of crisis we may well fear that the frenzied Jews who followed this cult would not hesitate to go so far.

Indeed, the very denunciations of the prophet point in this direction. We know that the Prophet of Jehovah after referring to some idolatrous practice constantly says a similar fate shall fall upon the whole nation.[a] For example, in this very passage Ezekiel, after referring to these slayings, says that the men who did them shall in their turn be slain. Moreover, a few chapters later in denouncing Judah he says:—

" Thou hast taken thy sons and thy daughters, whom thou has born unto Me, and these hast thou sacrificed to devour them.

Thou hast slain my children and delivered them to cause them to pass through the fire for them."[3]

The combined effect of these two passages indicates quite clearly that not only were the children sacrificed by means of fire, but they were actually eaten.

In verse 13 of chapter 2, Ezekiel tells us that Pelatiah died. Perhaps herein we receive a hint as to who was the silent corpse in the secret chamber, for there Jaazaniah alone is mentioned by name.

But there were other incidents connected with these rites of Adonis, for " He said also unto me,[4] Turn thee yet again, thou shalt see greater abominations that they do. Then he brought me to the door of the gate of the Lord's house which was towards the North;[b] and behold there sat women weeping for Tammuz. And he said unto me, Hast thou seen, O Son of Man ? turn thee

---

1. The High History of the Holy Graal. Trans. by Dr. S. Evans. Everyman ed. p. 76.
2. J. L. Weston, " The Quest of the Holy Graal."
3. Ezekiel, 16. 20 sq.
4. Ezekiel, 8, 13.
(a) See also the fate of the false prophets in Jeremiah 14, 15.
(b) Where stood the figure of Astarte and apparently the seething cauldron.

yet again, thou shalt see greater abominations than these. And he brought me into the inner court of the Lord's house, and, behold at the door of the Temple of the Lord, between the porch and the altar, were about twenty-five men with their backs towards the Temple of the Lord, and their faces towards the east; and they worshipped the sun towards the east."

We learn further that " they put the branch to their nose." This might appear to be only a sign of derision, but a branch or a tree is always closely associated with Tammuz, as we have already seen, and Mr. Stanley Smith of the Assyrian Department of the British Museum agrees with me that this also was one of the ritual practices of the cult. The soul of the slain man was supposed to enter into a tree, which symbolically grew out of the grave. The original idea was that the seed which was planted and died transmitted its soul to the plant or branch which grew therefrom.

That the Jews enacted a tree drama, similar to that in the Cult of Attis, is shown by Jeremiah. " For the customs of the people are vain: for one cutteth a tree out of the forest, the work of the hands of the workman, with the axe.

They deck it with silver and with gold; they fasten it with nails and with hammers, that it move not.

They are upright as the palm tree, but speak not: they must needs be born, because they cannot go. Be not afraid of them."[1]

This clearly indicates the ceremonial carrying in of a decorated tree, probably with an image of Tammuz fastened thereon, as we find elsewhere, particularly in the worship of Attis.

We know that they said of a stock, i.e., a pillar of wood, " Thou art my father." These stocks were plain pieces of wood, merely trunks of trees, and it is clear that they were not only symbols of the phallus but also the residing place of the Spirit of Vegetation. Among many primitive races the belief is current that the souls of those waiting to become incarnate dwell in the trees, so much so that many races think that a woman can become pregnant if the seed or flower of certain trees falls on her. Thus certain Central African races believe that if the purple blossom of the banana tree falls on the back of a woman, even though she be unmarried, she will have a baby.[2]

In this belief we have the cause and origin of many stories well known to the students of folk-lore in which a virgin gives birth to a child because she has smelt a flower, eaten a fruit, or perhaps merely handled either. For example, Attis himself is said to have been born because his virgin mother, Nana, placed a certain seed in her bosom. Nana, incidentally, means Mother, and is of course the name of the Great Mother. Probably the

---

1. Jeremiah 10. 3. sq.
2. Rev. J. Roscoe, " The Baganda," pp. 47 sq.

answer given to the inquisitive child to-day who wants to know whence the new baby has come, namely, that it was grown on a gooseberry bush, is the worn down tradition of this once almost universal belief. Fantastic as it sounds, even now many tribes do not know that a woman cannot become a Mother without the help of a man.[1] They say that she becomes a mother only when a soul which is waiting for the opportunity can slip inside her, and the most common method adopted by these waiting embryos is to hide themselves in a seed or flower, or merely fall from a bush on to a woman. Races who still hold these beliefs are the tribes of New Guinea and the Australian blacks. Hence to these people there is nothing very remarkable in a virgin birth.

Now all these tribes believe in re-incarnation, and their line of argument runs somewhat as follows:—We bury our dead in the ground, and lo, a tree or plant grows from the spot. This contains the life-principle of him who dies, his soul is in it, and from it he leaps into a woman and so once more is born. Frankly, the modern man who, while acknowledging that a human being has a soul, appears to believe that that soul is created by the same procedure that creates the infant's body is even more illogical, for how can a material act create an immaterial and immortal being ?

The doctrine of re-incarnation attaches to the Spirit of Vegetation in a much higher degree. The God dies and is buried, a tree springs up from his grave, and therein resides the soul which can again enter into flesh. So powerful is this divine soul that it can, as it were, eject, or at any rate overshadow, the ordinary human soul resident in a suitable body, and take its place. Therefore certain of the ceremonies of the Vegetation Cult include elaborate details for transferring the soul of the dead God-man into a strong and healthy physical body, which henceforth is supposed to possess the Divine Soul, and ultimately suffers the same fate as its predecessor. Among such rites are raising the Corpse and drawing in the dead man's breath; stepping over the corpse or over its grave, etc. Thus it would appear as though the transference of the Divine soul of Adonis in Judea was made by someone sniffing a bough, which had either formed part of the Adonis tree or had been planted on his grave. This fact explains the significance of the sprig of acacia in masonry.

We now understand why the Jews said of a tree trunk or " Stock," " Thou has begotten us." The actual passage is as follows:—

" Saying to a stock, Thou art my father:[a] and to a stone,[b]

---

1. Prof. Malinowski, " The Beliefs of the Trobriand Islands, New Guinea."
(a)   or " Hast begotten me,"
(b)   These seem to have been flat stones with a socket into which the "Stock" was set. These would symbolise Mother Earth, and the "Stock" the Spirit Vegetation. The Phallus and Yoni symbolism is obvious.

Thou hast brought me forth: for they have turned the hinder part of their necks to me and not the face."[1]

The authorised version says, " Backs " but the above is the literal Hebrew and conveys an important piece of information. " Their backs " might be merely allegorical, but the other phrase admirably depicts what the twenty-five elders were doing, i.e., with heads bent back gazing upwards, watching for the sun to rise above the horizon, which would indicate that the soul of the dead Tammuz had arisen and passed into the bough which his successor was about to sniff.

Thus we see in both scriptural passages a reference to the worship of the sun and to a tree, and in each case the primitive idea is clearly re-birth, or the resurrection of the slain God, Tammuz, over whom the women at the north gate were weeping, while the seventy and one elders in the tomb were by means of prayer and incense striving to raise him. We can have little doubt that a sprig, possibly of acacia, was sticking in the rock of sacrifice, beneath which lay the human representative of Tammuz, while the silent watchers waited for the golden dawn in the East to proclaim the great truth " Adonis, the Lord, hath risen from the dead; the whole earth will be fertilised through his Divine energy." Then, no doubt, the watchers seizing the bough or tree sniffed it ceremonially.[a]

Thus we see a tendency to unite in Tammuz, the Vegetation Spirit, or Corn God, and also the Sun God, nor is evidence lacking that he also gathered up details which in strictness belonged to the Moon. For example, the mourning for Adonis lasted three days, which is meaningless if he was either a purely Solar or a purely Corn God, whereas the Moon vanished from the sky for three whole days every month. On the other hand, this occurs thirteen times in the year and not once a year, as does the burying of the seed. Astarte also takes on, at quite an early date, the attributes of the Moon and of Venus, a point which is of some importance to us. It should also be noted that she was from the very earliest not only the Goddess of Love but of War and Destruction, therein showing her similarity to Kali, in India, and giving a good reason why her mate should bear such a title as " He who destroys."

The date of the mourning for Tammuz seems to have been near Midsummer in Judea, in other words, at the gathering in of the Harvest, which in Palestine takes place in two sections:—the barley in April and the wheat towards the end of May and the beginning of June. The second half of June and the first half of July is still called Tammuz by the Jews. The mourning synchro-

1. Jeremiah, 2. 27.
(a) Compare the ritual death and resurrection rite among the Australian Blacks. See Chap. XX.

nised with the threshing,[1] hence the significance of the fact that the Temple was built on the threshing floor of Arunah the Jebusite. It is generally believed that it actually occurred about Midsummer Day, or St. John in Summer, as we should call it, and Professor Jastrow says:—" The calendar of the Jewish church still marks the seventeenth day of Tammuz as a fast, and Houtsma has shown that the association of the day with the capture of Jerusalem by the Romans represents merely the attempt to give an ancient festival a worthier interpretation."[2]

We have thus learnt from the Bible itself a good deal about the Rites of Tammuz, and here and now we must note that 600 years later than the time of Ezekiel, namely in the days of Josephus, the Essenes worked a secret Initiation Rite of four degrees, and though regarded as good Jews, nevertheless prayed to the Sun just before the dawn as if invoking him to rise.[3] Surely this fact is most significant and suggests that in the Essenes we have at least one of the links by which the old Adonis Cult, cleansed and purified, was passed on to the Roman Colleges of Architects, and so, via the Mediæval Comacine Masons, to us.

Let us now recapitulate what we have discovered concerning the Rites of Adonis among the Jews, as revealed in their own writings. There were three courts in the Temple of King Solomon, which may hint at three degrees. The first was the women's court, beyond which they were not permitted to pass, and which therefore would symbolise birth. The second court was that of the men, and obviously symbolises life in this world of work and war. The third was restricted to the Priests, and it was here that the great natural rock altar of sacrifice stood; on this the burnt offerings were made, and beneath it was the mysterious rock-hewn chamber, still in existence. Is not this the open grave— the tomb, the symbol of death and also, be it noted, of sacrifice ?

Beyond this lay the porch, whence the twenty-five elders looked east towards the Sun. Here at times stood the throne of the King; may we not call it the chair of the Master ? Behind lay the enclosed part of the Temple, divided into two, and into the Sanctum Sanctorum only the High Priest himself might enter.

To us the porch would symbolise the Installed Master, the risen King, and beyond lay the mystery of the unity of the Godhead and the Sacred Name, while the innermost secrets were reserved for the High Priest, who would correspond to the J. of the R.A., and his ceremonies to the Masonic degree of High Priest, which seems to have been originally part of the secrets of J.[4]

---

1. Frazer, " Adonis, Attis, Osiris." 3rd ed. Vol. I. p. 231.
2. Prof. M. Jastrow, " The Religion of Babylonia and Assyria." pp. 547, 682.
3. Josephus, " The Wars of the Jews," 11. 8 : " Antiquities " 13. 5. par. 9 . 18. 1. par. 5.
4. Ward, " An Explanation of the R.A. Degree."

It will be noticed that if so, the King or Master sat in the West, which is precisely what we still find in an Operative Lodge, and the present position in a Speculative Lodge may be due to the increasing triumph of the Solar Cult over the old Vegetation Cult.

Students are of the opinion that the Kings of Judah were anointed, crowned and enthroned between the Pillars, and we know that Adonis in other Syrian Kingdoms was the Divine King of the city. His robes were red, like those of the Z. in the R.A., and when the Roman soldiery in mockery crowned Jesus they robed him in Royal red[a] in a manner similar to that in which the figure of Adonis lay in state.

The women were certainly not in the secret vault, that is clear, and therefore the regulation which debarred them from approaching nearer to the altar than their own court was not exclusively a Jehovistic command. It is thus quite probable that there were in Judah, just as there were in other ancient religions, an exoteric and an esoteric Cult. The ordinary worshippers never got further than the substituted secrets, which in this case would be an explanation that the ceremony was a magical one intended to increase the fertility of the soil; the Priests, however, who entered the Temple itself, learnt there, not merely an allegorical interpretation of the external ceremonies, but, still more important, that God was one, and one only. This teaching, which as masons well know, forms the essence of the R.A., is common to many faiths, but in Judea it seems as if some members of this supreme degree, filled with zeal for the true God, refused to remain silent. They shouted from the house tops their great discovery that there was but one God, and, despite persecution, and probably in many cases death itself, persisted in their teaching.

Nevertheless, there may have been other spiritually minded men who, while recognising that the old Adonis Cult as it then stood contained much that was repulsive, perceived that it also contained much that was good, and therefore set themselves to purge it of certain objectionable elements. And we shall see in the next chapter, in the writings attributed to King Solomon, there seems to be the beginning of an attempt to attach an allegorical meaning to some of the ceremonies. After the Captivity this school of thought, I suggest, used this Cult as an allegory, and by dramatic representations taught the great truth that death does not end all, for beyond the grave of the willing sacrifice lies the resurrection, and only by that path can men truly enter into the knowledge of God. These men, I consider, were represented in the days of Josephus by the Essenes.

(a)   Purple in Biblical and classical times means " Red " not the violet colour we now call purple.

Let us now concentrate on what the Adonis Rites were:

(1) There was a tree and the slaying of a God-man; which ceremony may in times of prosperity have been merely a dramatic representation, but in times of stress, as even to-day in India,[a] no doubt men were slain.

(2) There was a ceremony with a cauldron.

(3) The women offered cakes in the form of the phallus to Astarte, and wept for Tammuz, the cakes being clearly a substitute for the male organs of their husbands.

(4) Meanwhile in a secret cave under the altar of sacrifice the Elders were endeavouring to raise the slain man to life.

(5) In front of the altar, and facing the rising sun, twenty-five other Elders were invoking the Sun, waiting for it to rise, as that was the sign that he who had died as a man had entered into Heaven as a God.

(6) After that a branch of a tree played an important part and was sniffed by some of the worshippers. This branch was apparently growing out of the grave of the dead man.

(7) There was a sacramental meal consisting of bread and wine, symbolising the body and blood of the Vegetation God, which in all such Rites replaces a more cannibalistic feast, hinted at in the presence of the cauldron, which later appears in the Graal legend, even in the 12th century. This feast seems to have been an integral part of the Essene Rites.

Now all these features were, as we have seen, characteristic of the Rites of the Great Mother and her lover Son all over the world, and most of them in a more decent form survive in Freemasonry to-day, either in the Craft or in the higher degrees.

Moreover, we have not yet exhausted all the information concerning these ceremonies which we can obtain from the Bible itself, and in the next chapter we shall learn a good deal from two books which are supposed to have been written by King Solomon.

There existed, however, among the Jews not only the open Rites of Adonis but also an inner secret ceremony. Can we therefore trace any further features of the Adonis Cult, and in particular what was supposed to befall the Soul of the representative of Adonis during the three days between his death and resurrection ? This quest we will take up in the next chapter but one, for there is no doubt that the legend of Jonah deals with this theme.

(a) In January 1915, I stood in the Kaligat at Calcutta and saw the goats being slaughtered as a sacrifice in front of the door of the Temple of Kali. My Brahmin guide said, " Before the British came they sacrificed men to her, and even now when famine visits the land the people secretly offer a man to the Great Goddess." Kali represents the destructive side of Shiva, but she is also the Great Mother. She is the only Divinity in India still worshipped with blood sacrifices.

CHAPTER VIII

SOLOMON'S PART IN THE ADONIS RITES

Tradition ascribes to King Solomon the authorship of two books in the Bible and places them in the closest juxtaposition; these are Ecclesiastes and the Song of Solomon. Concerning the former the Rabbis relate the following tradition.[1]

Solomon trapped Asmodeus, a demon King, by making him drunk with wine, and then forced him to obtain for Solomon the Shamir, a magical worm, by means of which the King of Israel was able to cut the stones for the Temple without using metal tools. The Shamir in reality seems to have been a hard stone used for cutting other stones, and was probably a king of whetstone with which the stones of the building were dressed. At Seringham near Trichinopoli, in Southern India, I watched native masons carving a design on tall stone pillars, which were to be used in repairing a Temple to Shiva. Instead of using metal tools they had what looked exactly like a small whetstone, with which they were grinding away the face of the column in such a way as to leave a raised pattern thereon. It was a laborious, but quite effectual, method.

No doubt the wild legend now associated with the magical Shamir originated from a similar procedure. The Smiris, or Sh Mir, occurs in certain passages in the Bible,[2] where it is translated as Diamond and Adamant respectively, which substances can be similarly employed for grinding or cutting.

Having obeyed Solomon, much against his will, Asmodeus in return persuaded the King to remove the chain with which the demon was bound, and to give him the signet ring from his finger. No sooner had Solomon done so than Asmodeus seized him, *swallowed him*, and then " vomited him up " at a place 400 miles distant. Solomon now found himself unknown and penniless, and wandered through the land preaching the vanity of human greatness, at the same time trying to persuade the people that he was the real King. Meanwhile Asmodeus had by magic art assumed the form of Solomon and reigned in his stead. At length Solomon succeeded in convincing the chief men of Israel that he was the real King, and the usurper fled as Solomon reascended his throne. It was during this period of distress and misery that, according to the Rabbis, he composed Ecclesiastes.

Although the legend in its present form is absurd, it may nevertheless contain a germ of truth, and be a distorted memory

---

1. Hershon, " Talmudic Miscellany,"
   Dudley Wright, " Masonic Legends and Traditions," p. 51.
2. Jeremiah. 17. 1. and Ezekiel 3. 9.

111

of a Syrian Initiation Rite which included the symbolic swallowing of the initiate by a monster, on this legend represented by the
demon.   If so Ecclesiastes was no doubt part of the ritual then
employed, and represents truly and accurately the feelings of a
man who has mystically descended into Hell.

Every great mystic sooner or later passes through a period of
bitter disillusionment, wherein he discovers that his so-called
friends are false to him, and the great causes for which he has
laboured unceasingly are empty and vain.   Thus Ecclesiastes
rises to a height which so far we have not previously discovered
in the Fertility Rites of Syria, and indicates that behind a semi-
magical cult for the maintenance of the fertility of the soil great
thinkers had built up a higher and nobler message for the aspiring
soul.

It is, therefore, not without significance that in many Provincial workings, the last chapter of Ecclesiastes still plays an
important part in the 3rd degree in masonry.   Perhaps it has
actually wandered down to us in its appropriate place, a fact which
seems more probable if we compare it carefully with the Song
of Solomon.

Before doing so it may be worth while suggesting that though
Solomon was a real man, perhaps in Palestine he came to typify
the Master of a Lodge, who had passed through the various
grades, even as he still does in many masonic degrees.   Indeed,
the title of Most Wise may be a dim recollection of a time when
the ruler of a certain degree was called Solomon, and at any rate
every master of a Lodge is told that he is installed in the chair of
King Solomon.

If this be so, then the ascription of Ecclesiastes and of the
Song of Songs to the wise King is hardly surprising, even if he
himself did not write them, which may be possible.   If he did,
however, they must have been composed by him after he had
passed through certain ceremonies, a possibility which amounts
almost to a certainty when we realise that the King of Babylon
annually took the part of Marduk in mimic drama, descended into
the grave as representing Marduk [1] and was rescued therefrom by
the High Priest, who represented Nabu, the *Mason God.*   There
is therefore nothing unreasonable in supposing that Solomon may
have done likewise.

We can, however, go further, all the Kings of Phoenicia,
including Hiram of Tyre, claimed to represent the " Dying God,"
and a legend of a Dying God is associated with the Temple of
King Solomon, the King subsequently becoming accepted as the
Master instead of Hiram who became known as the Architect.

---

1.   Sidney Smith, " The Relations of Marduk, Ashar and Osiris."   Journal
     of Egyptian Archæology.   Vol. 8., parts 1 and 2.   April, 1922.
     Prof. Heinrich Zimmern, " Zweiter Beitrog zum Babylonischen Neu-
     jahrsfest."   (Leipzig, 1918).

Let us now turn to the Song of Solomon. The death of Tammuz resulted from his being wooed by Astarte, and the last chapter of Ecclesiastes clearly refers to death and to the feelings of a man who has mystically descended into the Underworld: with these facts before us this Song at once becomes intelligible.

At one time it was customary to explain the Song of Solomon as a prophetic vision of Christ and His Church, and the translators of the authorised version accepted this view and emphasised it by the brief summaries which they placed at the head of each chapter. To-day no serious or reliable Biblical scholar accepts this view and all agree that it is an erotic Eastern love song, but this fact, although now fully recognised, only raises a further problem, which is, how did an erotic poem come to be included in a volume of Sacred Writings ?

The explanation at first sight may appear startling, but is nevertheless correct. The Song of Solomon is a ritual song of the old Fertility Rite of Astarte. The key to the problem, as is usually the case, lies within the Poem itself, in chapter 2, verse 12, but before we go into this point it may be necessary, for the benefit of some of my readers, who do not claim to be Biblical scholars, to prove that the Song is erotic and of the earth,—earthy.

" He shall lie all night between my breasts "[1]
" His left hand is under my head and his right hand doth embrace me."[2]

I hardly think it is necessary to quote any further examples to prove that the lady's feelings towards " her beloved " were neither mystical nor platonic ! When we turn to consider its connection with the Fertility Rites we cannot fail to be struck with the continual reference made to the Spring and to plants, especially the vine, the palm tree, the pomegranate, etc., but any doubt as to the true purpose is set at rest by chapter 2, verse 12, which is supposed to be spoken by the man, and which in the authorised version runs as follows:—

" Rise up, my love, my fair one, and come away. For the winter is passed, the rain is over and gone; the flowers appear on the earth; the time of the singing (of birds) is come, and the voice of the turtle is heard in our land: the fig tree putteth forth her green figs, and the vines with the tender grapes give a good smell. Arise, my love, my fair one, and come away."

That the period is Spring is obvious, but the pregnant passage is " the time of the singing," etc. The words inside the brackets are, in the authorised version, printed in italics to show that they are not found in the original Hebrew and have been

---

1. The Song of Solomon, 1. 13.
2. Ibid. 2. 6.

inserted by the translators in order to make sense. Unfortunately they did not know the exact meaning of the Hebrew word "Zamir" which they translated "singing," but to-day we do know, owing to the existence of a similar word in Babylonia. "Zamir" means "Ritual Song" and has nothing to do with singing birds. Moreover this word occurs only in ritual songs, and in Babylonia it is found employed in the ritual songs connected with Tammuz.[1][a]

Thus the line should read, "the time of the ritual song is come and the voice of the turtle is heard in the land." The turtle dove is the bird of Astarte, and the lines call together the people to sing the liturgy of the wooing of Tammuz by Astarte. The woman in the piece is Astarte herself and the man is Tammuz, or perhaps more accurately the human representative of that God.

So the Song of Solomon is the liturgy of the wooing and marriage of Starte and Tammuz performed every year in Palestine in the Spring, which inevitably led up to the death, or loss, of the male God in order that the land might become fertile. In consequence, many strange and otherwise inexplicable features in the poem become intelligible. If it had been merely an ordinary love song why suddenly break off and in an aside say:—"Take us the foxes, the little foxes which spoil the grapes."[2] As a song to promote fertility by means of sympathetic magic the "aside" becomes perfectly intelligible, and means, "O Goddess, destroy these vermin which would render abortive the magical ceremonies we are now performing to aid thee in thy task."

But there is hardly a line in the Song which does not bear out this explanation, e.g. "Our bed is green, the beams of our house are cedar, and our rafters (or galleries) of fir."[3] The Song, however, has more than a hint of the impending and inevitable tragedy. "My beloved had withdrawn himself, was gone: my soul failed when he spake: I sought him, but I could not find him: I called him, but he gave me no answer. The watchman that went about the city found me, they smote me, they wounded me: the keepers of the walls took away my veil from me."[4]

Here we have the death, the lamentation and the seeking of Ishtar for Dumuzi, even to her being deprived of her clothing, as she passed on her quest through the Underworld, by the Guardians of the Gates thereof.

Neither are we left in any doubt as to what had befallen the body of the slain Tammuz, for the poem says:—

---

1.   T. J. Meek, Univ. of Toronto in "The Song of Solomon. A Symposium," delivered before the Oriental Club of Philadelphia, 1924.
(a)   The above work edited by H. Schoff contains articles on the subject dealing with it in a most thorough and scholarly manner, and the contributions include six of the leading authorities of the day, who leave no doubt on these points.
2.   Song of Solomon. 2. 15.   3.   Ibid. 1. 16 sq.   4.   Ibid. 5. 6 sq.

" Stir not up, nor awake my love, till he please . . . .
Behold his bed, which is Solomon's; three score valiant men are
about it, of the valiant of Israel.   They all hold swords, expert
in war, every man hath his sword upon his thigh because of fear
in the night." [1(a)]

Here then we have the funeral cortege with its armed guard
of honour, and the swords, may be, were used for other and more
sinister purposes than to render honour to the corpse, real or
feigned, which lay within the golden litter.   Lucian tells us that
even in his time c.150 A.D. at Heirapolis in Lebanon men who
came to these feasts, carried away by excitement, would seize the
swords which stood ever ready for that purpose and castrate
themselves as a dedication rite to the Great Goddess.   Those
who have never seen an Eastern mob worked up to religious
frenzy at such times have no conception of the length to which
men will go.

We have a careful description of the litter, or bed of state,
on which Tammuz lay.   " King Solomon made himself a bed (or
chariot) of the wood of Lebanon.   He made the pillars thereof
of silver, the bottom thereof of gold, the covering of it of purple." [2]

Finally, the chapter closes with this dramatic peroration,
" Go forth, O ye daughters of Zion and behold King Solomon
with the crown wherewith his mother crowned him in the day of
his espousals and in the day of the gladness of his heart." [3]

If the Kings of Judea, like the Phoenician Kings of Cyprus,
had annually to marry the Goddess of Fertility, the above passage
becomes clear.   If, like the great Kings of Babylon they had also
to enact the part of the dying God, the full significance of the
phrase is obvious.

If it was only a mimic death no doubt it was performed by
the King himself, but it it was still necessary that one man should
die for the people, then, as elsewhere, a humbler person probably
a Prince of the royal blood, was for a short time made titular
King of Israel and paid the price.

Thus interpreted the verse would run as follows:—" Behold
the Divine King, still wearing the crown with which he was
crowned when he was wedded to the Goddess Astarte, amid pomp
and glory.   Behold, and weep, O ye daughters of Zion, for the
vanity of human greatness and the fleeting days of joy."

---

1.   Song of Solomon, 3. 5 sq.
2.   Ibid. 3. 7.
3.   Ibid. 3. 11.
(a)   In the legend already quoted from J. Hershon, " Talmudic Miscellany ''
      we are told that King Solomon, despite his recovery of his throne,
      was always afraid lest Asmodeus should again carry him off, and there-
      fore always slept with three score fighting men around him to protect
      him.   Herein, no doubt, we have a dim and distorted memory of the
      original ritual connection between the Monster of the Initiation Rite
      and the Lying in State.

With such a picture before our eyes we can well understand the real Solomon sitting down to write Ecclesiastes. It may be that here we can trace the first beginnings of a process which gradually turned a magical Fertility Rite into an allegory of the vanity of human greatness. We have indeed a striking analogy from ancient Mexico. Every year a man was chosen to represent a divine King and was married to four beautiful wives, who represented Goddesses. For a year he lived in the greatest pomp and splendour in a magnificent palace, with everything that man could possibly desire, and honoured by the people as if he were both God and King. But at the end of the year the unfortunate victim was taken from his palace and cruelly sacrificed on an altar on the top of a Pyramid (a high place), in full sight of the very people who but a few days before had literally bowed themselves to the ground whenever he passed. And the priests explained his tragic story as an allegory of the vanity of human greatness.[1]

As the account of these ceremonies given in the Song of Solomon may not be very clear to my readers, I will now describe the festival of Maharan, nominally a Mahomedan festival in honour of Hussain and Hussan, but really only the old Tammuz festival under a new name.

It is dark, and down the streets pours a frenzied crowd of men. No women dare appear, for if they did they would be liable to outrage, if the strong hand of the British Raj should not be close by to protect them. But they too have their allotted place which is in the Mosques, where they are wailing in front of replicas of the tombs of the murdered Hussain and Hussan, even as the Jewish women once did outside the gates of the temple. Down the narrow streets, filling them from side to side, comes the procession to the sound of strange oriental music and the beating of tumtums. A wild frenzied mob sweeps by, waving burning torches in their hands, and chanting a strange, weird litany. Then come men armed with naked swords who dance wild fantastic dances, and sing songs which seem to stir men's blood to madness. Here and there one more fanatical than the rest has gashed and cut his flesh so that the blood is streaming from a dozen wounds, just as the High Priest of Cybele did in days of yore.

Then come the replicas of the tombs, great towering structures of gilt wood and paper, which in the dim light of the torches seem as if made of gold and gems. On they come, borne high on the shoulders of men, and woe betide any who rouse the fury of the worshippers at that solemn hour ! On through the livelong night, under the silver beams of a tropic moon, floating in the velvety blackness of the night, from place to place the great procession sweeps. As the excitement increases men forget all about

---

1.   Prescott, " The Conquest of Mexico." Ch. 3.

the regulations which forbid the discharge of fire-arms in the public streets, and the night is punctuated by the crack of guns, which echo from side to side of the narrow native streets, while the dancers whirl and shout and howl for Hussain and Hussan slain.

Place after place is visited, where the more fanatical fearlessly walk through huge pits of fire, and on, on till dawn. At long last it is over, and the great gilt " Tombs " are carried to some convenient lake and there flung into the water to sink, even as in Alexandria Adonis was flung into the sea.

No man who has not seen such a night, who has not heard the intoxicating sounds of the wild, terrible, barbaric music can have even the faintest conception of the mad frenzies into which the worshippers are swept at such times. If fifteen hundred years of the fierce zeal of Islam has failed to obliterate such a ceremony, we can well understand that the Hebrew Prophets found it no easy task to destroy the Cult. It is just such a scene as this of which these verses in the Song of Solomon give us a hint, verses which themselves form part of the liturgy of the Festival and contain still a vivid picture of the closing scene of the drama.

With this scene still before our eyes, let us turn back to the last chapter of Ecclesiastes, which may well have been chanted over the still form which represented Tammuz slain.

" And the grinders cease because they are few." [1] Why are they few ? Among the Arabs in the tenth century a Festival of Tammuz was still kept. It took place at the harvest and during it the women refused to grind corn, for as we have already shown they could not grind the body of the Corn God under the grind stones at the very moment when they were ostensibly lamenting his death. [2]

But let us read still further what Ecclesiastes says,—
" And they shall be afraid of that which is high, and fear shall be in the way, and the almond tree shall flourish, and the grasshopper shall be a burden and *desire* shall fail."

Why should desire fail because some man dies ? This one line alone is sufficient to tell us who it is who is dead ! According to the old legend desire failed among beasts and men when Ishtar went down into the Underworld in search of her lost Dumuzi. And thus we can interpret the line " Because man goeth to his long home and the mourners go about the streets." It means, because Tammuz, the Divine Man, goeth to the Underworld and the people mourn for him in the streets. It is clear that we herein commemorate the death of Tammuz, who represents firstly, the Spirit of Vegetation, and especially of Corn, and *then* Man himself.

What spiritually minded man watching such a ceremony

---

1. Ecclesiastes. 12. 3. sq.
2. Frazer, " Adonis, Attis, Osiris." 3rd ed. Vol. 1. p. 230.

could fail to draw comparisons between the fate of the human
representative of Tammuz and the general lot of man, and sum-
marize them in the dark words of despair, " Vanity of vanities,
all is vanity," words which we can hardly doubt were spoken
over the form of the initiates who in the secret ceremonies of the
Cult, as distinct from the popular festivals, enacted in a dramatic
form the tragic story of Tammuz.   We may even suspect that in
the phrase, " They shall be afraid of that which is high," we have
a hint of the title of Hiram, which means " The Exaltation of
Life," and in any case may feel sure that as in the Song of Solomon
we had a fragment of the ritual of the external Cult, so in Ecclesiastes we have the allegorical teaching, reserved for the fully
initiated men, of the inner meaning of the death of Tammuz.
If so, its retention in modern Freemasonry is significant and
appropriate.[a]

(a)   Those who would like still further evidence on the point should note the
       repeated use of the phrase " My Beloved," one of the most charac-
       teristic titles of Tammuz, and also the emphatic reference to Lebanon,
       the great shrine of Astarte—Adonis, in chapter 4, verse 8, bearing
       in mind the fact that Lebanon was never part of the kingdom of Israel.
       Furthermore, the damsel is stated to be black (Ch. 1. 5.), and Cybele
       was represented in Rome by a black stone which formed the face of
       the image of the Goddess.

CHAPTER IX

THE HIGH GRADES OF TAMMUZ

The story of Jonah[1] has always been a matter of speculation, but one factor has ever been recognised by the Christian Church, namely that Jonah was the prototype of Christ, for just as Jonah lay for three days in the belly of a whale[a] and yet came forth alive, so in like manner Christ was in the tomb for three days and then rose from the dead.

This fact supports the view now widely held by scholars that the story is an allegory of the journey of the soul through the Underworld, and is probably a somewhat distorted account of an initiation ceremony once practised in Phoenicia and Syria, which taught of life beyond the grave.[b] If we compare Isaiah 26. v. 19 to 27. v.1. we shall see that the resurrection of the dead is associated with the destruction by God of Leviathan and the dragon that is in the sea.

The Jews themselves had no doubt that the story referred to death and resurrection, as is clearly indicated by the eleventh question of the series put to Solomon by the Queen of Sheba.[2] I shall indicate presently that Balkis, Queen of Sheba, seems to have replaced Astarte in the Biblical and Masonic legends, and the questions she puts to Solomon strongly resemble the riddles put to initiates in certain primitive initiatory rites, such as those of the Yaos. Many of those put by her, like similar questions put by the savages, are grossly obscene, thereby clearly indicating her true character, as representing the Great Mother, Astarte. Not all, however, are of this objectionable type and the questions themselves number 22, the exact number of the picture cards in the Tarot pack, whose use for the purpose of Divination, and in connection with initiation rites, is well known, a most significant fact. This legend of Solomon is not in the Bible and is of late Jewish growth, which increases its value throughout, for it indicates that Solomon, Sheba, Jonah and the rest were figures associated with initiation rites. The important question for us here is No. 11.

---

1. Jonah 1. 1 sq.
2. Dudley Wright, " Masonic Legends and Traditions," p. 130.
(a) It is popularly called the whale but the Bible merely calls it a " great fish."
(b) I must express my indebtedness to Mr. N. M. Penzer, the editor of " The Ocean of Story," for much valuable help on this subject, and especially for drawing my attention to Simpson's " The Jonah Legend " in which that author produces strong arguments in support of the view that it was a rite of Initiation. See also note on Jonah on pp. 193-194 vol. II. " The Ocean of Story."

SHEBA. The dead lived, the grave moved and the dead prayed. What is that ?

SOLOMON. The dead that lived and prayed, Jonah; and the fish, the moving grave.[1]

The fact that the date of the book of Jonah is much later than the time of Solomon proves nothing. The rite may have been working in the days of the great king and its legend only committed to writing at a later date. On the other hand, it may have been evolved out of older material about the time that it was written down.

Another important detail is that Jonah in Hebrew means " A Dove," and it was at Harran, which some scholars consider to have been his birth place and which was a city sacred to the moon god, that the dove, we are specifically told, was never sacrificed. The dove was also sacred to Astarte.[2] Tammuz in time absorbed some of the attributes of the moon, like whom he lay " dead " for three days. Furthermore, the dove among many races symbolises the soul of the Dead, whose astrological identification with the moon is well known. One example of the close association of the dove with the soul and the Underworld must suffice. When Aeneas was seeking the " Golden bough " which would admit him to the Underworld he was led to it by two doves.[3] Here we have not only the dove but also a branch, which, as we have previously seen, was closely associated with the dead. Therefore the dove, which symbolises the moon and the soul, enters the fish's mouth and yet comes forth alive.

Now in many primitive initiatory rites the initiates are supposed to be swallowed up by a monster and killed, but ultimately this monster opens his mouth and restores them to life, no longer boys, but fully initiated men. This system prevails among the Kai, Tami, and several other tribes who dwell around Finsch Harbour and Huon Gulf, in what used to be German New Guinea. The initiates are swallowed and subsequently disgorged by a mythical monster whose roar is simulated by means of bull-roarers. This monster consists of a huge hut 100 feet long, specially built for the purpose, and in Chapter XX I have given full details. These facts may enable us to understand better the story in the Bible which runs as follows:—

THE STORY OF JONAH

Jonah was told to go to Nineveh and warn its citizens that the wrath of God was kindled against it because of its wickedness, but Jonah was afraid to do so and decided to flee to Tarshish.[a] He

1. D. Wright, Ibid. p. 130 quoting Dr. Lewis Ginzberg, " Legends of the Jews."
2. Frazer, " Adonis, Attis, Osiris." 3rd ed. Vol. I. p. 33.
    J. Selden, " De dis Syris." (Leipsic) pp. 274.
3. Virgil, " Aeneid." Bk VI, line 199 sq.
(a) Where Sandon was burnt.

took *boat* at Joppa and paid the *fare* thereof. The Lord thereupon raised a great storm and the sailors prayed to their gods to save them. They were astonished to find Jonah asleep instead of praying, and discovered that he was the cause of the wrath of God. He advised them to throw him into the sea, and ultimately they did so, whereupon the storm ceased. Jonah, instead of being drowned, was swallowed by a great fish and remained for three days in its belly.

Before proceeding with the narrative, let us note certain significant details. We are carefully told that Jonah paid for his passage, a procedure which at first sight seems so obvious that we may be quite sure that it is mentioned for a specific reason. In like manner it is carefully recorded that Gilgamish had to pay a fee to Ur-Shanabi, the boatman who carried him over the waters of death, before he could enter his barque.[1] The fee that Gilgamish paid consisted of tree trunks which he was told to cut down from the forest with an axe, and as a tree trunk cut in the forest and carried into the city was a regular feature of the rites of Adonis and Attis, this tree would symbolise the spirit of vegetation.

The careful mention of the fact that Jonah paid a fee implies two things. Firstly, that it was believed that the dead had to pay a fee to the gate keeper, or ferryman, of the Underworld, and secondly, it suggests an initiation fee. With regard to the former, there are numerous examples of this belief. Among the inhabitants of the Trobriand Isles, New Guinea, the dead must give a fee to Topileta, the Keeper of the Gate of the Underworld,[2] and every classical scholar knows that a small coin was laid on the eyes of the dead by Greeks and Romans to enable the corpse to pay the fee to Charon. This custom survived in England up to the beginning of the 19th century, and may not even yet be quite extinct. In modern times people explained that they placed pennies on the eyes of the corpse to keep the lids shut, but this is quite a recent explanation, invented when the original reason had been forgotten.

The boat in the story represents the Solar barque into which the souls of the good were permitted to enter, and to journey with the sun through the Underworld, along the underground river of Ocean.[a] Here we have a hint that the wicked were not permitted to travel by this boat,[b] but had to make their way over

---

1. " Epic of Gilgamish." Brit. Mus. p. 53.
2. Prof. Malinowski, " Baloma : The Spirits of the Dead in the Trobriand Island." Pub. R. Anthro. Inst.
(a) See Ward, " The Hung Society," vol. 2. for details re " geography " of the ancient Underworld and the voyage of the Solar Barque.
(b) The Solar Barque is not peculiar to the ancient Egyptians. It occurs in the Babylonian legend of Gilgamish, in the mediæval legends of the Graal, in the ritual of the Hung Society in China, and elsewhere.

land in the Underworld, and this was the fate which befell Jonah
when he was swallowed by the big fish or monster.

Thus the story of Jonah fits in perfectly with what we know
was supposed to befall the dead after death among most of the
ancient Eastern races, and the fact that he subsequently returned
to life on earth and went to Nineveh indicates that the story does
not relate the actual death but a symbolic death; a journey
through the Underworld, and a symbolic resurrection. In short,
he seems to have had to undergo a special initiation in order to
qualify him for his work as a prophet. Now a precisely similar
course has to be followed by an Australian Bushman of the
Arunta tribe who wishes to become a medicine man and a seer,
although he has already passed through the ordinary initiation
rites of the other bushmen. Before he can be admitted into the
ranks of the acknowledged medicine men he must go through a
kind of higher degree, beyond the craft, and thereafter he is entitled to preside as a Master of Ceremonies at the initiation of boys
into manhood. The ceremonies of the ordinary tribesmen consist
of three degrees, and in the last of them a man lies in the grave
and a tree appears to grow out of him. Thus we have a degree of
death and resurrection, which in the case of a Medicine Man is
followed by a degree which is supposed to reveal to him what
befalls the dead in the next world.[1] We shall return to this
degree at a later point in the book.

The true nature of Jonah's experiences are graphically
depicted in his own words, for when he was in the belly of the big
fish he prayed, and said, " I cried by reason of my affliction unto
the Lord, and He hears me; out of the belly of hell cried I, and
Thou heardest my voice."[2]

Hell here means the Underworld, and not necessarily the place
of the damned, and we thus see that Jonah himself states that
the belly of the fish represents the Underworld, and the part
mentioned—belly—reminds us that according to old accounts in
the centre of the Underworld there was supposed to be a pit into
which the more wicked had to pass. Jonah then tells us other
geographical features of this Underworld and says, " I went down
to the bottom of the mountains, the earth with her bars was about
me for ever; yet hast Thou brought up my life from corruption."[3]
. . . . " And the Lord spake unto the fish and it vomited out
Jonah upon the dry land."[4] After which Jonah was again
ordered to go to Nineveh, and obeyed.

When we come to consider this story the conviction grows

1.   B. Spencer and F. J. Gillen, " Native Tribes of Central Australia."
       (London, 1899). pp. 523 sq.
       Id. " Across Australia." (London, 1912). II. 335.
2.   Jonah, 2. 2.
3.   Jonah, 2. 6.
4.   Jonah, 2. 10.

that it is an allegory of the journey of the soul through the Underworld, and chapter 2 seems to be an explanation of the meaning
of the initiation ceremony. The Jews themselves in ancient
times regarded it as an allegory.

We learn from it that the soul on its journey after death was
supposed to pass by mountains and to be shut in by bars. These
mountains are the mountains of sunset, which were believed to
stand like twin pillars on the Western edge of the world, and
between them the sun passed out of the sight of men on earth into
the Underworld. The setting of the sun often causes bars of
light and darkness to appear in the West, which would quite
naturally be regarded as the bars of the Gates which shut in the
denizens of the Underworld.

The statement that God " brought up my life from corruption," reminds us of certain prayers in the Egyptian Book of the
Dead which ask that the deceased may not see (or experience)
corruption of the body.

The three days denote the period during which the soul is in
the Underworld, and the exact period thus allotted must be based
on the disappearance of the moon from the sky at the end of each
lunar month for three days, before it reappears as the New Moon.
In like manner Adonis was mourned for three days, but in some
variations of the Rite of the Dying God ten, or even twelve, days
are allotted for his journey through the Underworld.

The outstanding fact, however, is that the god was slain only
once a year, and thus corresponds with a definite agricultural process which occurs only once annually, and not with an event like
the vanishing of the moon from the sky which occurs every month.
Neither can we say that anywhere outside the Arctic circle does
the sun entirely vanish annually for three days. The Vegetation God dies at the harvest when the corn is reaped, is buried in
the Autumn, and resurrects in the Spring. In Syria the harvest
is all over by the Summer Solstice and we therefore find a tendency
to confound the attributes of the sun with those of the vegetation
god. The adoption of the three days of the moon comes about
equally naturally, for the moon in its waxing and waning is
supposed to influence the growth or decline of vegetation.

Not only, however, is corn sown in Autumn, but all the wild
plants shed their seeds at that time, and these fall to the ground,
become covered by the dead leaves and are thus buried. There
is therefore at least three months between the harvest, or the
slaying of the spirit of the corn, and the planting, or burial.
But three months is far too long a period for primitive man to
keep as a time of mourning, and a day to represent a month
would soon be substituted. This period, representing the three
days of the lost moon, whose influence on vegetation was universally accepted, leads naturally to a tendency to identify the
slain god with the moon.

So the same god at various times and from differing stand-points represents Sun, Moon, and the Spirit of Vegetation; a bewildering contradiction to the modern student, who expects a logical meaning throughout the symbolism, oblivious of the fact that primitive man is not at all logical and that the slain god as we now know him is the result of a series of racial evolutions and religious conceptions, whose general development seems to have been out of the worship first of all, of the vague forces of nature, later, of the Moon, and finally, of the Sun.

That all these cults have left their traces in the Jonah legend is clear.   Jonah originally represented the spirit of vegetation, his three days in the fish are based on the moon's vanishing, his boat is the Solar Barque, and in later times he was definitely considered to represent the sun.   In a personal letter to me dated, Oct. 3 1924, Sir John Cockburn, M.D., K.C.M.G., P.Dept.Gr.M. of, South Australia writes, " You ask . . . a question regarding Jonah as a sun type.   There is no room for doubt on this subject.   The three days and three nights of the Solstice indicate it.   The proof is to be found in Sadi's Gulistan,[a] ' Now the first watch of the night was gone, the disc of the sun was withdrawn into the shade and Jonah had stepped into the fish's mouth.' "

The reference to the Solstice is because at both winter and summer solstice for three days the sun appears to stand still, i.e. the days appear to be of exactly the same length, and the ancients supposed that at such times the sun in his journey met with more than usually fierce opposition from his enemies.   This idea gave rise in some rites to the existence of three gates, or stages, through which the initiate had to pass, and at each of which he had successfully to undergo certain tests.

Such gates are represented in masonry by the first three veils in the Excellent Master degree, which in Scotland precedes the R.A., and similar gates also appear in the ritual of the Royal Order of Scotland.   They likewise occur in the ritual of the famous Chinese secret society, " The Hung League."[1]   As this Chinese ritual also represents the journey of the soul after death, and includes a Solar barque, the existence of these gates is most significant.

We thus see that Jonah from one standpoint typifies the Soul (the dove), and from another the Sun.   As the souls were supposed to accompany the sun in the solar barque, we can see that there is no real contradiction in this twofold or threefold character, for he not only represents the soul of every initiate but especially the experiences of Tammuz, the representative of men, and even of plants, who die and yet come to a greater and more glorious life thereby.

---

1.   See Ward and Stirling, " The Hung Society."   Vol. I. for full details.
(a)   Sadi's Gulistan is a famous Persian work translated by Sir R. Burton and published in 1888.

The Jonah legend therefore represents " a higher degree " of the Tammuz rites, and we can recognise even at this early date a tendency to turn the old magical Tammuz ceremony into an allegory of the death and resurrection of man.   As time wore on this aspect increased in importance, and the old magical significance of the rite, whose purpose was by means of sympathetic magic to assist the forces of nature in producing an abundant harvest, grew less and less.   For all that, this magical aspect never entirely disappeared from the " open " ceremonies, and still survives in certain parts of Europe.   We may, however, postulate that even in the days of Ezekiel there were men in that secret chamber under the altar of sacrifice who saw, in the ritual of the death of Tammuz, the deep spiritual truth that the dead shall rise from their graves.

Before leaving Jonah it is worth while drawing attention to the fact that, according to Jewish legends, he was the son of the widow of Sarepta, whom Elijah restored to life.   Again and again we find that the representative of Tammuz is called the son of a widow, and the tradition that Jonah had actually been raised from the dead, therefore, makes the whole of his legend of peculiar interest.

Fortunately we are able " to pick up " the story of this Syrian initiation rite many hundred years later.   The exact date of the story of Jonah as given in the Bible is a matter of dispute amongst Jews.   The traditional date is about B.C. 862, but students are inclined to place it somewhat later, whereas Lucian lived A.D. 120—180.

Lucian was born at Samosata on the Euphrates, in Northern Syria, and was a hardened cynic who mocked at the contemporary religions and philosophies, but amid his mockeries we can discover the subjects at which he mocked, and as a Syrian born and bred he was in a position to know a great deal about Syrian beliefs.   One of his most important works was " *On the Syrian Goddess Mylitta*," the Moon goddess, i.e., Aphrodite or Astarte, in which he gives us much genuine information on the Galli, her eunuch priests, and other valuable details to which we have already referred.   Therefore his information on Syrian religious beliefs is worthy of the most careful consideration, even though in the " True History " he is but scoffing at them.

His " *Golden Ass*," in like manner, is a travesty of the *Metamorphoses of Lucian of Patroe*, which book was also the source of the " Golden Ass " of Apuleius, who was born A.D. 125, and in it he avowedly deals with the initiation rites of Isis.   With these facts in our mind we shall see that his story in the " *True History* " of the ship which was swallowed by a whale is nothing less than a cynical parody of the old Syrian initiation legend of the soul being swallowed by a huge fish.

In this account we are able to collect a number of details of the ceremony over and above what we have learnt from Jonah, and the fact that the voyagers reached the Isles of the Blest is a valuable hint as to the true nature of the story, despite his own declaration that it is all lies, for we know from Josephus that the Essenes of Palestine also believed that the righteous went to the Isles of the Blest whereas the wicked passed to a place of torment, which is also described by Lucian.[1]

---

1.   Encycl. Brit. 11th ed. (1911).   Vol. 17.   p. 100.
      H. W. and F. G. Fowler, " The Works of Lucian of Samosata."
      H. W. L. Hime, " Lucian, the Syrian Satirist."

CHAPTER X

LUCIAN'S ACCOUNT OF THE RITES OF TAMMUZ[1]

Lucian gave his book the title of *The True History* because, according to him, it contained nothing but lies, and he expressly says that it is fiction intended as a jibe at those professedly serious historians who related as true, what was pure invention. If, however, he intended his readers to believe that he invented, " de novo," all the incidents in his narrative, it is to be feared that he himself was not telling the truth, for though some no doubt are the product of his fertile imagination, others are old myths and current beliefs, at which he was jeering.

Moreover, in two or three cases he related things which were, and still are, actually true, such as the Frozen Sea and the Forest in the Ocean, which latter is merely a mangrove swamp such as exists off the West Coast of Africa and also in the West Indies. In like manner his continent beyond the great ocean which he calls *The Antipodes*, is undoubtedly a tradition of what was later rediscovered and called America.

In the case of the first island visited, wherein he says he found traces of Hercules, we have a very fair description of the Island of Madeira, namely " a steep, wooded island." As to the giant footprints, it must be remembered that in Ceylon visitors are still shown a gigantic footprint called " Adam's Footprint," on Adam's Peak. The Buddhists, however, call it Buddha's Footprint, and in many Pagodas in Burma so-called casts, or models, of this footprint are shown. The one which I saw at the Shwe Dagon Pagoda, Rangoon, was over six feet long and was undoubtedly a relic of some almost forgotten myth, or custom, which had been transferred to Buddha. In India similar " casts " exist and are called " Footprints of Vishnu," but here it is impossible to discuss the origin and meaning of these objects, although it is important that we should realise that herein we have definite proof that there was a solid basis for the wild story of footprints of Hercules and Dionysius, even though Lucian was making fun of the stories he had heard and misunderstood. In like manner the story of the Vine-maidens on the island is an old legend, and testifies to the age-old belief that the vine had a soul or spirit whose blood formed the wine.

From the above facts embedded in his story, we can see that the " Vera Historia " is really a somewhat heterogenous collection of current myths and beliefs, at which the cynical and witty Syrian is poking fun. That he has added pieces, embroidered

---

1. See in addition to references given above, Bohn's Translations and Wilson's " Lucian's Wonderland."

the legends, and twisted them in order to make them seem
the more ridiculous, is no doubt true (he did the same with Christianity), but sometimes he treats them much more respectfully,
merely adding humorous incidents to enliven the narrative.
This reticence is peculiarly marked in his treatment of the " Isles
of the Blest," where his description fits in fairly accurately with
contemporary classical beliefs. But he " livens things up " by
inventing such incidents as the third elopement of Helen.

His book, however, is of great importance to students of folklore and initiatory rites, as it is one of the chief links whereby
the ancient beliefs, traditions, and legends of Asia were transmitted to the Middle Ages, and so down to us. For example, it
seems probable that St. Brenden's Voyage is a distorted memory
of certain incidents in the " Vera Historia," although in the
process they have been distinctly spiritualised and given a higher
allegorical meaning. The alternative theory, however, cannot
be lightly dismissed, namely, that St. Brenden's Voyage is the
Christianised version of the old Syrian initiation ceremony at
which Lucian pokes fun.

Whether St. Brenden's Voyage is the son or the younger
brother of the " Vera Historia," one thing is certain. Both are
descendants of the Syrian Initiatory Rite of the Solar Barque, and
the great monster who swallows the candidates. It seems,
indeed, as if the original framework went Westward, and became
Christianised, Eastward, and became the foundation of the ritual
of the Hung Society in China, and found an abiding place in the
Mahabharata in India. It has analogies with primitive savage
rites as far afield as New Guinea and the Yao of Nyasaland.[a]

THE VOYAGE

Lucian set sail in a boat *Westwards*, into the Great Ocean, and
first called at a mysterious island covered with trees, where he saw
the footprints of Hercules and Dionysius. He also came across
vine maidens, the upper half of whom resembled women whilst the
lower half consisted of the twisted stems of the vines. When
some of the sailors broke off their fingers, wine, instead of blood,
came from the stumps, but the vine-maidens screamed with pain.
This was the origin of the rivers on that island which consisted of
wine instead of water.

This section seems to be a travesty of the rites of Dionysius
who was, of course, the Asiatic fertility god, originally similar to

---

(a)   The similarity of these various rites may, however, be due to their descent
from a much more primitive form of the ceremony, such as that which
still exists in New Guinea. From that form the ceremonies may have
developed in various areas according to the standard of civilisation
in each. If we accept this view it does not necessarily follow that
the Hung ritual is derived from Syria, but Lucian's story certainly is,
for he was a Syrian.

Tammuz, to whom we have previously referred. It is possible that his name, Iacchus, may be the origin of the name of one of the pillars of King Solomon's temple, which in the Bible is said to be called Jachin; as we should expect, one of his emblems was the Phallus.

The Vine-maidens are the spirits of the grapes and so represent the female spirit in the vine, as Dionysius does the male. Thus they may be regarded as descendants and representatives of the great, all-embracing spirit of fertility, Astarte.

The reference to Hercules is also significant, for, as we have seen, he was originally Melcarth of Tyre, whose statue was burnt each year by the Phoenicians. According to the Greek legend, he was burnt to death on a pyre and his soul ascended to Olympus. For all that, Lucian afterwards tells us that he found the shade of Hercules on the Isles of the Blest, and learnt that it was only his divine soul that had gone to Olympus. This statement is important as it indicates the belief, found among many races, that the god-men only differed from other men in that they had two souls, one human and the other divine. It was the divine soul which either returned to heaven or was transferred to the successor of the slain god-man at his death. These three points at the very beginning of Lucian's work show clearly its connection with the Syrian cult.

After a number of adventures the ship was caught by a whirlwind and carried up to the moon, where the travellers found a fierce war in progress between the men of the moon and those of the sun over a proposal to colonise the planet Lucifer, i.e., Venus. Here we obtain a reference to the conflict between the moon and the sun over Venus. In many of the Asiatic legends Tammuz tends to become closely identified with the Moon, and Astarte with Venus, while the Sun is hostile to her lovers, as is shown by the story of the shepherd Marsyas who was flayed alive by Apollo.

Having thus come in touch with the Moon, the boat returned to earth, and almost immediately was swallowed up whole by a huge sea monster or whale. Herein we are reminded of the fact that Jonah is said to have come from Harran, a city sacred to the Moon. It will be noticed, however, that whereas in the Jonah legend the ship representing the solar barque goes on its way to safety and only Jonah enters the fish, here the ship itself is swallowed up, therein portraying more accurately the old beliefs as to the journey of the solar barque through the Underworld.

At first all was dark inside, but when next the whale opened its mouth the travellers saw that there was land formed out of the sediment which the monster had swallowed, and thereon was a forest and even signs of cultivation—in other words they were in the Underworld.

The travellers then made a fire by friction with *fire sticks*, a very old and magical ceremony. The ordinary method at this period was by flint and steel, and the specific mention of the ancient method clearly implies that it was a religious rite in which metals might not be used.   If the Rite was associated with the vegetation god we can quite understand why the initiates should avoid using metals, for with them the trees are cut down and the corn is reaped.   Naturally men desirous of propitiating a tree or corn god would avoid using the material, namely iron, which was usually employed to destroy him.

They then began to explore the belly of the whale and found an old man and a boy, both Greeks, who, like them, had been swallowed alive.   The old man had built himself a hut and had cultivated the soil, but complained that he was sore oppressed by the original inhabitants of the whale's belly, semi-human, semi-animal monsters of a most repulsive type.   These remind us of the creatures which Ezekiel saw painted on the walls of the secret vault in the Temple and undoubtedly represent the demon host of the Underworld.

Lucian and his companions agreed to help the old man and a series of battles took place, in which the monsters were exterminated.   The battles were fought on three successive days.   Here we have a distorted account of three days testing of the initiates, who probably had to pass through three mimic battles and gain entry into three separate chambers, just as to-day in some of the Higher degrees three rooms are necessary and three veils must be passed, their guardians being overcome by means of signs, passwords, etc.

In some primitive rites initiates have to pass through an artificial tunnel in the ground and there are niches in the sides from which men, clad in the skins of beasts, step out and challenge, or even fight with, the candidate.   Students of the Egyptian religion are aware that the Solar Barque was supposed to be attacked on its journey through the Underworld by the Demon inhabitants, and we may therefore feel fairly certain that these three battles are a humorous travesty of similar incidents in the Syrian Rites.

In order to get out of the whale they set fire to the forest inside it, which resulted in the death of the animal.   They then got their ship out undamaged through the monster's mouth.

Fire as a concluding incident in an initiation ceremony plays an important part in most primitive rites.   Usually the candidate has to lie on a smouldering fire or else pass through it, and in Phoenicia we know that there was a ceremony of walking the fire associated with the Astarte rites.   In addition to the numerous references in the Bible to passing children through the fire to Moloch we learn that the King of Tyre himself had to walk up and down amid the fire.[1]   Thus here again we have a hint as to what

1. Ezekiel. 28. 14.

these Syrian Rites contained, one point being a symbolical purification by fire before the initiates " came forth by day," symbolically rising from the dead after having passed through the Underworld.

The ship sailed on over a sea of ice and amid various strange and fantastic adventures, which are probably interpolated here and have nothing to do with the initiation rite.   Ultimately we pick up the theme once more, for the vessel reached the " Isles of the Blest " which although clothed in the vesture of Greece, nevertheless correspond with the Isles of the Blest in which the Essenes believed.   The first adventure here reminds us of what is said to have been the fate of a certain traveller in a degree now working in England, for they were arrested and brought in chains before the King of the Island—Rhadamanthus—the Judge of the Dead.   The description of the city is really very beautiful, and for once the scoffing old cynic seems to have forgotten his cynicism and dwells with tender and poetic language on the walls of gold and emerald, and the seven gates of cinnamon.   The streets were paved with ivory, the temples of the Gods built of beryl, and their altars formed of solid blocks of amethyst.   It almost seems as if he had heard, in the stately language of some age-old ritual, a wonderful description of the Holy City.   Gone is the scoffing cynic, while the half-forgotten words flow from his pen as he tells of the happy dwellers therein.   They neither grew old nor died, therein was neither night nor day, but the soft twilight of the dawn in an eternal Spring.   The meadows were filled with the fragrance of countless lovely flowers, the orchards were full of fruit trees and the rivers flowed with milk, wine and honey.

But soon he is back in his old strain and tells a humorous tale of an intrigue between Helen and another hero, which ultimately led to their expulsion from Paradise.   They therefore visited the Isles of the Damned and had to cross a bridge over a ditch full of fire.   Even Lucian does not venture to laugh at the horrors and anguish of the lost.

The rest of the story contains many curious features, some of which seem to be connected with initiatory rites.   Thus at one point the mast of the ship buds and vines and ivy covers it, which reminds us of the story of Dionysius.   On another occasion it has to pass over a mysterious bridge of water which spans a chasm in the Ocean itself, and reminds us of a certain bridge in the Red Cross of Babylon and in the Royal Order of Scotland.

Enough has been written to show that in the *Vera Historia* Lucian has embedded many details of the mythology of his time, and among them a rite of Initiation.   This took the form of being swallowed by a monster and being spewed forth therefrom, in order that the candidate might have dramatically depicted to him the fate of the good and bad after death, and so learn of the resurrection and of the life of the world beyond.

CHAPTER XI

SUMMARY OF THE SYRIAN RITES

We have seen that in Syria there were external ceremonies performed in the presence of the whole populace and secret rites which tended as years rolled on to become more and more exclusive. The popular ceremonies were originally of a magical nature, and aimed at sustaining the fertility of Mother Earth in order that she might bring forth an abundant harvest. These may be sub-divided as follows:—

1. At the festivals there was promiscuous intercourse between the sexes, intended, according to the rules of primitive magic, to encourage the productivity of the Great Mother and therefore of the earth itself. Even to-day similar festivals take place all over the world.

2. A man representing the mythical lover of the Goddess was slain. Originally he died from a brutal form of castration and later more humane methods seem to have been employed.

3. Sometimes he was burnt, and in such cases an eagle was released at the time of his death to symbolise the return of his soul to heaven.

4. Such victims were originally divine men and Priest-kings, though probably humbler substitutes were very often accepted.

5. Certain modifications of these ghastly ceremonies took place as men became more humane.

6. At first the Priest sacrificed his virile member but was not allowed to bleed to death.

7. Circumcision of all the males of the tribe was introduced which represented the giving of a part of the virile member instead of the whole of it, but this did not exempt the God-man from carrying out his duty.

8. In addition every year at the date when the god Tammuz was slain, i.e., the Harvest time, the women presented cakes to Astarte made in the form of the virile member of their husbands, in lieu of the member itself, which technically was claimed by the goddess.

9. The death of the god-man could not, however, be omitted, and so at first merely the brutality of the method was mitigated, i.e., he was hung on a tree and speared in the side, or else knocked on the head.

10. In cases where he had been burnt alive, subsequently a figure of a man was burnt.

11. In some cases where other methods of slaying had been employed the figure of a man was also substituted, over which the people mourned.

12. The slaying may also have been play acting, but although we know this took place in Babylon it seems as if this "dramatic form" in Syria was used only in the secret initiatory rites.

13. There was a sacramental feast which at first consisted of the body of the slain god, probably broiled in the cauldron, to which our attention has been directed.

14. Later, bread, representing the flesh, and wine, representing the blood, were certainly substituted. Probably the bread originally consisted of the obscene cakes, and the wine was what was left over after a portion had been poured as a libation to Astarte.

15. The corpse, real or substitute, was regularly mourned for by the people for three days, during which time the Divine soul was supposed to be in the Underworld.

16. The adventures of that soul were not revealed to the populace but were a closely guarded secret of the inner circle of initiates.

17. After three days the dead god was supposed to arise, and the exact hour was marked by the rising of the sun and by the fact that at the same moment the planet Venus was visible as a day star in the East, and not as an evening star in the West.

18. When this happened, the Elders who were celebrating the festival smelt the branch of a tree into which it was supposed that the soul of the slain god had ascended. It is not quite clear whether this ceremony was restricted to one man or was performed by all the watchers, but in any case it was supposed to transfer the divine soul of Tammuz to a new human body, wherein it again became incarnate until the ceremony had to be repeated.

In addition to these points there are one or two other details whose exact place in the sequence is uncertain. Of these the most important was a ceremonial baptism or bathing of the figure of Tammuz, or of his coffin, in the sea or river. According to most accounts it marked the end of the ceremony, as it does in India to-day, and probably it originally represented the throwing away of the now empty husk of Tammuz, whose divine soul had been satisfactorily transferred to a new and vigorous body. In the main it was undoubtedly a magical rain charm. In some cases, however, it seems to have been a purification after sexual intercourse between the dead Tammuz and the still living goddess.

THE SECRET RITES

We have learnt that undoubtedly there were certain secret rites taking place in the days of Ezekiel, and shall learn that in the time of Josephus the Essenes were a sect with elaborate initiatory rites, penal oaths, and so forth, whose obligation was strikingly like the charge given in the first degree in masonry. Included in their rites was a preliminary baptism with water, a special regalia, a sort of sacramental meal, and, above all, prayers to the sun which, though alien to the orthodox Jewish faith, were an integral part of the ceremonies connected with the death of Tammuz.

We have also seen that the story of Jonah and the adventures of Lucian indicate a definite " High degree " initiation ceremony which was Syrian, and dealt with the period represented by the three days during which Tammuz was supposed to be in the grave.

Throughout the whole world there still survive death and resurrection rites which help us to piece together the fragments of the Syrian system into an intelligible whole.   The two chief types are " A Grave and Tree Drama," and " The Swallowing by a Monster."   The former is represented in the external rites of Tammuz, and the latter by the system which accounted for the three days in the tomb.   Taking the grave and tree drama first[1] we have the following details:—

1.   Initiates have to be circumcised because this is a substitute for the whole:—the great fertility goddess claims every man's virile member.   She is a lustful, jealous goddess, and the savages trick her by means of elaborate ceremonies and make her believe that the initiates have died and surrendered to her their virile members.   If, however, there is any carelessness the goddess will see through the fraud, and this explains why so many boys die during these rites; needless to say it has nothing to do with the lack of adequate medical dressings!   Therefore instead of the whole member, the foreskin is buried in the earth as a sacrifice to the great mother, and at the moment of the operation in British East Africa the boy has to make the sign of G. and D.   It is hardly necessary to remind our readers of the important part circumcision played in the Syrian and Jewish religious systems, or of the fact that the foreskin was similarly buried.

2.   In Australia a man is placed in a sham grave, a tree with leaves on it is placed on his stomach or chest, and then he is covered with leaves and rubbish.   This symbolises the fact that at death the soul passes into a shrub or tree which grows from the grave and there waits until someone cuts it or even touches it, when the soul enters into that person.   In this way the soul of the dead man is raised to a new life.   Therefore in the Australian Rite the man in the grave rises from it.   This ceremony may also be a method of depositing the " External soul " in a safe and secret place outside the body, and be closely linked with totemism.   This ceremony explains the meaning of the branch mentioned by Ezekiel, and also of the sprig of acacia.

3.   Another method employed to transfer the soul of a dead man and bring it once more into incarnation,[2] i.e., to raise it

---

up, is to step across the grave. This method is particularly effective if the person who steps over it is a woman, for she will then become pregnant, but when a semi-divine soul is involved, this can enter into a man, who then becomes the spiritual successor of the dead man and inherits his doubtful privileges.

4. The soul, according to primitive beliefs, can also be transferred by sniffing or drawing in the breath of the dead person, as for example by raising him in one's arms in such a way that the raiser's mouth comes near that of the corpse.

5. According to the Red Indians the soul of a dead chief can be transferred to a suitable candidate by raising a living man from the ground in a peculiar way, at the same time calling him by the name of the dead chief.

The above facts, which are dealt with fully in chapters XX and XXI, will help us to understand what was taking place in the secret vault. Although we have little direct and specific information as to what was happening, we do know that the sniffing of a bough formed part of the external ritual, and are justified in believing that some, and possibly all, of the above ceremonies occurred in the vault. In any case we perceive that they are the origin of certain peculiar ceremonies well known to masons.

When we turn to the form of ceremony in which initiates are swallowed by a monster we are on firm ground so far as Syria is concerned.

a. The soul set out symbolically in the Solar Barque.

b. The good kept in that Barque as it entered the Underworld, which is described as a monster who swallows the ship. The wicked, however, were cast from the Solar Barque and had to go on foot through the Underworld. No doubt their subsequent adventures were rather similar to those which befell the Solar Barque, but as a rule the wicked did not reach the Golden City.

c. The soul had to pass a number of barriers or veils. In the Babylonian version of Ishtar's descent there were seven, but apparently later these were reduced to three or four. In any case, there was considerable opposition to be surmounted before the soul could enter each of these Halls. These gates or barriers may conveniently be compared with the veils in the Excellent Master.

d. The soul then came forth by day, that is in the east.

e. In its journey it had to cross two bridges, one of which led into Hell, i.e., the place of torment, and the other from Paradise,[a] here called the Isles of the Blest, into the City of the Gods.

f. The soul was bound in chains and brought before the judge of the dead, i.e., the king of the Heavenly City, which in the

---

(a)   This second bridge is represented in Lucian by his water bridge. It has perhaps deliberately been misplaced by him, but from a close comparison with other rites and Legends, e.g., the bridge in the Triad Ritual and Byfrost in the Norse legends, we know that it connects the mountain of the Dawn with the Celestial city.

Syrian version was in the centre of the Isles of the Blest. In most other Rites, however, it was separated therefrom and stood on the top of the Holy Mountain or Olympus. The soul, if good, was released and admitted to the Heavenly City, if bad, it was cast into the place of torment. Apparently in the Syrian ritual the good were then permitted in dramatic form to see the place of torment as a terrible warning.

g. We also learn that the Solar Barque sailed between the mountains of Sunset, which were the gateway of the Underworld, and came out therefrom through the gateway formed by the Mountains of the Dawn. (See Jonah).

In connection with these points we must bear in mind that the Essenes seem to have carried forward into their system features which must have been drawn from one or other of these initiation rites.

1. They insisted as far as possible on continence, which was no doubt a substitute for the barbarous custom of mutilation.

2. Unlike the Sadducees, they believed in a place of torment for the wicked.

3. They taught that the souls of the good went to the Isles of the Blest.

4. They believed that the souls of all, both good and bad, were in due time reborn in earthly bodies, therein differing from the Pharisees, who held that it was only the good who thus returned and that the bad suffered for ever.

5. Their peculiar veneration for the sun would to some extent be derived from the important part it played in the Tammuz Rites, and in part from their belief that in its barque the souls set forth on their long journey.

6. They had a mysterious founder, to revile whom was blasphemy and punished by death. We can but suspect that this founder was originally Tammuz, for whom another name was probably substituted when Tammuz became anathema to the more orthodox. Perhaps the substituted name was Hiram Abiff.

Before going further let us now indicate places where these important landmarks seem to have survived freemasonry.

1. The mutilation, which in some cases was replaced by circumcision, among masons was until recent years represented by a running noose, as already mentioned, especially among the Operatives.

2, 3, 4, and 5, are so easily recognisable by all masons that they need very little further comment. We may as well point out, however, that Tammuz was the lion god and born of the lion goddess, hence the lion's grip. The double-headed eagle was associated with these two sufficiently to explain not only the alternative name for the grip but also the use of that emblem in the A. & A. Rite, while the word Kadosh is the same as that used for the sacred men and women of Astarte.

When we turn to the Higher Degree or monster ceremony the following points occur.

a.   The Solar Barque seems almost lost, but the boat whose captain refused to take the three miscreants on board and who plays such an important part in the American ritual no doubt represents it.   We also find a boat which is wrecked, but whose passengers are all saved, in the Knight of Malta.   The Solar Barque with its full significance survives in the Hung or Triad ritual.

b.   The journey, but on foot, through the Underworld occurs in the 18th degree and in the R.O.S., in both of which there is a symbolical descent into a place of misery or a dungeon. It is also hinted at in the R.A.

c.   There are three veils in the Excellent Master which must be passed before a candidate can take his R.A. in Scotland.   The fourth admits him into that degree.   There are three " sentries " to be passed in the R.O.S., and three rooms in the 18th degree. There are three stages in the K.T. and in the Knight of the H.S., in both of which there is a sepulchre reminding us of the sepulchre of Tammuz.

d.   The coming out of darkness into a brilliantly lighted room is an incident well known to those who have taken a certain degree.

e.   In another degree the candidate crosses a bridge, is bound with chains and brought before a king.   The association of this degree with Truth is significant, for Lucian tells us that those who failed to satisfy Rhadamanthus on this point were by him consigned to the Isles of the Damned, wherein were those who were lacking in truth, using that term in its widest sense. In the R.O.S. there is a similar binding, release, and emphasis laid on truth.

f.   The Holy City is minutely described in the R.O.S.

g.   We obtain references to the Holy Mountain in the 18th degree and elsewhere, while in the R.O.S. the members, like the Solar Barque, go contrary to the sun.

Thus it will be seen that despite its apparent unfamiliarity the Syrian system of initiation has numerous striking points of similarity with Freemasonry, and those points are essentially " Ancient Landmarks."   They grow out of its remote and savage past and seem to have been transmitted to us as its heirs and successors.   Nor is this list exhaustive, for we have seen that the description of the temple of Solomon with its two pillars with globes, the temple dome, and so forth, correspond with the sacred fane of Paphos where they have a clear meaning, rather than with the account of the Temple as it now stands in the Bible. But how did this ancient system come to be transmitted to modern Freemasonry ?   The links which connect it will be considered in the next three chapters.

CHAPTER XII

THEIR SURVIVAL UNDER THE ESSENES

The Jews, like the nations around them, had a mystery system at the beginning of the Christian era. This consisted of the four degrees of the Essenes[1] and has always been a problem to students of antiquity, for our knowledge is, alas, somewhat limited. What we have, however, is definite enough and will bear recapitulating here.

They were a celibate order among the Jews, first mentioned in the time of Jonathan Maccabee (161-144 B.C.), but although this is the earliest record of their existence the authorities agree that they were of a far earlier origin. The three earliest authorities are Philo,[2] Pliny the elder,[3] and Josephus.[4] Eusebius quoting a lost book of Josephus also gives us some interesting details, and one of the last references to them is in Epithanius, who died in A.D. 402.

Our best account is that given by Josephus, in which he tells us that the Essenes were mostly celibates but that a few of them did marry. That they formed a king of brotherhood and could recognise each other, so that when travelling from city to city they neither took food nor money with them because their brother Essenes would always supply them with the necessities of life. They held all goods in common, despised riches, and led very frugal lives. As he seems to have been admitted to the first degree, although he went no further, he undoubtedly knew of what he was speaking. He says, " As for their piety towards God, it is very extraordinary, for, before Sun-rising, they speak not a word about profane matters, but put up certain prayers, which they have received from their forefathers, as if they *made a supplication* for its rising."

On ceremonial occasions they clothed themselves in a white garment and we are also told that they assembled in " an apartment of their own, into which it is not permitted to any of another sect to enter; while they go after a pure manner into the dining room, as into a certain holy temple." We learn that they were famed for their fidelity, truthfulness and mercy, were particularly charitable to the poor and distressed, while they abominated lax conduct or profanity.

---

1. Encycl. Brit. Vol. 9. p. 779, also Vol. 2. p. 457 sq.
2. Philo, " Quod omnis probus."
3. Pliny, " Nat. Hist." V. 17.
4. Josephus, " The Wars of the Jews." 11. 8. " Antiquities." XIII. 5. para. 9 : XVIII. 1. para. 5. etc.

THE INITIATIONS

" Now if anyone hath a mind to come over to their sect, he is not immediately admitted, but is prescribed the same method of living which they use for a year, while he continues excluded, and they give him also a small *hatchet* and the forementioned *girdle* and the *white garment.*[a] And when he has given evidence during that time that he can observe their continence, he approaches nearer to their way of living, and is made a partaker of the waters of purification; yet is he even now not admitted to live with them; for after this demonstration of fortitude, his temper is tried two more years and if he appears to be worthy, they then admit him into their society.

And before he is allowed to touch their common food, he is obliged to take *tremendous oaths,* that in the first place he will exercise piety towards God and then he will observe justice towards men, and that he will do no harm to anyone, either of his own accord or by the command of others; that he will always hate the wicked and be assistant to the righteous; that he will ever show fidelity to all men and especially to those in authority, because no one obtains the government without God's assistance.

. . . That he will neither conceal anything from his own sect, nor *discover any of their doctrines to others; no, not though anyone should compel him so to do at the hazard of his life. Moreover, he swears to communicate their doctrines to no one any otherwise than as he received them himself;* that he will abstain from robbery, and will equally preserve the books belonging to the sect and the *names of the Angels.*[b] These are the oaths by which they receive their proselytes to themselves.

But for those that are caught in any heinous sin, they cast them out of their society. . . . What they most honour, after God Himself, is the name of their legislator,[c] whom if anyone blaspheme, *he is punished capitally.*[d] They also think it a good thing to obey their elders and the majority. Accordingly, if ten of them be sitting together, no one of them will speak while the other nine are against it."

Now if my brother masons will cast their minds back to their

(a) Note the axe, the emblem of Sandan, etc., and the same as the gavel, likewise the cord and the badge of innocence.

(b) The phrase, " Names of the Angels " has always puzzled the commentators, who suggest " messengers." A more probable explanation is that the names of the angels were the pass words of the degrees.

(c) Some commentators suggest that this legislator was Moses, but without producing the slightest evidence. On the contrary, had it been Moses undoubtedly Josephus would have said so. Who this semi-divine legislator could have been we can only surmise, no doubt he was a reputed founder of the Order, perhaps Solomon—possibly Hiram Abiff.

(d) This means having the head cut off. Clearly the legislator who could be " blasphemed " must have been semi-divine.

own ob. and to the charge after initiation they cannot fail to be struck with the similarity.

Josephus further informs us that the society was divided into four distinct degrees, one above the other, that the members believed that man had a soul which survived death, therein differing from the Sadducees, and that after death the souls of the righteous go to Paradise, whereas the wicked are " in a place of punishment." His words are:

" But when they are set free from the bonds of the flesh they then, as released from a long bondage, rejoice and mount upwards. And this is like the opinion of the Greeks that good souls have their habitations beyond the ocean in a region . . . . such as is refreshed by the gentle breathing or a *West wind*, that is perpetually blowing through the ocean; while they allot to bad souls a dark and tempestuous den, full of never ceasing punishment. And indeed the Greeks seemed to me to have followed the same notion when they allot the Islands of the Blest to their brave men, whom they call heroes and demi-gods; and to the souls of the wicked, the regions of the ungodly, in Hades."

From the concluding lines it is clear that Josephus means that the Essenes, like the *Greeks*, believed that the Paradise of the good was in the Isles of the Blest. Later on he tells us that the Pharisees also believed in the immortality of the soul. " They say that all souls are incorruptible, but that the souls of good men only *are removed into other bodies*, but the souls of bad men are subject to eternal punishment."

This passage seems to imply that whereas the Essenes believed in the ultimate re-incarnation of both bad and good after a period spent in Purgatory or Paradise, the Pharisees believed that only the good were ultimately reborn on earth (in a body); the wicked remained in perpetual torment. He further tells us that the Sadducees did not believe in any form of immortality at all.

If the Essenes were descended from the old worshippers of Adonis we should certainly expect some trace in their beliefs of re-incarnation, since that doctrine underlies the whole of the beliefs associated with Tammuz. In any case Josephus' account is of great importance to us for it records several details which indicate that the Essenes were really a reformed version of the old Tammuz cult, and that they are a very probable link in the chain of the evolution of that cult into modern Speculative Freemasonry.

Firstly the worship of the sun is very remarkable in an *orthodox* Jewish sect. Ezekiel thundered against it at the time of the Babylonian Captivity, and yet we thus find it still going on among a recognised sect of the Jews, circa 70 A.D. More significant still, his denunciation of the Solar Worship is linked up with a denunciation of women weeping for Tammuz. And from that account we learn that Ezekiel either in the flesh or, more probably, in a vision saw three sets of heathen practices taking place about the same time in the Temple itself.

(a) The elders of Israel in a secret underground chamber offering incense to all the Gods of the Syrians and Canaanites.

(b) The women weeping for Tammuz at the North Gate.

(c) Twenty-five Elders of Israel, with their backs to the Temple itself, looking towards the East and invoking the Sun.

Thus we see that the worship of the sun and the lamenting for Tammuz were closely interlocked, and yet we find the Essenes invoking the Sun *at Dawn*. Moreover, Ezekiel accuses the King of Tyre of claiming to be a God, a claim which the King would certainly consider himself entitled to make as an incarnation of Tammuz. Therefore we are bound to conclude that Ezekiel was attacking a semi-secret cult of Tammuz, or Adonis, popular in Jerusalem, which acknowledged the King of Tyre to be the living representative of Tammuz.

It is obvious that Hiram of Tyre, who lived in the days of King Solomon and David, could not have been alive 500 years later, and yet Ezekiel speaks as if it were the same man who had helped to build the Temple. He even says that he walked in Eden, which itself seems to imply that he knew and believed the Rabbinic legends which say that Hiram was allowed to enter Paradise alive because of the important service he had rendered to King Solomon. The only feasible explanation is that Hiram, like Pharoah, is a title, and that Ezekiel, hearing men speak of a Hiram, King of Tyre, thought that he was the same man as had helped Solomon, and this probably explains why he seemed so distressed at having to denounce him for what he regarded as a falling away from the light.

What, however, we must now realise is that a rite which involved invoking the sun at dawn, and which was denounced by Ezekiel in the 6th century B.C., was still being performed in 70 A.D. by an Order which had secret initiation Rites, and taught the doctrines of the resurrection and of re-incarnation. This Order, I suggest, was merely a reformed and purified survival of the old Tammuz cult. If this be so we can well understand why they tested their candidates so rigorously and bound them by tremendous penal oaths.

The more closely we investigate the Essenes the more clear it becomes that on the one hand they were derived from the old Cult, and on the other passed on some of their ceremonies to kindred secret societies, such as the Dervish rites, which still survive in Palestine. The ceremonial bathing or kind of baptism which the Essenes practised was always associated with the Adonis and Attis rites. It has survived in the Operative rituals to-day, although it is no longer enforced. According to the ritual the candidate has to step right into a bath, after which he is clothed with a long white garment, opening in front. I know quite a number of men who had to go through this ceremony only ten or twelve years ago. Although the bathing has now been omitted the white robe is still used, and similar robes were in use in old Dundee Lodge, a Speculative Lodge, in the 18th century, and were still in existence, though not in use, up to 1904, when they were destroyed.[1] Similar robes were in use in Boston, U.S.A. in 1914.[2] The convenience of these robes when testing a man's virility is obvious, and this was a custom which had not died out in Wales 40 years ago.[3]

The celibacy adopted by the majority of the Essenes was almost certainly a mild substitute for the emasculation at one time demanded by the Great Mother, which still at this date (A.D. 71) was exacted from the Priests of the more primitive forms of the cult at Heirapolis and elsewhere.

The four degrees have a striking similarity to the Masonic arrangement of the three Craft degrees and the R.A. It is also worth mentioning that the Essenes had a strong objection to slavery, and protested against it as unjust and a violation of the brotherhood of man. Have we here the origin of the Masonic objection to receiving into the Order anyone who is not free ? At any rate we may feel sure that any slave made an Essene was immediately set free, and therefore the Order would contain only free men. It may be noted that this humanitarian attitude was unique at that time in the ancient world. Even the best Pagans saw no harm in slavery, indeed accepted it as inevitable.

The very name Essenes presents an interesting problem. The commentators have been entirely unable to suggest its derivation, except that it may come from a Persian word, and here their arguments are far from convincing. Now Diana, or Artemis of Ephesus, who was of course merely another form of Astarte, had an order of Priests who were either called *Essenes* or at any rate had a High Priest over them known by the title of *Essen*.[4] These priests were eunuchs, and the common name by which they were known was Megabuzio, which indicates a Persian origin. It therefore seems probable that this Jewish secret society derives its name, not from a Hebrew word meaning the " Pail," as some have suggested, but from the name also applied to the Priests of the Great Mother at Ephesus, who like them were naturally celibates. The emblems of this goddess were the bee, the lion, the goat and the bear, and three of these are closely associated with Freemasonry.

The striking similarity of their obligation to ours and to our E.A. Charge seems to link this order with Freemasonry. That

---

1.   A. Heiron, " Ancient Freemasonry and Old Dundee Lodge," pp. 49 sq.
2.   Ibid.
3.   Ibid.
4.   See " Artemis."   Encyl. Brit.   11th ed. vol. II.

all traces of the old fertility cult were not extinct even among the orthodox Jews is shown by the Festival of Purim.   This feast, right down into the 18th century at any rate, had nearly all the characteristics of the Roman Saturnalia, and one of the most extraordinary features was the hanging of a figure of a man on a tree or cross.   The man was said to be Haman, but modern critics are agreed that this is a substitute for the old fertility god. [1][a]

---

1. Frazer, " The Scapegoat."   p. 392 sq.
(a) The double-headed Eagle of the Kadosh is also the insignia of a Patriarch in the Eastern Church, and five years ago was bestowed on the Arch- bishop of Canterbury by a vote of the Eastern Synod.   In short, it is still the badge of an Eastern Priest-King.

CHAPTER XIII

THE SURVIVAL OF THE ADONIS CULT IN CHRISTIAN TIMES

THE TWO ST. JOHNS

We have already seen that the Adonis cult was not extinguished by the triumph of Christianity. Finding that they could not stamp out these old heathen rites, the Church authorities seem to have adopted the policy of transferring them to the various saints. Indeed, to such an extent was the policy carried out that to-day there are scholars who question whether Christ Himself lived, for they can point to numerous incidents in His life which are clearly the same as certain events in the Myth of Adonis.

Such a corollary is, however, quite unnecessary and fails to account for the greatest of all Christian miracles, the rapid growth and ultimate triumph of the Christian faith. No great religious movement, such as Christianity, has ever arisen without a human leader with a great and evolved spiritual soul, who by his life and teaching aroused the aspirations of his followers and created a new and higher religious conception. We might as well doubt the existence of Mahomed as of Christ, and the fact that He may have gathered around Him legends of the past is no valid argument against His existence.

There is, moreover, another possible explanation of certain of these old traditions. They may have been deliberately attached to Him by His enemies, and a careful study of the account of His crucifixion makes this seem almost certain. On Palm Sunday He is brought in triumph, amid universal rejoicings, into Jerusalem, riding upon an ass, and with people waving palms and strewing them before Him, proclaiming Him, saying, " Blessed be He that cometh in the name of the Lord: blessed be the kingdom of our father, David, which cometh in the name of the Lord."[1]

Now in this scene we have a distinct counterpart to the proclamation of the God-man, Adonis, as a king and spouse of Astarte. The ass certainly played an important part in the Eleusinian Mysteries and was associated there with Dionysius, who is but a Hellenised form of Tammuz, while the waving of palms, etc., reminds us of the important part that plants and greenery played in the marriage of Adonis at Alexandria up to the end of the 4th century, or later. Further, the people proclaimed him king as coming in the name of the Lord and this, as we have

1. Mark 11. 1 sq.

144

previously seen, was originally the title of Tammuz and in its form of Adonis was the usual name by which he was worshipped at that very time.

Moreover, the triumphal procession was followed by the solemn cursing by Christ of a fig tree, which immediately withered away.[1] Now this incident has puzzled many worthy people, for, as we are told that the time for figs had not yet come, it seems like a fit of foolish childish passion and quite inappropriate to a man of Christ's patient character.

When we recollect, however, that as a result of the parting of Tammuz from Astarte the earth ceased to bring forth its increase, we see that the incident is one which would, by the populace, be associated with Him if they had decided to regard Him as the living representative of Tammuz. That He never cursed the tree at all is most probable, but that such a legend should subsequently be attached to Him, in view of His tragic fate, is perfectly natural. As never once otherwise did Christ curse any living thing even when justly provoked, we may feel sure that there is the very best of reasons for refusing to believe that Christ would ever have descended to such an exhibition of childish spleen. His whole life is a standing protest against the story.

When we come to His trial and death, again and again, we are struck by the similarity of the incidents to those which occurred when the Syrians mourned over a figure of Adonis slain, and it seems as if the brutal Roman soldiery were in mockery enacting the drama of the death of the Priest-King, the Divine Adonis.

He was scourged, as the unfortunate " Criminal " King at Babylon was scourged before he was taken out to be crucified. He was robed in the royal purple (red) robes of Adonis. He was crowned with a crown of Acacia thorns.[2] In his hand was placed a reed as a sceptre. What more appropriate emblem could they find to symbolise a God of Vegetation. Then they struck Him on the head with it. Does not this remind us of how another was knocked on the head ? He was crucified on a tree, as was the figure of Attis at Rome, and as was the " Criminal " King of Babylon, and probably in like manner Adonis in Syria.

Over His Head they placed His title " King of the Jews," which at once brings to mind the fact that the earthly representatives of Adonis were Priest-Kings. Finally, He was stabbed in the side just as was the human victim among the Albanians, and the man fastened to a tree by the people of the Philippine Islands, when they sacrificed him in order that the ground might be fruitful. Again the traditional date of Good Friday was the 23rd

---

1. Mark XI. 13 and 20.
2. O. D. Street, " Symbolism of the Three Degrees," p. 162 (London 1924).

March, the very day when similar ceremonies in a modified form were enacted in honour of Attis at Rome. There are other points which have not escaped the notice of scholars, and to some it has seemed that the story of Calvary is merely a form of the Adonis myth. To them, however, I would suggest another and, I believe the true explanation. Christ lived and died precisely as recorded, but the details of His death were arranged by His enemies. They were the official priests of Jehovah who for generations had fought against the old fertility cult which, for all their efforts, still gripped the imagination of a large part of the Syrian population, and probably of the less educated Jews.

If, as we have cause to believe, the Essenes represented a reformed and spiritualised form of the old cult, which while not denying Jehovah, yet stressed the loving mercy, instead of the severe and harsh justice, of God and taught it in their Mysteries, then the problem is solved. St. John seems to have been an Essene, certainly some of the disciples were, and so probably was Christ. Possessed of these facts, we can picture the priests in council saying " This man claims to be a divine king. He says he is God incarnate. There is one such claimant; we know of Tammuz or Adonis, whose living representative was originally slain each year. To-day this cult has substituted a figure for a man, but it would not be difficult to work up the ignorant mob into a state of frenzy in which they would insist on the old ceremony being done according to ancient form. We have only to whisper the words ' It is expedient that one man should die for the people ' and this dangerous opponent of ours would be removed for ever."

This explanation fits the facts exactly and accounts not only for the similarity of the details to which I have drawn attention, but also for the extraordinary phenomena of the same people within five days proclaiming Christ as King and then clamouring for His death.

If so, it also explains the fervour with which the small sect of Christians subsequently went forth to convert the world and were ready to die for their faith. Men will not readily die to propagate what they know is a myth, but the followers of Christ, who had actually seen Him martyred and afterwards seen Him alive again, would indeed be inspired with that spirit of self-sacrifice and devotion which they hereafter showed. I repeat, there is no more justification for doubting that Christ lived and died than there would be for doubting the existence of Mahomed or any other great historical character.

These facts are of considerable interest to us, but since they eventually became interwoven with the history of Christ's life, their survival will not help us greatly. Of an entirely different character are the numerous fragments of the fertility cult which were incorporated at a later date by the Church. We have already seen that in Cyprus certain ceremonies of Astarte have been transferred to the Virgin, and that even the title of the Goddess is applied to S. Mary[1] who has also inherited the crescent moon, and even the stars, of her great predecessor.   But it is those ceremonies which have been handed on to the two St. Johns which most clearly indicate an unbroken tradition.

Masons must not overlook the fact that for some apparently inexplicable reason these two saints are always associated with Freemasonry, despite the fact that the real patron of masons in the Middle Ages was S. Thomas.   There is nothing in Holy Scripture to warrant this association and yet, even as late as the time of the formation of Grand Lodge, the association was so strong that Anderson is careful to say that the famous meeting was held " on S. John the Baptist's Day."[2]   Even still, Craft Masonry in Scotland and also in many other parts of the world is always called " S. John's Masonry."

S. John in Summer and S. John in Winter really represent the old Fertility Festivals of the Summer and Winter Solstice, and when the Church found that she could not stop the Pagan feasts she fixed the feasts of the two S. Johns at the same period and so changed these festivals into nominally Christian ones.   For all that, it is difficult to see why people should jump through the fire[(a)] on S. John's day in summer, seeing that the saint was not burnt, but beheaded.   No doubt one reason why S. John the Baptist's day was fixed at midsummer was because on that day people bathed, just as the Romans did when they washed the figure of Cybele.

The ceremony is an old magical charm intended to produce rain, and when the Church found she could not stop it she reminded her somewhat lax followers that S. John baptised in the River Jordan.   Thus a heathen rite was sanctified.   For all that, people continued the custom in order that the fields might be fertile, which was certainly not the reason why S. John baptised, although he and the Essenes probably inherited the custom from a similar magical rite of the Adonis cult.

We have, however, many other survivals of the old Adonis cult associated with S. John.   There are the gardens of Adonis, later renamed " Gardens of S. John."[3]   There are the trees and flowers which, if plucked on S. John the Baptist's day, bestow various magical powers and are clearly descendants of that mysterious branch associated with the death of Tammuz.   We have too, the numerous customs which the Pope has taken over from the High Priest of Attis, such as the three knocks, the testing of his manhood, the eunuch choir, and so forth.

We thus see that the only reason why the two S. Johns could

---

1.   See Chapter IV.
2.   Ward, " Freemasonry and the Ancient Gods," p. 168.
3.   Frazer, " Adonis, Attis, Osiris."   3rd ed. Vol. 1. pp. 236 and 244 sq.
(a)   In many of these fires figures of human beings were burned !

have become associated with Masonry is because, in like manner, they represented older gods, or their cults, and that cult must have been the old Fertility Cult, the central feature of which was the myth of a dying god. Indeed, the two straight lines between a circle, called the two S. Johns, avowedly represent the summer and winter Solstices, while the curious ceremony still enacted by the Masons of Melrose every midsummer[1] attests to the direct connection between modern Freemasonry and the old Fertility Cult.

It must not be supposed, however, that the rites as transmitted to our mediæval ancestors were still in the crude and savage form which disfigured them in the days of Solomon. They had passed through many purgings, not the least of which was that of the Essenes, and doubtless the ceremonies performed in the Temple of the Roman Collegia at Pompeii were much nearer to our own than to the original form which existed in Syria in the days of Hiram of Tyre.

The Roman Collegia had an initiation rite and the discovery of an inlaid marble tablet containing certain symbols suggests that Attis was their hero. On a ground of grey-green stone is inlaid a human skull in grey, black and white. The skull has one peculiarity; although it is a true skull, it nevertheless has an ear. Above it is a square in coloured wood with brass points. There is a cross-piece a little above the points of the square, and from the apex hangs down a plumb line. This tool can be used as a square, a level or a plumb line. Beneath the skull is a moth, not a butterfly, as it is sometimes described, which rests on a six-spoked wheel. On the right side of the skull and wheel is a crooked thorn stick which reminds us of the crook of the priest-king at Bognaz-Keui and the acacia thorn. On the stick hangs a ragged, old, brown cloak tied with a cord, and over it a leather knapsack.

On the left side is a staff with a kind of knot at the top and at the bottom it comes to a sharp point. By some it has been described as a spear, but the point does not seem large enough for the blade of a spear. To the top, just beneath the knot, is a strip of white material with a line of dots or holes along the middle, and beneath is a robe of royal purple (red) fastened to the stuff by a cord.[2]

There is little doubt that here we have the " tracing board " of the degree of Death and Resurrection worked by the Roman Collegia. Why the skull should have an ear is difficult to say, unless it implies that the dead can hear us, though they cannot see or speak to us. The thorn staff with its crooked handle no doubt refers to old age, which needs to walk with the aid of the stick, and the old cloak reminds us of the worn-out body. The meaning of

---

1. See Chapter IV. p. 58.
2. See Transactions of the MSS. Vol. I. (1921-22) ill. op. p. 45, and
   S. R. Forkes, " Rambles in Naples."

the scrip or knapsack is obscure, but it is obviously the reverse of the strip of cloth on the staff, the meaning of which is equally uncertain. The staff is, however, clearly the staff of the conductor of the dead, and the royal robe reminds us of the robes in which they clad the figure of Adonis slain. The thorn staff also seems to refer to the Acacia tree, and we cannot forget the fact that Adonis was not only the God of Corn but also of Trees.

The fact that the royal robe is attached to the staff of the Conductor of the Dead clearly indicates that the initiate was symbolically raised from an old worn-out physical body to a perfect spiritual body fit for habitation by the Divine King.

Moreover a sculpture on the walls of their temple shows that the Roman Collegia not only attached a symbolic meaning to their working tools but associated them with a drama of death. The symbol consists of a spade, a trowel, a combined square, level and plumb line, such as is depicted on the tracing board, a pair of compasses, a chisel or crowbar, the head of a gavel, the skirret and, most important of all, an urn reversed. This last refers clearly to death, the urn containing the ashes of the dead being often buried with the mouth turned down.

When we remember that in Rome the death of Attis was regularly commemorated every year and that there were also secret rites of initiation, can we have any doubt as to what these symbols imply ? Neither can we forget that similar secret rites took place in a subterranean chamber under the altar at Jerusalem in the time of Ezekiel.

Moreover, ears of corn are constantly found carved on the water troughs in Pompeii, and as if to prove that this was not an accidental coincidence, on a fresco painted by the members of the college in what is usually called the House of the Tragic Poet a figure is depicted making a certain sign, which may well be considered to be associated with an ear of corn near a fall of water. This sign was reproduced by the lineal descendants of the Roman Collegia, the mediæval masons, in sculptures, mosaics, etc., and continued to be used in an appropriate way right down to the eighteenth century.[1] We thus see that a peculiar sign and a drama of death and resurrection were employed by the Roman Collegia, and there can be little doubt that it is through them that a reformed version of the old Tammuz ritual has passed down to modern times.

There is, however, another line of descent which probably reinforced and strengthened the tradition just at the time when it was likely to be tending to fade away. There are unmistakable signs of a fertility cult ritual in the legend of the Graal and also among the Templars. This aspect of the problem we shall

---

1. See Ward, " An Outline History of Freemasonry," for numerous examples.

consider in the next chapter, but here we must show that in the country of its origin the old Tammuz cult survived the Mahomedan conquest, and even to-day in a reformed guise survives in the secret rites of initiation among the Dervishes. It is probable that the Templars picked up the tradition, which afterwards cost them so dear, and reinfused it into the masonic lodges.

We have previously seen that as late as the 10th century the " pagan " Syrians of Harran were still annually celebrating the death of Tammuz, and even to-day at the harvest it is customary among the Arabs to bury a figure made of corn stalks, which they call the " old man." Hence there seems little doubt that the Dervish rites which have such a close similarity to Freemasonry are derived from the old Fertility Cult.

The most precise information available is that supplied by Henri M. Leon,[1] based on information obtained by him in Turkey. There are thirty-three Orders of Dervishes, each with their own ceremonies of initiation, special signs, pass-words, etc. Some of these ceremonies and signs are very similar to those known by Freemasons. Thus the " Lion's grip " is used by the Mevlevi Dervishes, the Scotch form of the sign G. and D. is known to most of these Orders, even as far away as the Senusis of Lybia, who used it during the War,[2] and by the Arab tribes who live near the Red Sea, who likewise employ the peculiar sign which was associated with the Roman Collegia at Pompeii and their successors, the Comacines. Their highest degree has a striking similarity to the R.A. and it is called the Kardashlik or " The Builders of the Kaaba." This title is of special interest to us since there is little doubt that the black stone of the Kaaba, which is supposed to have fallen from heaven, originally represented the " Great Mother," and is a " close relation " to the black stone which the Romans brought to the Holy City when they established there the rites of Cybele. It is, however, very much larger in size. The " Three Principals " in this degree are called " Our Lord Abraham," " The Exalted Ishmael " and " Isaac."

The title of " Our Lord Abraham " is particularly appropriate. First of all " The Lord " was title of Tammuz; secondly, the original name of Abraham was Abram, which is the same as Abiram, and so the same as Hiram Abiff. It consequently means " The Father of He that destroys " or " The Father of the Exaltation of Life "—titles whose tremendous significance we have already perceived; thirdly, Abraham, according to Jewish tradition, was about to offer up his son, Isaac, as a human sacrifice, but according to the Mahomedans it was Ishmael who was the destined victim.

---

1. Henri M. Leon, " The Masonic Secretaries' Journal," Sept., 1918. Ward, " Freemasonry and the Ancient Gods." p. 1. sq.
2. This information was supplied to me by an English soldier who fought against them.

These facts seem to suggest that the old Biblical patriarch's name has been used to replace that of Tammuz. In any case it is of masonic interest to know that the Dancing Dervishes make the sign of Rev. as used in the R.A. when they change their chant in the ceremony from " Allah " to " Jahuwe," which is obviously Jehovah.[1]

Abraham is also the Sheik or Master of the degree of Al-Kair-or (" Covenant,") in which the novice represents Ishmael.

The Bektashi Dervishes, whose ceremony we shall now consider, have a special girdle to distinguish them from the un-initiated. My readers will remember that the Essenes likewise had a girdle, and one of the charges made against the Templars was that they wore a girdle which had a heretical import. The charge is significantly explicit— " in their girdles was their Mahommerie."[2]   The ancient Order of the Assassins also had a girdle, which was red, and these four examples suggest that the Dervish girdle is the lineal descendant of that worn by the Essenes and that the Templar girdle came from one of the Syrian sects.

The Bektashi girdle usually has attached to it a flap covering a small bag, called the " jilband," and in it is carried a stone, the *pelenk*, which has seven points called " *terks*." It is said to symbolise the seven heavens, etc., for Allah said, " We have created the seven heavens and the seven earths in the same form, all of light."

Before an assembly is opened an altar of " rough, unhewn stones " is erected. The members then exchange the word, or the " Terjuman," (the interpreter) in groups of threes, in a manner familiar to R.A. masons. When all is ready the candidate, or Mureed, is deprived of nearly all his clothing, and of all metals or minerals. This latter detail suggests a rite connected with the spirit of vegetation, whose " death " is caused by metal tools. He is blindfolded and has a rope with a running noose placed about his neck. This, of course, conveys the idea that he is a victim being led to the altar for sacrifice. This cord is called " Deh-bend," or " Taybend." The candidate is then led in by two guides, named " Rehpehler," who each carry a weapon called " tebber."

He then makes seven journeys round the " tekkieh," or Lodge room, and after each circumambulation the Sheik, or Master, places one point of the pelenk (which he has taken from his own girdle) against the candidate's naked left breast and says, " I tie up greediness and unbind generosity," etc. The sentence varies with each round.(a)

---

1.   The Rev. A. Wigram, D.D., actually saw this incident in Irak and is my informant.
2.   Chronicle of S. Denis.
     Ward, " Freemasonry and the Ancient Gods," p. 279.
(a)   The whole seven are given in " Freemasonry and the Ancient Gods," p. 4

The candidate then takes the solemn obligation of secrecy at the stone altar on which is a copy of the Koran open at Sura 16, An-Nahl (The Bee) at the verse which begins " Perform thy covenant with God." As the Mureed or candidate kneels, his knees must touch those of the Sheik, who holds his right hand in his with the grip of a M.M.M., which grip is said to form the Arabic letter " Alif " or A, the first letter in the Arabic and Turkish alphabets.

The candidate, who is still blindfolded, is next asked what he most desires and on his replying " Light," the bandage is removed.

The Sheik then gives a very fine mystical lecture on the inner meaning of the word " Light," which is further elaborated by the Wazir, or second officer, who sits opposite the Sheik, the latter being in the East, or, at any rate, in the direction of Mecca.

When the Wazir has finished his lecture he advances from West to East by seven processions of seven steps each, in the manner adopted in a R.A. Chapter, and, taking the Mureed by the hand, asks the Sheik to invest the candidate.

The Sheik does so, the first article being the white girdle, and other garments follow in a way similar to the investiture of a masonic Knight Templar. Each garment is put on with an appropriate sentence indicating that the initiate is thereby consecrated to Allah.

Then follows the " historical " lecture in which the candidate is told that the first founder of the Order was the Angel Gabriel, who at the command of Allah initiated Mahomed. After this comes the mystical charge, in which the new member is told that " to know thyself is to know Allah." He is taught the word and signs, and is then proclaimed a member by blowing a horn at the four points of the compass and at the centre of the room.

Among the signs taught him is that sign which was used by the Roman Collegia, and also the p.s. of a M.M. Of course all Mahomedans continue the old fertility rite custom of circumcision, though too much stress must not be laid on the survival of one custom.

Perhaps, however, the most interesting fact about this and similar Dervish rites is that they have a tradition that because Richard I. admitted Saladin into the Order of Chivalry (this seems to be a fact) the latter repaid his courtesy by initiating Richard into some of the lower Dervish degrees. The King in his turn initiated a number of his knights, including some of the Templars, who on their return to Europe initiated some of the masons, who built their churches. " In this way " say the Dervishes, " you have our lower degrees but not our higher, for these Richard never received."

As to whether the Dervish higher degrees are quite different from the high degrees of Masonry, I cannot say, but it is obvious that as many of these masonic degrees are based on the Cross, the Mahomedan ones would naturally differ. The hostility to the Cross which fanatical Mahomedans feel would inevitably lead to the elimination of a symbol, which, though not originally Christian, in their eyes has become identified with our faith.

The tradition, however, is important, for, although I consider that the masonic ceremonies have come down to us from the Roman Collegia, there is every reason to think that a fresh infusion of the old cult into Masonry, via the Templars, occurred in the 12th and 13th centuries.

In addition to these Mahomedan rites there are the Druses, who not only have secret ceremonies and use some of our signs but actually claim to be descendants of the men who built the Temple.[1] They believe in one God and have a system of initiation very similar in some ways to Freemasonry, and it is important to remember that their chief centre is Lebanon, the centre of the Adonis cult. Their degrees are the Jakels, or Jahils, into which boys[a] and women are admitted, but the former are only admitted to the second degree, of Akils, when they are adults, and the women apparently are not admitted at all. Jahil means " The Ignorant," and Akil means " The Intelligent." There is a third, inner degree which constitutes the priests, who are called Khateels, concerning whom very little is known.

Above these there are a few members of a higher degree who are regarded as seers, or prophets, and deal with the higher flights of Astrology.

We can correlate these degrees with the Craft and the R.A., and in their sacred book, "Testimonies of the Mysteries of Unity," this condition is laid down for a candidate for the Akil degree. He must be " of full age, free from servitude and sound in mind and body." The Rev. Haskett Smith found that some of their grips and signs were similar to those used in Freemasonry, so much so that a Druse once asked him how he knew the signs of the Druses. They have inner and outer guards to their temples, which are adorned with the double triangle, and in general the Order seems to have many points of similarity to Freemasonry.

---

1. See Rev. Haskett Smith's articles in Quatuor Coronati, Vol. IV., pp. 7-19.
   Ward, " Freemasonry and the Ancient Gods," p. 8.
   Article " Druses " Encyclopædia Brittannica, 11th ed., Vol. VII. 1910, pp. 603 sq.
   C. H. Churchill, " Ten Years' Residence in Mount Lebanon " (1853) id. " The Druses and Maronites " (1862).
   H. Guy, " Le Theogonie des Druses " (1863), id. " La Nation Druse " (1864).
   G. L. Bell, " The Desert and the Sown " (1907).
(a) Apprentices were boys in mediæval times.

The Druses are not orthodox Mahomedans and derive their present form of faith from a heretical Mahomedan, named Hamze, of the 10th century A.D., that is to say, at the date when the old Tammuz rites were still alive in Syria.

Their faith is peculiar in that, like the old followers of Tammuz and unlike orthodox Mahomedans, they believe that God has been constantly reincarnated in a series of semi-divine prophets. Altogether they consider there have been seventy such incarnations, the last and final one was Hakim, the sixth Fatimate Caliph, after whom there will be no others, for the final revelation has, they say, been made. Among these incarnations they acknowledge Christ as one, but not Mahomed. They believe moreover in a second advent of Hakim, who shall return to conquer the world.

There are clear traces of Phallic and Fertility worship in the Druse religion and they pay great veneration to certain angelic intermediaries between God and man, which reminds us of the peculiar clause in the obligation of an Essene, not to betray the names of the angels. They have a number of " high places " in the Eastern Hauran, or shrines on the hilltops, which each contains a black stone to which goats and other animals are sacrificed. It is said that they also venerate the image of a calf, but this has been queried. It is, however, quite possible, for it is clear that the Druses, whose chief centre is Lebanon, the old centre of the Adonis cult, were followers of that cult who were converted by Hamze, the apostle of Hakim, who found them easy to convert because they already believed in the repeated incarnations of a Deity.[1]

Their belief as to what befalls the dead is, moreover, very similar to that held by the Essenes, and quite opposed to that of orthodox Islam, being based on the doctrine of Reincarnation. They hold that " the material world is a mirror " of the Divine Intelligence. The good after death pass through a series of fresh incarnations, each of a higher spiritual nature than the last, till they are absorbed into God Himself, whereas the wicked are reborn either as men in a miserable condition or as animals.

Now we have seen that the branch which the Jews used in the rites of Tammuz, and the whole fabric of that faith, all point to the doctrine of reincarnation. These facts therefore suggest that in the Druses, with their secret initiation rites and masonic signs, we have one of the many scattered and reformed descendants of the old Fertility Cult of Tammuz; if not, why do they venerate the black stone, which is the emblem of the Great Mother ?

Those Druses who have come into close contact with Europeans often maintain that they are connected with the Rosicrucians and with Freemasonry. As they are in a position to enter these Orders and we are not permitted by them to join theirs, it is

---

1. See Encyclopædia Brittannica, Ibid., p. 605.

obvious that they are in a better position to speak on such a point than are those who hastily deny the truth of their statements.[1]

The Ismailites are another heretical Mahomedan sect which still survives in Syria and in India and Persia. They too believe in a kind of reincarnation of the Deity, and since their twelfth Imam, Mahommed, vanished mysteriously, in Persia the Shah is the temporary substitute for this "hidden Imam."[2] This revival of the belief in a Divine King (the Imam) is instructive. In general Persia seems to have retained much of the old cult of Tammuz, as is shown by the importance of the festival of Maharan, held in honour of Hassan and Hassain. These heroes, by their duplication, remind us of Castor and Pollux, but otherwise the ceremony is similar to the old " Lamentation " of Tammuz.

The survival of the Ismailite sect in Syria, and especially in Lebanon, is therefore another example of the persistence of the old belief of the indigenous population.

The Assassins, who were a sect of Ismailites, are, however, for our purpose, most important, for they were in constant contact with the Templars, not only as enemies but also, strange to say, as allies, and even as feudatories. Indeed, in 1236 Pope Gregory IX. threatened the Templars and the Hospitallers with excommunication because he found they were negotiating a treaty of alliance with the Assassins.[3] We shall consider further this strange connection between a secret Infidel Order and the Champions of Christendom in the next chapter and here will confine ourselves to a brief account of its organisation.

The Assassins were a sect of Ismailites and, like the parent body, believed that God was incarnated in a series of great teachers, but in their case they considered Hassan,[a] their founder, was one of these and that to some extent he transmitted his divine nature to his successors. His real power dates from 1090 when he seized the mountain stronghold of Alamut, in Persia,[4] and there organised his followers into a secret society.

At the head was Hassan, who was called " The Sheik-al-Jabul," i.e., " the Chief or Old Man of the Mountains." Under him were three Provincial Grand Masters, called Da'i-al-Kirtal. Then came the highest degree, the Da'is or Masters, who were

---

1. Article " Druses " in Encyclopædia Britannica, ibid.
2. See article " Shiites " Encyclopædia Brittanica, 11th ed. (1911). Vol. 24, p. 867.
3. Article " S. John of Jerusalem," Encyclopædia Brittannica, Vol. 24, (11th ed. 1911) p. 15, quoting Cartul ii. No. 2149.
4. Article " Assassins," Encyclopædia Brittannica (11th ed.) (1910-11) Vol. 2. pp. 774 sq.
   A. Jourdain in Michaud's " Histoire des Croisades," ii. pp. 465-484.
   R. Dozy " Essai sur l'histoire de l'Islamisme " (Paris, 1870). ch. IX.
(a) It is certainly curious that so many of these reincarnate deities had as the first letter of their name the letter H. While it would be dangerous to build on such a foundation we cannot help suspecting that it is not due to " coincidence."

fully initiated into all the secrets of the Order. The Refigs may be compared with the Master Masons; they knew part of the secret doctrines and normally became Masters in due course.

The Fedais (" the devoted ones") correspond roughly to the Fellow Crafts. It was these men who were used as assassins when the Sheik desired the removal of any enemy. The Lasigs, or Novices, probably knew very little, and were merely men selected out from the common people with a view to testing their character.

There were also a large number of " common people " under the temporal sway of the Sheik from whom recruits were drawn, but these were outside the Order altogether.

The Sheik used the dagger of the assassin so effectually that his Order became a power in the land, and his victims were more often orthodox Mahomedan princes than Christian crusaders. We know very little about the actual ceremonies of initiation into the Order save that the distinguishing badge was a red cord, or girdle, but we do know that these semi-divine leaders were nearly always assassinated by their successors.

While this may, of course, be merely due to the ambition of an unscrupulous successor to obtain power, it is strange that in the majority of cases the assassin seems to have been accepted at once as the lawful successor. Indeed, although Mahomed II. was poisoned by his own son, Hassan III., the latter stands forth as one of the most pious rulers of the sect, and one who during his whole reign entirely abstained from assassinating anyone else. He in his turn was murdered and his son, a mere child of nine years old, was placed on the throne. Indeed, there is hardly a Sheik of the Order who did not obtain the throne by murder, and die by being murdered, and we are forcibly reminded of the Priest-King of Nemi, and similar divine kings who, in like manner, were killed when they began to grow old.

The name of the founder, Hassan, is also that of one of the two brothers who are annually mourned over at Maharan, and although this may be merely a coincidence, it seems more likely, since Hassan II. openly claimed to be the Imam, or an incarnation of the Deity, that the name was deliberately adopted with that end in view, and we may suspect that he thus proclaimed openly what the first Hassan had taught secretly to the fully initiated.

The other important centre of the sect was Lebanon, which means " whiteness," and comes from the Semitic word " Laban." [1] This brings to mind the fact that Hiram also means " whiteness."

It was during the reign of the successor of Hassan II., viz., Mahomed II., that the Syrian branch made itself independent, and remained so for the rest of its history. It was with this

---

1. See article " Lebanon " Encyclopædia Brittanica. Vol. 16. (1910-11 p. 346.

branch that the Templars came into contact, and to all the crusaders " The Old Man of the Mountains " meant the Sheik of the Assassins of Lebanon.

We thus see that this secret Order, which had three distinct degrees and a super degree corresponding to Master of a Lodge, or possibly to the R.A., was strongly entrenched on Lebanon, the old site of the Adonis cult, and that its doctrines included that of the reincarnation of a Divine Being as Priest-King, which kings were usually murdered.   Furthermore, this cult was organised at about the same time as the Druses, at a period when the old Tammuz cult was not even officially extinct, and has, undoubtedly, a direct connection with the Knights Templar.

To sum up this chapter, we find herein that Lebanon in the 10th, 11th and 12th centuries was the centre of a series of secret societies which carried on, more or less *sub rosa*, certain doctrines of the old Adonis cult, in direct opposition to the orthodox Monotheism of Islam, and while we cannot definitely say that these secret rites included one of Death and Resurrection, in view of the nature of their beliefs and of such fragments of their organisation as we can trace, we can have no doubt that they were the descendants of the cult of the Dying God.   This being so, we may be practically certain that this central feature of the old cult was not omitted.   Indeed, the story that those who were to be sent out as assassins were first brought into the gardens of the chief, which they were told were Paradise, suggests that before being sent forth to certain death they were, by a ceremony of Death and Resurrection, given a sure and certain hope that their souls would rise from their dead bodies and enter Paradise.

We have also seen that numerous details of the Fertility Cult were retained by the mediæval Christians and attached to S. John, a fact which suggests the real reason why the two S. Johns have become associated with Craft Masonry.   Finally, we have seen that in addition to the heterodox Mahomedan secret societies there are also orthodox Dervish rites which bear more than a superficial resemblance to Freemasonry.

With all these facts before us, let us turn to consider briefly the connection of the Templars with Freemasonry, a tradition, be it remembered, which is enshrined in the very heart of the modern masonic Order.

CHAPTER XIV

THE KNIGHTS TEMPLAR AND THE HOLY GRAAL

I have in a previous work[1] given a brief history of the Templars, and so need not devote any space to that subject here, this is the less necessary since the literature on it is extensive and exhaustive.[2] In my former work I said that in my opinion, although the charges of gross immorality and impiety were unfounded, according to orthodox mediæval views the Order *was* tainted with heresy. Since then I have read more authorities on the subject and have considered carefully the conflicting views they set forth.

As a result I adhere to my original view that many of the secret ceremonies of which they were accused did take place and, although they had not the impious meaning their enemies alleged, were certainly not orthodox. It is probable, however, that the majority of the Knights did not understand them at all, but merely did them because they were the custom of the Order.

The fact that the admission of members was done secretly, behind closely guarded doors at daybreak, and that initiates were forbidden to reveal anything that had transpired, *even to another member*, under the penalty of expulsion, shows that there *was* a secret ceremony of initiation. This feature was peculiar to the Templars, and is not found in any other of the regular orders, and while this does not justify us in believing all the accusations made it does show that there was a secret ceremony.

Now we know that the great centre of secret initiation rites was Palestine, the only alternative source being one of the great building guilds, such as the Comacines, concerning whose precise ceremonies little is known. As the great centre of the Templars was Palestine, the most obvious source of their secret rites was that country. Let us, therefore, consider briefly those ritual practices which in my opinion were proved. The charges against the Knights were nine in number.

(1) Denial of Christ and the defiling of the cross.
(2) The adoration of an idol.

---

1. Ward, " Freemasonry and the Ancient Gods," pp. 268 sq.
2. Michetet, " Proces des Templiers." (T.1. 1851) and (T.2. 1861).
   Maillard de Chambure," " Regle et statuts secrets des Templiers, prec. de l'hist. de cette ordre." (Dijon-Paris, 1840).
   H. de Curzon, " La Regle Temple," (Paris, 1886).
   C. G. Addison, " The Knights Templars." (London, 3rd ed. 1854).
   Fred. von Hammer-Purgstall, " Mysterium Baphometis revelatum." (1818).
   Ibid, " Die schuld der Templer," 1955.
   H. C. Lea, " History of the Inquisition," (1888).
   Also the works by Wilh. F. Wilcke, Loiseleur, Prutz, Fuike.

(3) A perverted form of the mass.
(4) Ritual murders.
(5) The wearing of a cord of heretical significance.
(6) The ritual (or obscene) kiss.
(7) Alteration in the words of the mass and an unorthodox form of absolution.
(8) Treachery to the other sections of the Christian army in Palestine.
(9) Immorality.

Of these numbers four, eight and nine may be quickly dismissed.   There is no reliable evidence for number 4.   Number 8 merely indicates that as a result of the internecine jealousy which rent the Latin kingdoms of the Holy Land the Knights did not always act as promptly as they should have done, but their heroic resistance to Islam, proved on many a blood-stained field, shows that they far outshone most of their detractors in loyalty to the cause of the cross.   As to number 9, no body of men, much less soldiers, ever existed for long without some of them wandering from the strict paths of vritue, and even the ordinary clergy in the Middle Ages were not always above reproach, but there is no evidence to support the monstrous charges levied against the Order as an Order.   The other points must be considered in detail.

5.   THE WEARING OF A CORD OF HERETICAL SIGNIFICANCE

The inquisitors may have been knaves, but they were certainly not fools, and as their object was to discredit the Templars in the eyes of the orthodox, the stress that they laid on this cord shows that neither they nor the populace regarded the Templar cord or girdle as orthodox, or in any way similar to the Cistercian girdle with which some modern critics have compared it.   The " Chronicle of St. Denis " emphatically states that " in their girdles was their mahommerie."   Now we have seen that the Essenes invested their novices with a girdle, that the distinguishing badge of the Assassins was a red cord or girdle, and that in the Dervish rites, as still practised, the candidate is first encircled with a girdle.   Furthermore, among the Dervishes this piece of ceremonial marks the formal investiture of the novice, and is accompanied by appropriate phrases, implying that thereby the novice dedicates himself to Allah.   The " Chronicle of St. Denis " says of the Templars that in their gridles was their Mahomedanism, for that is the clear meaning of the phrase, and implies that they had dedicated themselves to the service of Mahomed.   It must not be forgotten that the Mediæval ecclesiastics regarded the Mahomedans not as members of an alien or non-Christian faith, but as heretics, and in consequence Dante placed Mahomed in the Hell reserved for schismatics, and not in that of the Pagans.   The Cathari also used such a cord, fastening it round the breast of their " Perfecti " at the completion of the ceremonies, and these " heretics " undoubtedly derived their original ideas from the Near East, as their doctrines show.[1]

Thus the Essenes, the Assassins of Lebanon, the Cathari, and the present day Dervishes use a cord to denote membership of a secret Order, and we can therefore have little doubt as to whence the Templars derived it. We may be perfectly sure that their ecclesiastic opponents likewise knew whence it came. The curious connection which existed between the Assassins and the Templars has already been mentioned. The " Old Man of the Mountains " actually paid them tribute, and when he offered to become Christian if this tribute was abolished the Templars killed the messengers who had taken his proposal to King Amalric of Jerusalem. This occurred in 1172 A.D. It seems that the head of this secret, heretical, Mahomedan sect had been paying tribute to the Templars since about 1149 A.D., while as late as 1252 A.D. the overlordship of the Templars over the Assassins was still intact, for in that year they rebuked the insolence of certain envoys of the Assassins to Louis IX. in a manner which leaves no doubt as to the close connection which existed between the two societies.[2] Thus both these Orders were secret societies with initiation rites, and wore a cord as a badge of membership. They were closely associated, although one was Christian and the other Mahomedan, and both were regarded as heretical by the orthodox members of their respective faiths.

This connection was well known, as is proved by the steps taken by the Pope to try to prevent it, to which we have previously referred. Their persecutors, therefore, would know precisely whence that tell-tale cord was derived, and, like them, I regard it as strong evidence of unorthodox tendencies, although probably the ignorant knights did not recognise it as such.

3. A Perverted Sacrament

There is no reliable evidence of a perverted sacrament, and it is most improbable. If, however, we unite this charge with number 7, we shall find that there is evidence that the form of the Mass celebrated was unusual, while the form of absolution was certainly open to suspicion. In some of the answers to this charge there seems to be indicated a peculiar veneration for the thief on the cross, which by a few was interpreted as a denial, not only of the divinity of our Lord, but even that He died unjustly.

6. A Ritual Kiss

The charge seems proven, but I regard it as no more than a method used to humble the proud spirit of a novice, and similar

---

1. Dr. F. W. Bussell, " Religious Thought and Heresy in the Middle Ages," p. 714.
2. Article " Templars," Encycl. Brit. 11th ed. Vol. 26. p. 596.

to the "lick my boots" of the school bully to the new boy.
It was usually given " in ano," but there is no reason to impute
anything immoral to the kiss.   It may, of course, be a survival
from the old fertility cult ideas, but even this is doubtful.

2.   THE ADORATION OF AN IDOL

The real points of interest in these charges are numbers 2
and 1.   With regard to the adoration of an idol, which is usually
described as a head, the question is more complex than most
defenders of the Order admit.   There does seem to be evidence
that one or two such " Heads " were found, one being at Paris,
and we cannot ignore the curious Templar legend of the head
which brought good luck.   It may be that this head represents
the head of Adonis, which was thrown into the sea at Alexandria
each year, and we also cannot overlook the fact that among the
" hallows " of the Graal is a bleeding head, sometimes described
as the head of St. John the Baptist.   We have already seen that
the two St. Johns, and more especially St. John the Baptist, took
over many of the rites and customs associated with Adonis, and
therefore we are entitled to suspect that the Templar head and
the head in the Graal legends both go back to the older cult.

Our suspicions derive considerable support from the Mabinogion wherein Peredur sees the Graal, the spear dripping blood
and the head, which latter he is told is that of a relation of his
who was murdered by witches.[1]   In this early version of the
Graal there is no hint that the head is that of St. John, neither
is the bleeding sword that of Longius, the soldier who pierced
the side of our Lord.

Remembering this, let us turn to a curious Templar legend.

" A noble lady of Maraclea was loved by a Templar, a Lord
of *Sidon*, but she died when young, and on the night of her burial
this wicked knight crept to the grave, dug up her body and violated
it.   Then a voice from the void bade him return in nine months'
time, for he would find a son.   He obeyed the injunction, and
at the appointed time opened the grave again and found *a head
on the leg bones of the skeleton*. (Skull and cross bones).   The
same voice bade him ' guard it well, for it would be the giver of
all good things,' and so he carried it away with him.   It became
his protecting genius and he was able to defeat his enemies by
merely showing them the magic head.   In due course it passed
into the possession of the Order."[2(a)]

Now, not only did the inquisitors find such a head at Paris,
but a number of the Knights admitted having paid reverence to it,
some adding that they thought it was a skull.   While it is possible,

1.   Lady Guest, " The Mabinogion," (Everyman Ed.) p. 219.
2.   Ward, " Freemasonry and the Ancient Gods," p. 307.
(a)   Compare a somewhat similar story told by Mandeville of Cyprus where
        a dead woman brought forth a Serpent.

of course, that it was some "relic," this hardly seems likely, for if so the Knights would have had a ready answer to the accusations of the Church.

The legend seems to be a garbled account of an initiation rite of death and resurrection, and, moreover, one reminiscent of the old legends of Adonis and Astarte, and also of the story of how Horus was begotten by the dead Osiris. This legend would represent a Templar ceremony of the mystic marriage, the age-old symbol of the attainment by the true seeker of Divine Union, and reminds us of the ceremonial marriage between the figures of Aphrodite and Adonis at Alexandria. The burial of the lady, not the man, is a curious variation, but it nevertheless corresponds with the death and burial of Adonis, while the appearance of the severed head brings to mind the head of Adonis, which was flung into the sea, and that of Orpheus, which was flung into the river. The magical properties of the head are similar to those possessed by the head of Vran in the Mabinogion, and to the bleeding head in the story of Peredur, perhaps in some later legends it becomes the head of John the Baptist. It may also be the origin of the various brazen heads which appear in numerous mediæval legends. One of these is the brazen head of Friar Bacon[a] which could speak, and but for the failure of the man who was watching it to report the fact to Friar Bacon, would have "walled all England with a wall of brass" and have rendered her invulnerable. In other words, this head, like that of the Templars, would have given England the victory.[1]

The Templar head is, therefore, magical in origin, a bringer of victory and prosperity, as we should expect if it was originally the head of Adonis, the fertility god. Such a head or skull might have appeared on the altar, just as a skull still appears in a certain masonic "Higher Degree," but it is quite probable that it was not worshipped and merely formed one of the objects used in the secret initiation.

My readers should note that novices were forbidden to speak of anything which occurred at their initiations, *even to another member*. The significance of this last clause seems generally to have been overlooked by students. If the prohibition had been merely forbidding them to tell anything to outsiders it would have been sufficient to show that, like Freemasons, the Templars

---

1. See " Famous Historie of Fryer Bacon " (London, 1615), reproduced in Thoms, " Early Prose Romances."
    R. Greenes, " Friar Bacon and Friar Bungay," (1587).

(a) Roger Bacon lived A.D. 1214-1294 and was one of the most profound and original thinkers of his age, for which reason he was suspected of heresy. He had certainly studied the Arabic scholars and may have learnt something of the magical side of the fertility cult. It is significant that he lived at the period when the Templars were at the height of their power and when the Graal literature was still a living force.

did have secret rites of initiation, but the fact that novices were forbidden to compare notes with other members indicates either that certain parts of the ceremony were not given to all, or else that different explanations of the meaning of the same ceremony were given. Probably both occurred, and this would explain why some Knights denied that a particular ceremony took place while others acknowledged it. It is clear, however, that the explanation of certain ritual practices varied considerably, and no doubt the purpose of the head was in like manner explained differently to different Knights.

To some it might be merely an emblem of mortality to others a magical head, bringing good fortune, and the genius of the Order, to whom reverence, though hardly worship, should be paid. In American Templar Lodges a skull is still used for ritual purposes and is called " Old Simon." Is this a corruption of the Lord of Sidon ?

I have in " Freemasonry and the Ancient Gods " shown that the claim made that the Knights Templar did enter Freemasonry, carrying with them certain of their rites, is not nearly so fantastic as some people think.[1] Only some 800 Knights out of 15,000 suffered death or imprisonment, and in addition there were thousands of Templar Clergy and also thousands of lay brethren, many of whom were masons,[a] and none of whom were persecuted. What happened to this huge body of men ? Is it not probable that some of them did take refuge in the Masonic Guilds ? If the masons also had initiation rites drawn from the Adonis cult the similarity of the two systems would naturally attract the Templars, particularly the Templar Priests, who, unlike the Knights, probably did understand what the ceremonies meant.

This connection becomes more probable when we consider other details of the secret Templar Rites. For example, the novices were deprived of practically all their clothing. " Geraldus de Pasagio said he took off the coloured clothes he was wearing behind the altar, except his shirt, breeches, socks and boots . . . . and put on a garment of camel's hair."[2] The use of a special candidate's robe reminds us of the old custom which survived till the 19th century at Old Dundee Lodge, No. 18, and the use of " camel's hair " suggests an Asiatic origin of the custom. The number 3 played an important part in the lives of the Knights, for example, the ritual kiss and the symbolic denial of the cross occurred three times in the ceremonies.

This brings us to the most peculiar feature of the secret

1.   " Freemasonry and the Ancient Gods," pp. 284-310.
2.   Proc. I. pp. 205-214.
       See also Walsingham, " Life of Edward II."
(a)   One of these lay brethren called Frere Jorge la Mason was expelled from the Order for misconduct. See " Freemasonry and the Ancient Gods,"
       p. 284.

ceremonies, the denial of Christ and the defiling of the Cross, which seems clearly proven and was, no doubt, a ritual practice very little understood by the Knights. Moreover, here again it seems as though different explanations were given to various novices, for while Petrus Picadi told the inquisitors that it was a test of fidelity and had he been brave enough to refuse to do as he was told he would have been sent to the Holy Land,[1] Gonavilla, Preceptor of Poitou and Acquitaine, said that the Denial was in imitation of St. Peter's having denied Christ thrice. A similar explanation was given for spitting at the cross, and that the procedure may have been merely part of a ritual drama is shown by the fact that in a Mediæval mystery play called " The Festival of Idiots," the character known as the Idiot, or unregenerate soul, spits on the cross.

Although such explanations as these may have been given in good faith by some of the Preceptors, it is more likely that in this incident we have a survival of the hatred of the cross which characterised certain Gnostic sects. These, instead of venerating the cross as a symbol of their salvation, declared it to be a loathsome thing, since it was the means whereby Christ was slain. We shall return to this point in a few moments, for a scene which occurs in the " High History of the Holy Graal " depicts such defilement of the cross, and therein the act is explained and justified. The incident shows very clearly that the Graal legends are connected with the Templars.

Some of the evidence suggests that the cross was at times painted or carved on the floor, and that the ceremony then partook of the nature of a ritual step. This brings to mind certain ritual steps in Freemasonry which constitute crosses and which, by ill-natured people, might be misconstrued and twisted into a charge of blasphemy, a charge which, however, would be utterly false. In our first r. step we trace out a tau cross, and thus trample on it; we do so as symbolising the trampling underfoot of our animal passions, and when in like manner we make the Latin cross it is to indicate the sacrifice of ourselves, or, in other words, that the novice treads the way of the Cross. Moreover, a careful study of the legend of our Master H.A.B. will reveal the fact that, as he staggered from point to point in the Temple with the blood streaming from his wounds, he must have made with his blood a Cross—the Consecration Cross, which is always made at the consecration of a Church and is subsequently blessed by the Bishop.

For all that, the ceremony was evidently a severe test of the obedience of the novice, for again and again we read that the other Knights had to threaten him with drawn swords.[a]

---

1.   Proc. I. 523.
(a)   In an old Masonic Templar ritual the cand. was threatened with a sword during his ob., and even in the Craft this occurs in many districts, including Bristol, which was always an important Templar centre.

We must remember that the Crusaders brought back to England many Eastern customs. Thus women adopted the wimple, which is merely the veil worn by Mahomedan women. Syrian details in capital and shape of arch were introduced into English Churches, and the Templars themselves adopted certain distinctly Asiatic customs. For example, Templar Knights were distinguished from all other knights by their beards, so much so that when the blow fell the Preceptor of Lorraine ordered the Knights to shave their beards, abandon their robes and escape into obscurity.[b]

The shape of the Templar churches, circular outside and octagonal inside, is peculiar to them. It may be copied from the Mosque of the Dome, which they thought was the Temple of Solomon, but if so this shows that they would be particularly drawn to a ritual which dealt with the building of that Temple if they found one still working in Syria. The shape of these churches, however, is such as to suggest that they were built for a special ritual purpose, in which the circumambulation of the " Lodge " round a central point or altar was an important incident. If that ritual included a dramatic representation of the death and resurrection of the novice " at the centre," the shape and plan adopted would be admirable.

The next important point is that according to tradition the Templars were Guardians of the Holy Graal, a tradition which appears to have a solid foundation as indicating that the Graal legends were originally a fertility cult carried on from ancient times, and only partially Christianised. So obvious was this to the Ecclesiastical authorities that they seem to have discouraged the growth and development of the Graal legend although they could not entirely prevent its popularity as a " Romance." We will therefore consider this great cycle of stories very briefly.

THE HOLY GRAAL

That the Holy Graal is a mystical allegory has been recognised by many great writers, but few seem to have realised that it was also a kind of initiation rite. J. Weston,[1] however, has made out a very strong case in support of this view and shows that in its original form the Graal itself was not even a Christian emblem, much less the Chalice, which it had become by the time that Malory incorporated the story in his Morte d'Arthur. Weston traces the Graal theme back to the old fertility cult of

---

1.   J. L. Weston, " The Quest of the Holy Graal " (Bell, London, 1913).
(b)   A certain sign which is used by the Masonic Knights Templar thus becomes not only intelligible but also an indication that this body may be connected with the old Order. Other points in the ritual which seem to have come down from the old ceremonies are considered in " Freemasonry and the Ancient Gods " in a manner intelligible to those entitled to understand.

Adonis, and suggests that to a large extent it came from the Templars. I do not propose to go over the ground thus admirably covered by this writer but will concentrate attention on certain points which have not yet received the consideration they deserve, and which tend still further to confirm the view that the Graal theme is derived from the Adonis cult and was propagated by the Templars.

1. The original versions of the Graal story all appeared between c. A.D. 1175 and 1225, then the source of the supply was cut off abruptly, as if the Ecclesiastical authorities had brought pressure to bear to prevent the publication of any more such material. Henceforth writers simply re-use the old material, adding chivalric stories of Arthur and his Knights. We find no further development of the Graal itself.

2. The original hero was Gawain, later Perceval. Galahad is quite a late invention.

3. Sir Perceval is always called the " Son of the widow lady."

4. The Graal is a talisman whose appearance brings *fertility* to the soil and feeds the worshippers.

5. It has many forms, the only thing in common between them being the fact that it is always a food providing object. These forms are, (*a*) A stone; (*b*) A holy object, whose form is not specified; (*c*) A reliquary; (*d*) The platter or cup used at the last supper; (*e*) A vessel in which St. Joseph of Arimathea received the Blood which came from the wounds of Christ, and quite late in its evolution it takes the form of (*f*) The Chalice of the Eucharist. Even in this form it is of no material substance whatever.

6. The original object of the Quest was to restore the vitality and also the virility of the Guardian of the Graal, who is known as the Fisher King, or the Maimed King, which being done fertility would return to the land.

7. We are told that the Graal is a mystery which must not be revealed to the uninitiated. This we learn from more than one author, including Blihis in the " Elucidation," whilst in " The High History of the Holy Graal " appears this pregnant passage.[1] " The Graal appeared at the sacring of the mass, in *five several manners that none ought not to tell*, for the secret things of the sacrament ought none to tell openly but he unto whom God hath given it. King Arthur beheld the changes, the last thereof was the change into a chalice. And the hermit which chanted the mass found a brief under the corporal and declared the letters, to wit, that our Lord God would that in such vessel should His Body be sacrificed."

The account adds that until then there had been no chalices known anywhere. Thus we see that there was an inner meaning to the Graal story and, moreover, as in the Templar ritual, the

---

1. Dr. Sebastian Evans, " The High History of the Holy Graal," (Everyman Ed.) p. 268. (Usually called by scholars the Perlesvaus).

meaning of the sacred object varied according to the initiate, the outermost meaning being that of the chalice.

8. The journey to the Graal castle depicts the journey of the soul through the Underworld to Paradise, as is made abundantly clear by the little explanations conveniently given from time to time by various hermits to the hero, when he cannot understand some incident.[1] It thus corresponds to the High Grades of Tammuz.

9. In Parzival, by Wolfram von Eschenbach, the Graal is a stone[a] which brings food to its worshippers, and is under the protection of a body of Knights Templars who are chosen by the stone itself. On the stone appear written the names of these guardians when they are yet children, also the destined wife of the King, whom alone he is allowed to marry.

10. According to Wolfram, Parzival's half-brother, who is the son of a *Saracen* princess, marries the maiden who bears the Graal and has by her Prester John. This incident clearly indicates an Asiatic connection.

11. In the Diu Crone Version Gawain achieves the quest, asks the long-awaited question, and thereby restores to life the *dead* King-guardian.

12. From some accounts it is clear that the wound from which the King-guardian is suffering is that of castration. On this point J. Weston says: [2]The " dead body on the bier, the Maimed King on the litter, correspond with the god, dead, or wounded in such a manner that he is deprived of his reproductive powers. This is an analogy which has hitherto been too much ignored, though certain scholars have evidently been aware of its existence. Vellay and other writers pointed out that the term ' thigh ' used in connection with the wounding of Adonis is merely a well-recognised euphemism, of which they give numerous instances; and while the majority of the Graal texts employ this term for the wound of the Fisher King (Parmi les cuisses), Wolfram von Eschenbach uses words which leave no doubt that here, as elsewhere, the term is to be understood in an euphemistic sense."

Even in the late form of the tradition preserved for us in the Morte d'Arthur, Sir Perceval " wounds himself in the thigh," namely, castrates himself, because he had nearly had carnal connection with the lady who came in a ship " covered with silk blacker than any bear," who is undoubtedly Astarte.

On being discovered and rebuffed by Sir Perceval she changed into a fiend.[3] This is what always happens to the old Gods in

---

1. See, " The High History of the Holy Graal," and also Ward, " The Hung Society," Vol. 2, for full details.
2. J. Weston, " The Quest of the Holy Graal," p. 80.
3. Mallory, " Morte d'Arthur." (Everyman ed.) Vol. 2. pp. 201-205.
(a) This form of the Graal reminds us of the stone in the Mark degree and the small cube still given in the Masonic K.T.

Mediæval Christian legends. The black hangings remind us that Cybele was black, and the bear, we know, was her animal form. We have thus seen that the Graal literature in some mysterious way is connected with the Templars on the one hand and with the old Adonis cult on the other, but one of the strongest pieces of evidence is still to come. In the " High History " we are told that Sir Perceval saw a " questing beast " torn to pieces at the foot of a wayside cross by twelve hounds, to which she had just given birth. Then there came a knight and a damsel and gathered up the fragments of the mangled snow-white beast, placed them in golden vessels which they bore, and departed.

After this came two priests to the cross, and the first ordered Sir Perceval to withdraw from the cross, and when he had done so " The priest kneeleth before the cross and adoreth it and boweth down and kisseth it more than a score of times and manifesteth the most joy in the world. And the other priest cometh after and bringeth a great rod, and setteth the first priest aside by force, and *beateth the cross* with the rod in every part and weepeth right passing sore.

Perceval beholdeth him with right great wonderment, and sayeth unto him' ' Sir, herein seem you to be no priest! Wherefore do you so great shame ? ' ' Sir,' sayeth the priest, ' It nought concerneth you of whatsoever we may do, nor nought shall you know thereof for us.' Had he not been a priest, Perceval would have been right wroth with him, but he had no will to do him any hurt. Therewithal he departed. . . . "[1]

In the first incident we seem to have a dim remembrance of the animal representing the dying god, which was torn to pieces by the worshippers, while in the defiling of the cross we have the exact counterpart of the Templar ceremony. Later on we obtain an " official " interpretation of these two incidents, given to Perceval by King Hermit, according to whom the white questing beast " signifieth Our Lord Jesus Christ, and the twelve dogs . . . . the people of the old law," i.e., the Jews. By his teaching Christ brought forth the twelve tribes of the Old Law into the light of the New Law, after which, unable to bear the unaccustomed light, they rent Him. Moreover, He also brought forth the twelve apostles and the official Catholic and orthodox Church, and one cannot help suspecting that the original explanation of this incident implied that the official church had mangled Christ's teaching, and that this " heretical view " has been amended by the orthodox cleric who compiled, or at any rate copied, this version of the Holy Graal.

As to the two priests, King Hermit explains that both of them loved Christ equally, and that he who beat the cross did so because it had been the instrument of bitter pain and anguish to

1. Dr. Sebastian Evans, " The High History of the Holy Graal." Branch XVII. Title 2. (Everyman Ed.) pp. 191 sq.

our Lord.   King Hermit adds that he who adored it was called *Jonas*, and he that reviled it was named Alexis.   Now this explanation can only have been inserted in order to justify and explain a ceremony known to the Knights Templar and as yet undisclosed to the outside world, for whereas " The High History" was written about 1220 A.D., the facts concerning the " Defiling of the cross " in the Templar Rites only became known at their trial in 1307.   The importance of the passage is obvious, for it shows that the ceremony was old, had a legitimate explanation in the eyes of those who took part in it, and that the man who wrote the " High History " was a Templar, probably a Templar priest, otherwise he would not have thought of such an incident. The whole of the " High History " is full of the crusading spirit. In it Perceval is all the time fighting the follwers of the old law ; and when he defeats them, in true crusader style, he offers them the alternative of baptism or death.

We have already seen that on quite independent grounds J. Weston had come to the conclusion that the Holy Graal legends contained the remnants of the old Syrian Adonis cult, and that these legends owe their origin and dissemination to the Templars. Here we have a distinctly Templar Rite coupled with an explanation which aims at justifying it.   As, moreover, one of the Graal stories specifically says that the Graal was protected by the Templars, we can have little doubt as to their connection with these traditions.

Furthermore, we cannot overlook the fact that Perceval, like Hiram Abiff, Jonah and Tammuz, was a widow's son, and the references to castration are further proofs of the connection between these legends and the Adonis cult.   Did those who persecuted the Templars also recognise the significance of the phallus in this connection ?   It seems more than probable, for with fiendish cruelty they attached heavy weights to that organ when torturing the unfortunate knights, as if to say, " Your rites centre round that member and so shall the tortures we inflict on you in order to extract from you damning evidence! "   That the men of the 14th century quite understood the principle of making the punishment fit the crime is shown by the fate of Edward II.   He was popularly believed to be addicted to a certain unnatural vice, and his murderers slew him by thrusting up a red hot iron into his bowels.

There are numerous other traces of the old fertility cult in the Graal stories, and even the " Hallows " themselves seem to be derived therefrom, as we have already seen.   The chalice has the attributes of the magic, Celtic cauldron which was supposed to have come from Syria[1] and like the Graal chalice restored the dead and brought fertility back to the land.   We will, however,

---

1. See Chapter VI., p. 78.

content ourselves with considering two more incidents, that of the cauldron, in the " High History," and a certain adventure which befell Lancelot.

Gawain went forth to rescue a King's son from a giant who had carried him off, but the giant when wounded by Gawain killed the boy. Gawain ultimately slew the giant, and brought back the giant's head and the boy's corpse to the king. After the King had lamented over his dead son " he maketh light a great show of torches in the midst of the city, and caused a great fire to be made, and his son set thereon in a brazen vessel all full of water, and maketh him to be cooked and sodden over this fire, and maketh the giant's head to be hanged at the gate. When his son was well cooked he maketh him be cut up as small as he may, and biddeth send for all the high men of his land and giveth thereof to each so long as there was any left." [1]

After this strange cannibalistic feast the King was baptised and gave Gawain the sword with which John the Baptist was beheaded. The peculiarity of this sword was that it became covered with blood each day at noon, because at that hour St. John was beheaded. [2] Later on Gawain arrived at the Castle of Inquest and asked the Master the meaning of the various strange things he had witnessed on his journey, and especially why the King cooked his son and " made him be eaten of all the folk of his land." " Sir," saith the priest, " already had he leant his heart upon Jesus Christ and would fain make a sacrifice of his flesh and blood to our Lord, and for this did he make all those of his land eat thereof. . . . . " [3] The explanation is of interest because, although it was obviously weak, it shows that the incident is old, and was naturally repulsive to the 13th century writer, who thus tries to make excuses for a custom he could not understand but certainly did not invent. It is, however, clearly the same custom as that connected with the cauldron in the Jewish rite, which Ezekiel and Jeremiah denounce so fiercely. It is a sacramental feast, and the victim, be it noted, is a *King's son*. My readers, moreover, must not ignore the association with this incident of the bleeding sword. In the Mabinogion this sword and a severed head are connected with a spear which drops blood, in the adventure of Peredur, and there is no hint there that either head, sword or spear are connected with St. John. We are told, indeed, that they are associated with the murder of a relation of Peredur by the witches of Gloucester. It should, however, be added that most scholars agree that the bleeding spear, at any rate, is phallic. I need not again remind my readers that St. John took over a whole host of symbols and customs belonging to Adonis.

The incident related of Lancelot shows that the Graal

---

1.   Dr. S. Evans, " The High History of the Holy Graal," pp. 75-76.
2.   Ibid., p. 74.
3.   Ibid., p. 82.

legends also retain a very clear memory of the slaying of a king for the benefit of his country. Furthermore, the death is by fire, which reminds us of the burning of Moloch. As Lancelot approached a city he was met by a great crowd playing *flutes* and other instruments, and told that he was to be the new king. They added that " this city began to burn and melt in one of the houses from the very same hour that our king was dead," and that it would not be quenched until another king was chosen who on New Year's Day would " be crowned in the midst of the fire, and then shall the fire be quenched."[1]

Naturally Lancelot tried to decline the honour, and even some of the onlookers said that it seemed a pity that so comely a knight should thus die, but others replied that through his death the city would be saved, which was a matter for joy. While Lancelot was still protesting a dwarf entered the city and offered to accept the throne on the terms set out, whereupon Lancelot was allowed to depart.

In this incident we have not only a specific account of the slaying of the king annually but also of the appearance of the substitute. As the " fire " in the city started when the last King died, it is obvious it would restart as soon as the new king died, and so there would have to be a series of Kings, each burnt on New Year's Day. The date, near that of the Winter Solstice, shows that it was associated with the Yule festivals, to which we have previously referred.

In the unpublished Merlin M.S., B.N. 337, there is a Graal procession which passes through a wood. " The procession is closed by a knight in a litter, borne by four little palefrois, while voices in the air above are heard singing: ' Honour, and glory, and power, and everlasting joy, to the *Destroyer of Death*.'[2] "

Here, then, we get the very name of Hiram in a Graal legend, given a Christian meaning. May it not be that for all that the meaning is the original one, and Hiram means, " He who by his death destroys the terror of death and proves the reality of the resurrection ? "

From the foregoing we see that on the one hand the Graal legends carry into the 13th century traditions and incidents associated with Tammuz, and on the other are connected with the Templars. We have seen that this Tammuz cult was still alive in Palestine in the 10th century, since we have a description of the mourning of the Arabs for Tâ-uz, and that in the time of the Crusades Palestine contained a large number of heterodox Mahomedan secret societies which were undoubtedly influenced by the old Tammuz cult.

We have learnt that the Templars had a peculiar, almost sinister, connection with one of these societies, namely the

---

1.   Dr. S. Evans, Ibid. p. 127-129.
2.   J. L. Weston, " The Quest of the Holy Graal," p. 154.

Assassins, and themselves had a mysterious secret rite, including a ritual of death and resurrection. Finally, we know that at least 14,000 knights survived the destruction of the Order and that the Templar Priests and serving brothers, who numbered some 25,000, were never persecuted at all. Among these serving brethren were numbers of masons, and therefore if the Comacine masons had not already the remains of the Tammuz cult they could hardly have failed to learn it from the Templars.

The black and white banner of the Templars, which represented dualism, or the struggle between good and bad, Light and Darkness, life and death, was itself the badge of heterodoxy gathered up in the Near East, and corresponds with the two pillars of King Solomon's temple and the checkered pavement of the masonic lodge. The badge of the Knights, two knights riding on one horse, represents the twin riders, Castor and Polus, who are still lamented in Persia under the names of Hassan and Hassain, with all the features of the wailing for Adonis.

If the Crusaders could bring back Syrian details in architecture which altered the whole style of Mediæval building, and they did: if they could introduce the Mahomedan veil for women, and adopt the Mahomedan beard for men, is it surprising that they should also adopt some of the old Syrian Rites ?

Thus we have traced the cult of Adonis from the days of Babylon down to 1307 A.D., and have shown that, despite all the vicissitudes through which it passed, and the modifications which occurred in it as men grew less barbarous, it retained a sufficient number of the ancient landmarks to show its true origin and to indicate that it is the source of modern masonry.

There are still many problems before us, and to these the latter part of this book will be devoted. What were the exact positions of Hiram Abiff and Hiram the King ? What were the parts played by Solomon and the Queen of Sheba ? Did the custom of foundation and consecration sacrifices survive among Mediæval Masons ? These and other questions will be considered next, and the answers will suggest that Hiram Abiff was a real man, the human representative of Tammuz, who was offered up by the workmen as a consecration sacrifice in order that the new Temple might stand firm for ever.

CHAPTER XV

HIRAM ABIFF AND HIRAM THE KING

We have now seen that throughout Syria and all the neighbouring lands the dominant religious cult centred round a Dying God, who represented the Spirit of Vegetation and especially of corn, and was supposed to be slain every year. We have seen that, despite their supposed monotheism, the Jews themselves were devoted followers of this cult, not only in the time of Solomon but down to the first captivity, and that traces of the cult lingered on among them in the secret ceremonies of the Essenes and the worship of Sabazius down to the time of the Roman Cæsars.

We can trace the survival of this cult of a Dying God among the Syrians down to the 10th century A.D., when it was swallowed up by a number of secret and heretical Mahomedan societies, with one of which the Templars were in alliance. We have likewise seen that this cult of Adonis, under the name of Attis, was very popular at Rome up to the date of the formal establishment of Christianity, and was thus contemporary with the Roman Collegia who, at Pompeii, had a mystery cult of death and resurrection. Even the formal establishment of Christianity did not entirely destroy the cult, many features of which were adopted and transferred to the cult of the two S. Johns.

We thus see that there are two lines of descent linking this ancient Tammuz cult with the 14th century, when the Templars were suppressed in 1313. In 1375 we find the first mention of the word "Freemasons," and about the same date appears the first of the Ancient Charges. So we have a double line of descent connecting Freemasonry with the ancient cult of a dying god.

We have learned that Hiram, King of Tyre, was the representative of a line of priest-kings who claimed to be gods, and that the god they represented was Adonis. Such divine kings were originally slain annually, or by substitute, and though at a later date a dramatic representation of the slaying of the king was instituted, when such kings grew old they still had to be murdered. As we shall consider this problem further in Chapter 17 we need not dilate on it here, and instead will try and fix the relative positions of the various Hirams we meet with in the Bible.

Hiram the King seems to have been the title of the reigning king of Tyre, just as the name Pharaoh was the title, and not the personal name, of the king of Egypt. Concerning this Hiram some strange legends are to be found among the Jewish Rabins, all of which point to his divine nature and to the fact that the name

Hiram was the *title* of the kings of Tyre. He was said to have lived from the time of David to the time of the destruction of the Temple, because he had helped to build the Temple. Towards the close of this period he became puffed up with pride, imagined himself a god, and built an artificial heaven in which he sat enthroned. At length God overthrew him because of his arrogant claim to be immortal.[1] Ezekiel denounced the King of Tyre for claiming to be a god and, though he does not definitely say so, seems to have thought the reigning king was the same as the man who helped to build the Temple. If so, the reason, no doubt, was that, like the earlier man, he was called Hiram. The pregnant verse is " Thou art the anointed cherub that covereth; and I have set thee so; thou wast upon the holy mountain of God."[2]

The ' mountain of God " must be Mount Moriah, and so implies that the King of Tyre was at the building of the Temple.

We also obtain from the same chapter the origin of the Jewish legend that Hiram the King was permitted to enter Paradise as a reward for his work on the Temple, till, becoming puffed up with pride, he called himself a God and was cast therefrom by Jehovah.[3] The Scripture passage is " Thou hast been in Eden, the Garden of God."[4] In the tradition that Hiram walked in Paradise we seem to have a distorted memory of the claim of these god-men that their souls were divine and ascended to the city of the Gods, a claim probably dramatically represented in the " higher grades of Tammuz " by the visit to the Isles of the Blest.

The title " Hiram " we have seen means, " He that destroys," " The Exaltation of Life," " Their whiteness or liberty; " all titles of a god rather than that of a mere man, and particularly appropriate to Tammuz. The significance of these titles has already been explained, but the title " whiteness " is peculiarly appropriate, not merely because it represents the flour made from corn and in India is the title of Shiva, the Destroyer, but because it is the same as the name of Lebanon, which means " The white mountain," and Lebanon contained the chief shrine of Adonis. We have also seen that the name " Hiram " occurs several times in the Bible, but have not pointed out the full significance of the original form of the name of Abraham, Abram, which means " The Father of the Exaltation of Life," etc.

(1) Abram tried to sacrifice his own son as did these Syrian worshippers of Adonis, and the changing of his name probably implied his reunciation of the cult of Moloch-Tammuz for that of Jehovan. The substitution of a deer for the daughter of Agammemnon when the king was about to offer her to Artemis (Astarte) is in striking analogy with the story of Isaac.

---

1. Dudley Wright, " Masonic Legends and Traditions," p. 97.
2. Ezekiel 28. 14.
3. Dudley Wright, Ibid. p. 98.
4. Ezekiel 28, 13.

Abram was, of course, a priest-king and had a very friendly reception from another priest-king, Melchizidech, who was one of the old Jebusite Priest-Kings of Jerusalem.

(2)   The next Hiram mentioned in the Bible is Abiram, who was a prince of Israel and claimed to be as good a priest as the Levites.   He perished by fire.

(3)   Hiram the King we know was a Priest-King who represented Tammuz, and his father's name was Abibaal, which name means " The Father of the God."

(4)   Adoniram means, " The Lord God who destroys," and he became the successor to Hiram Abiff.   He was set over the levies on Lebanon, which was not part of the dominions of Solomon but was the great sanctuary of Adonis.   He was later slain, like so many of those who had the ill-omened title of " He that destroys."   Just as Hiram of Tyre's father called himself " The Father of the God," so Adoniram's father called himself Abda, " The Father of the Beloved One," a title of Adonis, Moreover, the usual title of Tammuz was Adon, or, in Greek, Adonis, and we thus see that Adoniram must have been the local Priest-King of the sanctuary at Lebanon, who, like the Priest-King, Hiram of Tyre, helped Solomon by supplying timber and workmen.

(5)   Abiram, the eldest son of Hiel, was sacrificed by his father as a foundation sacrifice when he rebuilt Jericho !

(6)   Hiram Abiff is none other than Abibaal, who according to Josephus, was the father of Hiram of Tyre.   The biblical title of " Father of He that destroys " is precisely similar to that given to him by Josephus, " The Father of the God " (Moloch, the Destroyer).   It is therefore clear that Hiram, the so-called Architect, was the old, abdicated King of Tyre, whose divinity had passed on to his son Hiram, and who should in strictness have then been slain.   Having lost his personal name when he became the Priest-King and human representative of Tammuz, he lost the title Hiram on his abdication, but took that of " Father of the God " or " Father of the Destroyer."   Why, however, did the neighbouring Priest-King of Lebanon flaunt the full title of Adoniram ? Perhaps he is so named to distinguish him from the other Priest-King of Tyre, but more probably it was because the great shrine at Aphaca was far more sacred than the commercial city of Tyre, and so its Priest-King was considered to have more of the divine nature in him than had the other.   He, above all these others, represented the Adon Hiram, the Lord of Destruction.

These facts show that the masonic tradition that Solomon treated Hiram Abiff as an equal, is correct.   No Oriental despot would treat as an equal a mere architect employed by him, but the former King of Tyre and the father of his ally, Hiram, *was* his equal, and would naturally be treated as such.

CHAPTER XVI

WHO WAS THE QUEEN OF SHEBA ?

Whether the Queen of Sheba was a real woman it is difficult to say, but probably she was. If so, she has gathered around her many of the attributes of Astarte. Indeed, so clear is this that one might say that she was simply the Great Mother, humanised at a period when it was no longer desirable to speak of the Goddess.

The important position she still plays in Masonry, particularly in connection with the successor of the Architect, is very remarkable in an Order which, like the Essenes, debars women from participation in its secrets. The anachronism seems to have struck some of the leading masons of recent years, for of late there has been a marked tendency to eliminate her as far as possible.

This was not the attitude of the mediæval masons, who, in legend and sculpture, stressed her importance and associated her very closely with Solomon. In masonic tradition she is described in terms which imply that she was highly respectable and having but little in common with the wanton Astarte, but Jewish traditions retain far more of her original character and leave no doubt as to the true nature of the Queen herself.

First of all, she is said to be black, the colour of the Great Mother, Cybele, and similar therein to the " lady " in the Song of Solomon, who, by some Biblical students, is thought to be the Queen. We are told that she came to Solomon with the deliberate intention of obtaining by him a son, an object she achieved, and the Abyssinians proudly claim that their Emperors are descended from this child, who was named David or Dodo, the Beloved One; a title, as we have seen, of Tammuz.

All these details might be facts and not mythology, but the same cannot be said of the next legend. According to this, the Queen had legs which were covered with thick shaggy hair, like that on the legs of a donkey. Some mischief makers actually told Solomon that she had the legs and hoofs of a donkey, but this Solomon found to be an exaggeration. On discovering the true facts, Solomon, with the assistance of certain demons, pro-- cured a depilatory, and thus the offending " fur " was removed.[1]

In this story we have a distorted memory of the original animal form of the Great Mother. Probably, originally she had lion legs, for Astarte was a lion goddess, but the Ass was sacred to Dionysius, and may also have been more closely associated with Astarte than is usually supposed, for an ass is said to be one of the most lecherous of animals.

---

1. J. E. Hanauer, " The Folk Lore of the Holy Land " quoting Rabbi Mejr-ed-din.

That Balkis, Queen of Sheba, was very far from the respectable, modest woman some of my readers may have supposed, is shown by a whole series of Jewish and Arabic legends.

In Salaman and Absah[1] Balkis says that:
" Never night or morning
Comely youth before me passes
Whom I look not after longing."

The hard questions she set to Solomon seem almost to be a ritual catechism, but if so they contain a number of riddles which show that the lady who unblushingly asked them was not possessed of an overplus of modesty. Such riddles, however, appear in many primitive fertility rites and festivals, and are quite appropriate to the human representative of the great Fertility Goddess. As already pointed out, their number is 22, the same as that of the picture cards in the Tarot. Here are some characteristic examples:—

SHEBA: Seven there are that issue and nine that enter; two yield the drafts and one drinks.

SOLOMON: Seven are the days of a woman's defilement and nine the months of pregnancy; two are the breasts that yield the draft and one the child that drinks.[2]

Question 2 deals with the incestuous relations between Lot and his daughter.

Question 3 consists in making him decide who are men and women among a company of boys and girls whom she had dressed in the clothing of the opposite sex. This incident reminds us forcibly of the Galli of Astarte who were clad in female clothing.

Question 7 is a particularly indecent question.

Question 10 again refers to the incest of Lot.

Question 11 refers to Jonah and the great fish.

Question 17 refers to Tamar who had a son by her father-in-law.

These questions indicate the true character of the Queen, while not only question 11, but also questions 13, 18 and 22 refer to death.

Question 9 is very peculiar and, clearly refers to certain things used in the ritual of death and resurrection.

SHEBA. Which are the three that neither die, nor do they drink, nor do they have bread put into them, yet they save lives from death ?

SOLOMON. The signet, cord and staff are these three. The cord is clearly the cord or lariat with which the candidate is dragged into the Temple like a victim properly prepared for

---

1.   Ed. Fitzgerald's translation of " Salaman and Absah," by Jami, a
        Persian poet and Sufi of the 15th century.
2.   Dudley Wright, " Masonic Legends and Traditions," p. 128 quoting
        Dr. Louis Ginzberg, " Legends of the Jews."

sacrifice.   The staff is the wand or staff of the Conductor of Souls, who carried it with him through the Underworld.

The ring no doubt symbolises the visica piscis of rebirth, and probably the marriage ring with which the candidate was symbolically married to the goddess.   As question 11 deals with the legend of Jonah's descent into the great fish, there can be little doubt as to what is the meaning of the above symbols or that these questions are a fragment of the secret initiation ceremonies of Astarte-Tammuz.

We thus see that the Queen represents Astarte, and this aspect of her true nature is shown in a curious quasi masonic legend which says that the death of Hiram Abiff was indirectly caused by the Queen, who fell in love with him and decided to elope with him instead of marrying Solomon.   For this reason Solomon plotted his murder.   In this legend we have an exact analogy with the later form of the myth of Adonis, who was supposed to have been killed by Ares, who was jealous of the favour shown to Adonis by Aphrodite.   Unfortunately the origin of the story is a matter of dispute and its antiquity queried by many able masonic students.   It does, however, fit in so admirably with the above fact, that I feel that it is really old and not a comparatively modern invention, and therefore include it here in the hope that one of my readers may be able to trace it back to its original source which, I suspect, is Jewish or Arabic.

The story is briefly mentioned by Bro. Dudley Wright[1] and is given in full by C. W. Heckethorne,[2] but unfortunately, so far I have not been able to identify its exact origin.   Neither author gives his authority, a fact which is the more regrettable as Heckethorne was not a mason and clearly obtained much of his information on masonry from unauthorised " exposures," whose reliability is open to the gravest question.

W. Bro. W. Wonnacott, Grand Librarian, whom I consulted, very kindly drew my attention to the following facts, and to him I am deeply indebted for all the trouble he took to help me. Bro. Rylands[3] says that G. de Nerval wrote a story which he called " The History of the Queen of the Morning and Soliman, Prince of Djiners."   Afterwards he sandwiched it into another book of his, " Voyage en Orient."   It was then turned into an opera by Meyerbeer, who wrote the music about 1848, and called it " La Reine de Saba."   Despite the vicissitudes through which it has passed, which prevent us placing too much reliance on the details therein, I think that it contains a core of genuine tradition, and that tradition fits in remarkably well with what we know concerning the old fertility rites of Palestine.   Sheba in

1.   Dudley Wright, " Masonic Legends and Traditions," p. 111.
2.   C. W. Heckethorne, " The Secret Societies of all Ages and Countries."
      Vol. II. p. 3.
3.   A.Q.C.   Vol. XIV. p. 179.   See also Vol. 19, p. 118.

that case represents Astarte, and the sons of fire would be the followers of Moloch and Astarte, in contradistinction to the strict worshippers of Jehovah. Dr. Oliver seems also to have known of the tradition.

According to Heckethorne, Hiram Abiff was descended from Cain, whose father was one of the Elohim, and begot Cain by Ebe. Jehovah thereupon created Adam and married him to Eve, from whom was born Abel. Thus Cain was generated by fire and Abel from earth, in consequence of which there was bitter discord between the two, which reached its culmination when Jehovah refused the sacrifice of Cain, consisting of the fruits of the earth, and accepted that of Abel, which consisted of domesticated animals. Cain slew Abel and Jehovah thereupon declared that he and his seed should henceforth be subject to the sons of Abel. Despite this, the sons of fire were the real inventors of the arts and sciences. It was Enoch, a son of Cain, who taught men how to cut stone and construct bricks. Irad, his son, and Mehujal, his grandson, taught men the rudiments of irrigation and how to turn cedars into beams.

Methusal was another of the descendants of Cain and he invented " the sacred characters, the books of Tau and the symbolic T. by which the workers descended from the genii of fire recognised each other."

Lamech had four children: Jabal, who taught men how to dress camel skins; Jubal, who was the first to play on the harp and thus became the originator of music; Tubal-Cain, the first smith; and a daughter, Naamah, who invented spinning and weaving.

At the flood all this gifted race were destroyed except Tubal-Cain and his son. The wife of Ham fell in love with this son and by him became the mother of Nimrod, who was not only a mighty hunter but the founder of Babylon. From Nimrod was descended Hiram Abiff, who is really the same as Adoniram.

Although Hiram was acknowledged to be the greatest Architect and worker in metals of his time, he was lonely and unloved by most men, no doubt because of his strange parentage. He was even envied by the great Solomon, who was jealous of his marvellous skill.

When Balkis, Queen of Sheba, visited Solomon, she accepted his offer of marriage, but soon after was taken to see the Temple, and there, being introduced to its architect, Hiram, repented her promise to the King for she had fallen in love with Hiram, which aroused the jealousy of Solomon. The Queen then asked to see all the workmen at once, and Solomon declared it was impossible to call them all together at a moment's notice, but Hiram Abiff with his right hand drew the symbolical Tau in the air and immediately all the workmen hastened to the place where he stood.

King Solomon, however, determined to have no rivals in the Queen's affection, and he therefore got in touch with three fellow crafts, who hated Hiram because he would not make them Master Masons and who wished to bring about the ruin of the Architect. Their names were Amen, a Phoenician carpenter; Fanor, a Syrian mason; and Metusael, a Hebrew miner. They determined to cause an accident which would ruin the casting of the brazen sea. The plot was discovered by a young workman named Benoni, who at once informed Solomon, but the treacherous monarch deliberately abstained from taking any steps to defeat the plot, which was, of course, really instigated by him.

On the appointed day the doors which held back the molten brass were opened, and the red-hot liquid overflowed the top of the mould and sped on over the ground, driving before it the terror-stricken onlookers. Benoni himself perished in a fruitless effort to stop the disaster, and though Hiram turned jets of water on to the advancing mass of molten metal, in a last desperate effort to stay its progress, this was of no avail.

Suddenly the distracted architect saw before him a gigantic human form which said, " Come, my son, be without fear, I have rendered thee incombustible, cast thyself into the flames." Hiram at once leapt into the molten mass and instead of being burnt felt himself being dragged down into a bottomless abyss. He cried " Whither do you take me ? " and received the answer " Into the centre of the earth, into the soul of the world, into the kingdom of Cain, where Liberty reigns with him. There the tyrannous envy of Adonai ceases; there can we, despising his anger, taste the fruits of the tree of knowledge; there is the home of thy fathers."

" Who then am I, and who art thou ? " asked Hiram.

" I am the father of thy fathers, I am the son of Lamech, I am Tubal-Cain."

Hiram afterwards talked with Cain and others of his ancestors, learnt that they were descendants of the genii of fire, and ultimately returned to the upper air, bearing with him as a gift the hammer of Tubal-Cain with which, he was told, he could in a moment repair the damage wrought by the malignity of his fellow workmen.

Hiram immediately used the hammer on the brazen sea, which next morning was whole and perfect, to the amazement of all who had witnessed the disaster.

The mutual love of Balkis and Hiram increased till at length they agreed to elope together, but on the very day fixed for their flight the three workmen, again encouraged by Solomon, brought about Hiram's death in the Temple. The rest of the story is well known, the only interesting details being those connected with a golden triangle which he wore suspended round his neck. On this triangle was engraved the Master's word, and before he was overcome by his attackers Hiram managed to fling it into a well. It was later discovered by King Solomon, who had it placed on a triangular altar set up in a secret vault built beneath the Temple. It was then covered by a cubical stone on which was engraved the sacred law, and the vault, the existence of which was known only to 27 elect masons, was then sealed up completely. The three culprits committed suicide rather than fall into the hands of their pursuers.

It must be admitted that Solomon does not appear in a very favourable light in this story, but neither does he in another, and undoubtedly old, Jewish legend, according to which he had all the workmen who had been engaged upon the Temple slain lest they should subsequently build another in honour of a pagan god.[1] Similar stories are related of other great buildings, even as near home as Ireland, although in these it is usually stated that the prince who paid for the building had the architect slain to prevent him building as fine an edifice for anyone else.

The above legends concerning the Queen of Sheba all indicate that she represents Astarte, and her survival in the peculiar position she occupies in craft masonry in connection with the promotion of Adoniram to the vacant office of Hiram Abiff confirms this view. That many of the more objectionable features of the Great Mother are no longer in evidence, is what we should expect, considering the old rite has been thoroughly purged of its early barbaric features. Perhaps the Craft G. or R. sign, the origin of which in the Scotch ritual is associated with this Queen, was originally the manner in which her worshippers offered to her their prayers and adoration.

1.   Dudley Wright, " Masonic Legends and Traditions," p. 53.

CHAPTER XVII

THE ANNUAL SLAYING OF THE PRIEST KINGS

One of the most amazing things about primitive races is the fact that at one time most of them seemed to have made a practice of murdering their kings. Such murders were a religious rite, not merely the assassination of a bad or weak ruler by a usurper. On closer investigation we find that these kings were priest-kings, and the living representatives of some god, usually the god of vegetation. The priest-king, Nemi is, perhaps, the best known example of these unfortunate potentates, but he was only a late survival in Italy of what seems to have been a wide-spread custom, and one which persisted until recent years in many parts of the uncivilised world, such as Central Africa.

The priest-king of Nemi was a priest of Diana and a nominal king. The post could only be obtained by murdering the old man according to a prescribed ritual, which achieved, the murderer became priest-king in his stead until another, in like manner, succeeded in slaying him. The most important ritual act of the would-be murderer was to pluck a branch of mistletoe from a sacred oak which grew within the precincts of the temple, and which the priest-king naturally guarded, sword in hand, by night and day.[1]

Originally it seems that the divine kings reigned only for a year, and in this form the custom survived in Mexico up to the time of the Spanish conquest, but practical considerations had resulted in the separation of the real headship of the State from the person of the priest-king. These annual priest-kings had most of the pomp and glory of sovereignty but little real power, and at the end of the year they were slain and sacrificed on the top of one of the Pyramid Temples.[2] In many other parts of the world we meet with similar divine kings, whose civil authority has been completely usurped by some non-divine noble. One of the most famous of these is the semi-divine Mikado of Japan, whose power for many years rested in the hands of the Shogun.

In Mexico, as we have seen, the annual king was a substitute for the real king, who not unnaturally preferred to retain life and real authority at the expense of the loss of a certain amount of dignity and pomp. This custom of finding substitutes seems to have been the usual one adopted among many races, but in other cases the fatal day was postponed until the virility of the king

---

1. Frazer, " The Magic Art and the Evolution of Kings," 2nd ed., I. 44.
2. Prescott, " Conquest of Mexico," Chapter 3.
   See also Chap. XX.

began to wane. Often, however, the annual slaying was enacted in a dramatic form, and at Babylon the king himself played the part of the victim.[1]

It seems clear that in like manner the king of Tyre by walking through a fire dramatically enacted his own death by fire and his subsequent resurrection therefrom. But although the evil day might thus be postponed, sooner or later the king grew old and feeble and no longer begat children. As the Syrian kings represented the Baal, or god of fertility of the land, and were its reputed husbands, in the eyes of their subjects they could not continue to fertilise it when old, and it would become barren. Therefore they must make way for a younger man into whom the divine soul of the god could enter.

If this transference were delayed too long the people feared lest the divine soul itself would become enfeebled and thus be unable to maintain the fertility of the soil of Mother Earth—the Great Mother. For these reasons as soon as it became clear that the old king could no longer beget sons, the hours of his life were numbered. We can thus see that the lamentations for Tammuz may have represented quite genuine grief for the death of an old and popular king who, nevertheless, the people felt must be slain for the good of the whole nation.

Among the Shilluks of the White Nile, the kings were always slain as soon as their wives reported that they could no longer " satisfy them." The original founder of this line was Nyakang, a real man, who after his death was worshipped as a god, and whose soul was transferred to each new king in turn by means of an image, in which it temporarily resided in the short space of time which elapsed between the killing of the old king and the accession of the new one, into whom the divine spirit of Nyakang then entered.[2] The custom was only abolished when the British occupied the country and put an end to this and other barbarous customs.

In the Pelew Islands when a chief grew old the heir, who was usually either his *brother*, nephew or cousin on the maternal side, had the legal right to murder him, and if he did so much further trouble was saved him. There was a regular procedure and the whole affair was carried through in a thoroughly business-like way.[3]

All over the world we find traces of this strange custom, of which a few more examples must suffice. The king, or Matiamvo, in Angola was not only killed but dismembered according to a

1. Sidney Smith, " The Relation of Marduk, Ashur and Osiris." The Journal of Egyptian Archæology. Vol. 8. April, 1922.
2. C. G. Seligmann, " The Cult of Myakang," p. 221.
3. D. Westermann, " The Shilluk People," pp. XLII.
   J. Kubary, " Die socialen Einrichtungen de Pelauer," pp. 43-45 and 75-78.

regular ritual,[1] which reminds us of the fate of Osiris. The
Dinka Rainmaker, when he grew infirm, was buried alive and his
soul entered the body of his successor.[2]   The kings of Calicut were
liable to be attacked and killed by their successors at the end of a
period of twelve years.[3]   This king had the title of " God in
Earth."[4] Among the people of Malabar, men were appointed
as supreme rulers for five years, at the end of which period the
holder of the office was decapitated and his head flung in the air.
Whoso caught it assumed the office of the dead man, and in like
manner perished at the expiration of another five years.[5] The
similarity of this custom to that of throwing the head of the
figures of Adonis into the water will be obvious to my readers.

At the installation of the Rajah of Keonjhur, a pretence is
made of killing a man, who disappears, and returns after three
days, having been miraculously restored to life,[6] but in Cassange,
in Angola, the victim, who was treated as if he were a king, was
killed, his heart was torn out and the real king was bathed in his
blood. The victim was subsequently eaten.[7] The similarity of
these proceedings to the blood bath of Cybele and the sacramental meal of Dionysius is likewise apparent. Among the
Yoruba, a certain chief was only allowed to reign for three
years and then was killed.[8]

We have seen that annually the king of Babylon went through
a ceremony wherein he enacted the part of Marduk and pretended
to be slain; it is therefore interesting to find the grim reality, of
which this ceremony was the civilised substitute, still taking place
annually in Babylonia in the days of Berosius.

There was a five days' Saturnalia during which time a condemned criminal was released from jail, clothed in royal robes,
placed on the royal throne, and actually allowed to enjoy the
king's concubines. At the end of his brief reign he was stripped
of his royal robes, scourged and put to death,[8] usually by crucify-
ing or hanging on a tree.

Thus it is clear that, like Tammuz, the Babylonian kings were
originally slain annually, and later substituted a criminal for
themselves. They nevertheless dramatically enacted their own

1.   F. T. Valdez, " Six Years of a Traveller's Life in Western Africa."
        (London, 1861). II. 194 sq.
2.   Frazer, " The Dying God," p. 33.
3.   W. Logan, " Malabar," (Madras, 1887). I. 162 sq.
4.   L. di Varthema, " Travels," Translated by J. W. Jones (Hakluyt Soc.
        1863), p. 134.
5.   Frazer, " The Dying God." p. 53.
6.   E. T. Dalton, " Descriptive Ethnology of Bengal," (Calcutta, 1872).
        p. 146.
7.   F. T. Valdez, " Six Years of a Traveller's Life in Western Africa."
        (London, 1861). II. 158 sq.
8.   John Parkinson, " Southern Nigeria, the Lagos Province." The
        Empire Review, XV., May 1908. p. 290 sq.
9.   Frazer, " The Dying God." p. 113 sq.

death, and we thus see both systems of substitution existing side by side. These ceremonies took place at different periods in the year: the dramatic ceremony no doubt corresponded to the reaping of the corn and the second to the planting of the seed, a fact which is proved by the right of the substitute king to enjoy the king's concubines who, doubtless, symbolised Ishtar.

The Babylonian custom explains the widespread habit of making the king abdicate for a few days and installing a temporary successor. Thus, in Upper Egypt on the tenth of September the real Governor is deposed for three days, and in his stead rules a substitute, who at the end of his reign is condemned to death, but instead of the man his mantle is burnt and he creeps out alive.[1] In this example we have not only a substitute for the real rulers, but actually a substitution for killing the substitute, which is, no doubt, a much later development.

In Persia, Shah Abbas, on being told by his astrologers in 1591 that he was in danger of death abdicated, and an unfortunate unbeliever was placed on the throne for three days. At the end of that period the unbeliever was slain and Abbas reascended the throne.[2] My readers should note throughout the constant recurrence of the number three days, corresponding to the three days which the soul is supposed to pass in the Underworld. In this last example we clearly have an example of a reversion to a primitive custom at a time of emergency.

Often we find that the king's son was sacrificed in his stead, and here again a mitigation of the old barbarous custom gradually evolved. For example, among the Indians of North Carolina in the 18th century there was a custom of holding a feast at which the King's son was *thrice* wounded, and at the last blow fell down as if dead.[3]

It is clear from the beliefs of many races that often primitive tribes think that the son possesses the soul of his father, who thus becomes a mere empty husk. So far did the people of Tahiti carry this view that their king had to resign as soon as a son was born to him. This son not only assumed the throne, but even the name of the king, who henceforth merely acted in the name of his son.[4] This fact explains why the father of Hiram of Tyre took the name of Abi Baal, and also why many of the Tahitians killed their sons as soon as they were born.

---

1. C. B. Klunzinger, " Bilder aus Oberägypten der Wüste und dom Rothen Meere (Stuttgart). p. 180.
2. Sir John Malcolm, " History of Persia." (London, 1815). pp. 527, sq.
3. J. Bricknell, " Natural History of North Carolina." (Dublin, 1737). pp. 342 sq.
4. Capt. J. Cook, " Voyages." (London, 1809). I. 225 sq.
   Capt. Wilson, " Missionary Voyages to the Southern Pacific Ocean." (1799). pp. 327 sq.

CHAPTER XVIII

FOUNDATION AND CONSECRATION SACRIFICES

The custom of burying a human being under the foundation of a building is still not extinct, and was at one time almost universal. It has been suggested that the purpose was to attach the spirit of the dead man to the place as a kind of " tyler " or guardian, as the spirit might well resent any attempt to disturb the place where its body was buried or the building which, as it were, constituted his monument.

Probably the explanation varied in different localities, but as we know that primitive races taught that a man's soul entered into a tree which grew out of his grave, it seems more likely that they thought that the soul of the victim entered into the post whose base was buried in his grave, and actually rested on his body. Early buildings were all of wood, and the custom would quite naturally be carried forward when stone replaced timber.

Now one of the chief reasons why a wooden building fails " to stand firm for ever," is that the main posts rot, and as felled timber rots more quickly as a rule than a living trunk, primitive races hoped by thus forcing a soul to enter into the post to ensure its long life, and thus the stability of the building. The Consecration sacrifice was in like manner associated with the roof tree, in my opinion, and this would explain the use of a cross at the consecration of a building even in pre-Christian times. Usually this cross is the St. Andrew's cross, or else the equal armed cross, both of which often occur in building the roof tree.

Be that as it may, examples of the custom abound and nowhere more plentifully than in Palestine. The Bible itself records one striking example, whose full significance few Masons seem to have realised. We are told that " in his day did Hiel the Bethelite build Jericho; he laid the foundations thereof in Abiram his first born, and set up the gates thereof in his youngest son Segub." [1] Now we have already seen that Abiram is the same name as Hiram Abiff, and the fact that the son had this name shows that *he* had begotten a son into whom his divine soul had entered. He was thus in precisely the same position as Hiram Abiff, who was, I suggest, offered up as a Consecration or Completion Sacrifice, like Segub.

In Bangkok, Siam, when the city gates were rebuilt three men were placed alive in a pit and then the great beam was lowered into position, crushing them to death,[2] while a similar

---

1. I. Kings, XVI. 34.
2. Mgr. Bruguiere in " Annales de l'Association de la Propagation de la Foi." V. (1831) pp. 164 sq.

rite was performed when the gates of Mandalay, Burma, were erected.[1] In Bima, a district of the East Indian Island of Sambawn, it was a pregnant woman, or young children, who similarly suffered.[2]

" In more civilised areas animals have replaced human beings, and in modern Greece a cock or a ram is the usual victim. But sometimes instead of killing an animal the builder entices a man to the foundation stone, secretly measures his body, or his shadow, and buries the measure under the foundation stone; or he lays the foundation stone upon the man's shadow. It is believed that the man will die within the year."[2]

A Bulgarian Mason measures the victim's shadow with a piece of string, places the latter in a box and then buries this under the foundation. It is believed that the owner of the shadow will die within forty days and his soul be kept captive in the box.[3]

In the above substitutes two facts should be noted. Firstly, the shadow is supposed to constitute the soul or life principle of the man. This belief is very widespread, and one of the commonest forms of black magic is to stab a man's shadow or reflection. That is why it is unlucky to break a mirror, for at some time it has caught your reflection, and so in breaking it you obviously shatter your own reflection or life. According to these primitive notions, even the picture of a man contains his soul or life principle.[4]

Thus we see that the modern custom of burying coins under a foundation stone has a sinister origin, for the image of the king thereon represents his life principle, and according to ancient, though long forgotten, beliefs, within a short time the King should die, his soul enter into the building and make it stand firm for ever. The connection between this modern practice and that of sacrificing a priest-king is thus perfectly clear, and directly bears on our subject. For these reasons Siamese Kings long refused to allow their images to be stamped on their coins.[5]

Secondly, the use of the foot-rule, which occurs likewise in the Hung ritual, is also obvious. In the Operative ritual the twenty-four inch gauge is replaced by a piece of wood which is called the " Straight-Edge," and with it the height of the candidate is measured. The straight-edge, like the twenty-four inch gauge, is retained by the Lodge, and according to this old belief the measure of the man remains attached to it and so his life principle is thus held hostage for his fidelity. Should he betray his trust,

---

1. A. Fytche, " Burma, Past and Present." (London, 1878). I. 251.
2. Frazer, " The Perils of the Soul." p. 89.
3. Ibid.
4. See also Ward and Stirling, " The Hung Society," I. Chapter 14.
5. See E. Young, " The Kingdom of the Yellow Robe." p. 140.

all that the indignant brethren need do is to bury that measuring stick under the next building they erect, and he will die.

This, and not the fanciful explanation now given in the Speculative ritual, is undoubtedly the true origin of the twenty-four inch gauge. That the custom of sacrificing a man did not die out till quite late, is indicated by a local story of Castle Rising, Norfolk. According to this the Norman Baron who ordered it to be built murdered the architect and had him buried beneath the foundations. Local gossips say that not many years ago the skeleton of a man was found there.

In like manner it was customary to sacrifice human victims at the Consecration or Completion of a building. The Bible says that Solomon Consecrated the Temple with *Burnt* offerings of sheep and of oxen, but Rabbinic legends relate that he killed all the workmen engaged on the Temple, ostensibly in order that they should not build another Temple to be used for idols.[1] As Solomon himself subsequently built several idolatrous shrines we can hardly accept this explanation as geniune. The wholesale slaughter is equally unlikely, but the tradition does point to at least one human sacrifice, although that may not have been officially ordered by the King. It might have been done by the workmen themselves. Even to-day there is a superstition that if a man is killed while a building is being erected that building will be lucky.[2]

The various legends of Mediæval times which relate how an apprentice was slain by his master because he did better work than he, perhaps point to survivals of this custom. The legends of the Apprentice Pillar at Roslin, of the two Rose Windows at Rouen, and the transept window at Lincoln are so well known as to need only a reference, but they all tend to show that even among Mediæval masons this barbarous custom was not entirely extinct, although no doubt the Church did all in its power by means of substituted ceremonies to wean the people from these old savage customs. With these facts in our minds let us turn to the Mediæval service for the Consecration of a Church as authorised by the Sarum and Roman Uses.

In the view of competent critics, the Mediæval service was largely based on the Jewish ceremonial, particularly that used by Solomon at the dedication of his temple, and the form used at the re-dedication by Judas Maccabeus in B.C. 168.[3] The most

---

1. Dudley Wright, " Masonic Legends and Traditions," p. 55.
    " Jewish Encycl." See article " Freemasonry."
2. Grant Allen in " Evolution of the Idea of God," on p. 98 gives an example
    of this superstition which occurred in the 19th century when a house
    was being built at Hindhead.
3. See I. Macc. iv. 36-57, and II. Macc. x. 1-8.

famous Use in England was that of Sarum, and the following is a summary of the most important incidents:—[1]

The Bishop vests outside the church and no one should be therein except a single deacon, who closes and guards the door from inside. The Bishop circumambulates the outside of the church, sprinkling the walls with Holy Water, and then *knocks once*. He again circumambulates, aspurges the walls, and returning, knocks on the door a *second* time. The same procedure is repeated once more, and at the *third* knock he is admitted, but the laity are still excluded. The Bishop proceeds *alone* to the centre of the Church where he fixes a cross, and then begins the litany. At this point the congregation enters.

Then with ashes he makes a St. Andrew's cross, and next inscribes the Greek alphabet on one arm thereof, commencing at the North East corner with the letter " Alpha " and ending at the South West corner with the letter " Omega." Next he inscribes the Latin alphabet on the other arm of the cross, beginning in the South East corner and ending in the North West.

After genuflecting to the altar he blesses water mingled with salt, *ashes*, and wine (symbolising blood) and sprinkles the inside walls thrice, going round East, South, West, North. Then he sprinkles the centre of the Church longwise and across, i.e. makes an equal armed cross. Next he circumambulates the church outside thrice, sprinkling the walls with this mixture, after which he re-enters and, taking up his position in the centre, sprinkles Holy Water to the four cardinal points and up to the roof (centre).

He then anoints with Holy Oil the twelve internal and the twelve external wall crosses, after which he again circumambulates the Church, thrice inside, and thrice outside, censing. Next he consecrates the altar with water and oil, washes it, censes it and then anoints the altar *stone* with oil. Finally he celebrates Mass.

The Sarum Rite is practically identical with the Roman Rite, except that there is no mention of " relics." Their use is Roman, and though often followed was always specifically mentioned as " Mos Romanus," but for all that it is very ancient even in England. After the consecration and aspurging of the four cardinal points in the centre, the Bishop prepares cement at the altar and then fetches the relics and deposits them in a cavity in the altar. The relics are ceremonially covered in and the cover censed and anointed. After this the consecration of the altar by washing, etc., follows.[2]

This ceremony can be traced back to the time of St. Ambrose and is almost certainly a substitute for a human sacrifice. By a decree of the Council of Celchyth (Chelsea) in A.D. 816 Cap. 2., if no relics were available, a portion of the Consecrated Elements

---

1. " Monumenta Ritualia ecclesiæ Anglicanæ." Sec. ed. I. pp. 195-239.
2. Enclycl. Brit. Article " Dedication." VII (11th ed.) pp. 918 sq.

of the Mass were to be similarly enclosed. In the Greek Church the ceremony of Consecration is very similar to that used in the West and includes the enclosing of " relics."

In this ceremony we see at once close analogies with Masonic ceremonies. The three knocks, the guarded door, the repeated perambulations, and so forth, are unmistakeable, but let us rather concentrate attention on the use of ashes. These are a substitute for the ashes of the victim, which were originally scattered over the land to produce fertility. Once, in a more barbarous age, those ashes had been a man, then animals were substituted, and by the Mediæval period no doubt they consisted of nothing more than wood ashes, yet even so they were appropriate, for was not Tammuz originally a tree god ? The setting up of a cross by the bishop reminds us of the manner in which the Can. approaches the ped. in the 3°.

The Consecration Cross is even still made in red, and was once made in blood. If my readers will study carefully the path Hiram Abiff traversed ere he met his final end they will find that it made a cross, marked with his blood, which in the above ceremony is represented by the equal armed cross made by the bishop after he has engraved the alphabet on the St. Andrew's Cross.

But the point to which I wish to direct my reader's attention is the depositing of " relics," i.e., the bones of the saints, in a hole in the altar. Clearly this was a Christian substitute for killing a man and burying his bones therein. The fact that, if relics were unobtainable, a part of the Consecrated Elements had to be buried, confirms this view. To the Mediæval Churchman these constituted the Body of Christ, and His Body thus completed the ceremony of consecration. Compare this fact with the statement that Hiram was buried as near the Sanctum Sanctorum as possible.

The aspurging of the four cardinal points and of the *centre* with Holy Water merely replaces the custom of sprinkling those points with the blood of the victim. As to the St. Andrew's Cross made in ashes, here undoubtedly we have a reference to the roof tree, and the ceremony brings to mind the sixth degree, or degree of a Passed Master, or Harod, among the Operative Masons. There, in the centre is placed a St. Andrew's cross, and on this a candidate, who is plumbed to the centre of the building. That is to say, he is held up on the cross under a plumb line which hangs from the centre of the roof and which must plumb true to *his* centre. He is also carried round the Lodge on the cross, contrary to the path of the sun, the age-old symbol for the journey of the dead. Thus just as they have a Foundation, so they have a Consecration Sacrifice, dramatically enacted.

This St. Andrew's Cross with the letters Alpha and Omega thereon was drawn by the Bishop who consecrated Liverpool Cathedral only last July (1924), and many other details of the old ceremony, such as the three knocks and the marking of the red Consecration Cross, were also observed, but there were of course no " relics."

Moreover, the Mediæval Church had a definite ritual drama of death which has escaped the notice of most writers. Even to-day the response " Alleluia " is omitted from Septuagesima to the Thursday in Holy Week, but in the Mediæval period there was an official ceremony called " The Burial of Alleluia," who was regarded as female. The choir boys had " to carry a clod of earth, as at a funeral, and go in procession to the cloister, wailing to the place where she (Alleluia) is buried." One MS. of this " Office " is contained in a diptych with an ivory cover whereon are depicted Ceres and Cybele. It is thus evident that the Churchmen substituted the mythical Alleluia for some descendant of Persephone, the corn maiden.[1] Is it surprising that in like manner the Masons should substitute for Tammuz, Hiram Abiff ?

Bearing these facts in mind, I consider that the Phoenician workmen, with or without the consent of Solomon, killed the old King of Tyre, Abibaal, or Hiram Abiff, as a Consecration Sacrifice. It may be that it was done secretly on their own responsibility, and that they were subsequently punished for it, but certainly the reason now given for the crime is totally inadequate. If the secrets of a M.M. were known to but three people, the miscreants as soon as they left Judea could have pretended that they possessed them, and no one would have been the wiser.

If they had attacked the chief Architect and succeeded in extorting from him those secrets, they would still have had to leave Judea for fear of punishment; why then risk their lives to obtain a secret which was useless, just because there existed no one save those three who could detect the fraud of a man who said he was a M.M. when he was not ?

On the other hand, the Phoenician and Jewish followers of the old Tammuz cult no doubt felt that the Great Goddess had been cheated of her just dues when Hiram Abiff was not slain, " according to Ancient Custom," on the accession of his son, and were confident that if he were not sacrificed when the Temple was completed its future and stability would be endangered. It is, however, quite possible that all three Kings, including Hiram Abiff, quite realised that the old King, the god-man, representing Tammuz, must be slain, and arranged to allow him to live until the Temple was finished so that he might have a peculiarly glorious end.

The Primacy among these Divine Kings then naturally passed to Adoniram, who was obviously older than Solomon or Hiram of Tyre, and, moreover, ruled over the peculiarly sacred Fane at Aphaca. He therefore became the successor of Hiram

---

1. J. L. Weston, " The Quest of the Holy Graal." pp. 101 sq.

Abiff, but for all that could not escape a similar fate and was killed in the time of Solomon's son.

Let us picture the last scene. The work is practically finished and Abibaal knows that his hour has come, and so at High Noon, the hour when according to ancient custom, the Divine man must die, he goes alone to the great Temple over whose creation he has presided for the last seven years. There, solitary and alone, he kneels and prays to his Father in Heaven. Whether he called him Baal or Moloch we know not, but for the last time he calls on Him as His son, the God-man Tammuz, ready to lay down his life for the sake of the people, as ancient custom prescribed. Outside the courts are crowded by a huge assembly of workmen. The messengers of death enter silently and alone,— and then comes the end.

CHAPTER XIX

THE BLENDING OF THE ANNUAL DRAMA WITH THE INITIATION CEREMONIES

Among the primitive races there is a clear distinction between their great fertility festivals, in which a representative of the Spirit of Vegetation is slain, and the rites of initiation. The former is a magical ceremony which aims at increasing the fertility of the soil, and all, both men and women, participate. The initiation rites, on the other hand, are semi-secret and restricted to each sex. In these, as a rule, there is very little, if any, reference to a hero and it is the candidates, or someone representing the candidates, who enact the part of the slain man, and not someone representing a god or hero.

It is clear, however, from Ezekiel's account, that in his time there were inner ceremonies, from which the women and the majority of the people were excluded, which took place in the secret vault at the same time as, above ground, the multitude were lamenting for Tammuz. It is also clear from his indignant words that these secret ceremonies were directly associated with Tammuz, and we herein see the beginning of the process of blending the annual drama with initiation rites, a process now complete in Speculative Freemasonry, but not complete in the case of the Operatives.

The reasons for the annual slaying of the human representative of the Spirit of Vegetation have been made abundantly clear; it was hoped thereby to transfer the Divine Soul to a fresh and vigorous human tabernacle, and was associated with " sympathetic magic."

The original purpose of the initiation rites was certainly different and has been a matter of dispute among scholars. Frazer considers that one of the chief reasons for the circumcision which always accompanied them was to create a nucleus which would facilitate the re-birth of the soul of the initiate when he died. To do this the initiate placed the severed foreskin either in the ground or in a tree, so that when he died his soul might go thither and await a chance of entering again into a woman.

The other school considers that circumcision was intended to preserve the member by sacrificing a part. Either of these views might explain the act of circumcision, but neither accounts for the elaborate ceremonies of death and resurrection which among primitive races usually accompany the surgical operation. The explanation I put forward not only does this, but in a sense shows that both schools of thought are right, but that the reasons they suggest are secondary and derived from the original motive.

I hold that it is clear that the Great Mother, even in her primitive form of a vague spirit of the earth, was considered to be like the Queen bee and required to be fertilised continually, and in doing so, tore off the virile member of her " lover." She claimed all men, and it was in order to save the majority of the tribe that these elaborate rites were performed. In short, thereby they tricked the greedy, lustful goddess of her rights, by giving her as substitute for the whole, a part, which was usually buried in the ground near some spot where edible plants grew, or, occasionally, actually in a tree in which edible grubs breed. By this sacrifice they assured the productivity of the Great Mother so far as that spot was concerned.

But the great goddess knew that her " lover " would die and if he did not actually die, she would discover the fraud. Therefore the initiate had to pretend to die and be reborn. As a baby the goddess could not claim him. He was safe till he reached puberty, and as, of course, he never did again reach puberty, he was safe till death really took him. Then his soul naturally went to the spot where he had planted a part of himself as a kind of seed.

If, however, you try to cheat the Great Mother, you must take every precaution possible to avoid detection, otherwise your fate, and indeed that of the whole tribe, is likely to be terrible. She will bring about famine in the land and sterility in the tribe. Hence the strict secrecy which surrounds these rites and, in particular, the exclusion of women. They are of the same nature as the Great Mother and may therefore be tempted to disclose to her the fraud that is being practised.

This, I suggest, is the original purpose; but on to this were grafted, at a very early date, subsidiary motives arising therefrom. Not only does the sacrifice of the part preserve the whole, but the part sacrificed is still in magical sympathy with the man. If an enemy can obtain control of it, he can injure the original owner by means of magical ceremonies. On the other hand, to the primitive mind it is obvious that this important fragment of the human body becomes a nucleus, which will enable the discarnate soul of its owner to return to earth and prepare for reincarnation, thus placing him at an advantage when compared with the uncircumcised souls in the underworld, who have no material necleus in the upper world. Then, too, in some cases, it seems as if the opportunity was taken during the rite of death and resurrection to deposit the soul of the initiate in some external object, so as to protect it from the wrath of the Great Mother or of fellow mortals.

Some of these rites are not mere play acting. The man undoubtedly goes into a swoon or trance. The savage considers that at such times the soul is outside the body, and tries by magical ceremonies to transfer it to some other object, whose nature he keeps a profound secret. Among these objects are trees, animals, stones, and a whole host of strange hiding places.

As men evolved they naturally tended to identify the candidate with the vegetation god, who was annually slain in order to satisfy the Great Mother. Such a process was a very natural one, and in time the candidate enacted the part of Osiris, Dionysius or Persephone as the case may be.

Out of these crude beginnings evolved the great mystery rites, and Freemasonry itself, wherein men were taught the doctrine of the resurrection of the soul and of life beyond the grave. The process was slow and gradual, but we can clearly see it evolving in the Jewish rites which Ezekiel denounced, and in the story of Jonah.

These rites always have associated with them certain " signs." At a later date these became a convenient method of proving membership, namely when the Mysteries had evolved and not every male was admitted. Originally they were part of the old sign language, which was necessary when man's vocabulary was limited, and became sacred, magical formula depicting certain wishes and prayers or, if you like, Mantras. Of these the H.S. of a F.C. and the sign of G. & D. are the most widespread and universal. They are almost invariably found in the primitive rites, and always have, respectively, the meaning of Preservation, and a desperate appeal to heaven for help or strength to bear the trial which awaits the candidate.

All these primitive rites are associated with the fertility cult, and in the case of the women their rites developed into a representation of the death and resurrection of the " corn maiden," called by the Greeks " Persephone," just as among the men it was the male spirit of vegetation, Tammuz, who predominated.

There were, however, a number of mixed rites, even among primitive races, a good example of which is the Ndembo Society in the Congo, and it seems probable that it was from such societies as these that some of the ancient mysteries and the modern Rosicrucians evolved.

To us, however, the most interesting rites are those restricted to men, and we will devote most of the next chapter to them, merely glancing at one or two of the other types in passing.

CHAPTER XX

INITIATION RITES OF DEATH AND RESURRECTION

" As already pointed out, these primitive rites may conveniently be divided into two main groups (a) burial in a grave, often associated with a tree, (b) being swallowed by a monster. The first is a simpler form than the latter, which in time developed into an account of what befell men after death.

There are, however, intermediate kinds of ceremonies, and even some which seem to have evolved so far away from the primitive form they can hardly be placed exactly. For all that, these various rites are linked together by the fundamental idea of a dramatic representation of death and resurrection, and in the vast majority of cases include circumcision.

Moreover, even among the primitive Australian blacks we find " advanced degrees," corresponding to the I.M. and the R.A., and usually the ceremony of death and resurrection, the very basis of the system, can only be approached after a series of preliminary ceremonies, some separated from the main by considerable periods of time, so that they may rightly be regarded as degrees.

AUSTRALIAN CEREMONIES

THE SACRED VALE OF BIAMEE. [1]

Only an hour's ride from Sidney lies what is really the ruined Temple of Biamee the God of Initiation, and the chief deity of the Kamilarois. It has been seen by but few, and those who have visited it will not reveal its exact location until they have been able to arrange adequate steps to protect it and secure its permanent preservation.

The walls of the temple, because of their strange character, have long since disappeared, but the floor remains intact and plainly inscribed with hieroglyphs eloquent to science. Because it was a temple of earth's most primitive people it was a primitive affair, but it was none the less a temple, and none the less a place of awe.

The ruins are hidden in a shallow gully north of the Pymble-Newport road and the setting is one of beauty. Within the valley a small stream springs from under a flat edge of rock, and, saunter-

---

1. For what follows I must express my great indebtedness to Bro. D. D. Harris, The Shire Office, Walpeup, Ouyen, Victoria, who kindly sent me these interesting details. He obtained them from an article in " Smith's Weekly," by B. Adamson, from information supplied by Mr. R. Smith and Mr. W. Robertson.

ing down, forms an unobtrusive little cascade, hiding its picture-
esqueness among the foliage.   At the base of this cascade there
are clear signs of its course having been diverted so that it would
flow over the southern portion of an immense rock, the surface of
which is flat and slightly sloping.   It is roughly circular, about
100 feet in diameter, and is formed by an outcrop of triassic
sandstone.

This was the floor of the temple.

The rites of Biamee, like all Bora ceremonies, require water.
For this, three ceremonial basins, in a terraced line, have been
hewn in the solid sandstone floor.   There is another basin at the
point where the diverted stream enters the floor space, but it is at
least partly natural.   From it a small carved channel leads to the
topmost of the three ceremonial basins, all of which are circular
hollows two or three feet across and about two feet deep.

These three basins are six feet apart, and the second and third
are double ones, the bottom of each being carved to form two
small, inner hollows.

Owing to the sloping surface of the rock, the basins have a
natural and continuous flow from one to the other, the water being
supplied by the diversion of the small stream.   Some six feet
below the lowest basin the water leaps the edge of the floor-rock
into a pool about ten feet across and of sparkling limpidity.
Slightly to the north of the line of the basins is what was presumably the sacred font, smaller than the others and carved in perfect
symmetry.

The Bora ceremony requires not only water but fire.   This
was apparently set in a large depression near the centre of the
temple floor, the remaining portions of which are carved with
tribal and mystic signs, some being remarkably plain.

The whole aspect of the locality now is one of quietude.
But for hundreds, and probably thousands, of years, this has
been a place of mystery, of awe, of stoic suffering, of barbaric
deeds, and often of death.   For in this primitive open-air temple,
the walls of which no longer exist because they were living
walls of men, the Kamilaroi youths were initiated into the tribal
secrets, the boy being carried to the centre of the sacred place
by an elder, who then left him to face the unknown.   As he
stood there he found himself imprisoned by the suddenly up-
reared walls of the temple.   Those walls were formed by the
grotesquely patterned bark shields of the initiated tribesmen who,
having secretly surrounded the huge floor of rock, leapt upright
with shields facing inward, so that they themselves would
remain invisible.

From this living wall came certain devilishly painted beings,
and within that ring of unseen men, with the central fire burning
fiercely, the boy was manhandled, tossed about, often perilously
close to the flames, and at one point compelled to leap that fiery

pit.   It was but the commencement of his ordeal, at a later stage of which he had to lie for several minutes on a log across the flames, doing his best to avoid a severe burning, and generally failing.   Before he was through the three degrees of bora, a process extending upwards of a year, a year of segregation from his tribe, there were further tests.   There was the scoring with stone instruments of the *left breast* and shoulder, and other trials of endurance, including the principal rite of circumcision.

If the boy got through the full ceremony he emerged proudly as a man.   But if at any time during initiation he gave the least whimper of fear or pain he came through with a brand of cowardice, still bearing the semblance of a man, but being one who could never reproduce his own cowardice because he could never become a father.   If his cowardice were too great, if the terror or the pain made him scream, then he died as being unworthy to live.

Those who came through, besides being acknowledged men, were able to read the meaning of those hieroglyphs on the temple floor, carvings which include an excellent drawing of a speared kangaroo, of a wallaby, of a chief's shield, of sacred circles, of girls dancing, and, in a more mystical degree, of the God, Biamee, himself.   Besides these there are carvings of mundoe, or ghost footsteps, and the footsteps of a bunyip.   At first two mundoe steps are shown, but only one gets past the bunyip, which seemingly turns and chases the remaining mundoe, but fails to catch it before the step reaches the line of the ceremonial basin.

The rites of this strange place, with its torture and mutilation and triumph, its savagery and death, were performed to the accompaniment of strange sounds.   This was the bellow of the bull-roarer, the voice of Biamee's son, warning the women and children to flee as far as possible from the valley of terrible secrets.

The use of a ceremonial bath and the pretence of burning the candidate are in close affinity with what we have seen of the Syrian rites of Tammuz.   The wounding on the left breast reminds us of the pretence of a similar act in other rites, as, for example, when a sharp stone is placed against the breast of the Dervish initiate.   In the Hung Society the candidate is still actually given a slight wound on the left breast and shoulder.

The mutilation of the boy, if he whimpered, is easily explained.   If he did so, he would disclose to the lustful Great Mother that she was being cheated, and to lull her suspicions to sleep again the full operation must be done, lest she discover the deception in the case of the other initiates.   The death penalty for extreme cowardice is merely the logical completion of the lesser penalty, for if really aroused the Great Mother would watch until the end.

In the foot-prints of the ghost we have the early beginning of those rites which later developed into a complete account of the

supposed journey of the soul after death. Let us now consider
further details of these strange rites.

" It is well known that the youths of the tribes are initiated
into the first stages of the Bora as they come to manhood, and the
primitive temple in the Sacred Valley of Biamee was one of the
places where those rites were performed. The ceremonial basins
and totem signs are unmistakable. But it does not follow that
this was the place where all the Bora mysteries, of which there
are three degrees, were performed.

Those degrees among certain tribes are known as the Bunda,
the Banjoor and the Barrang, the final division of the last being
the Turroine. That is the final and most secret revelation. No
white man has ever witnessed or been able to gather the least
whisper regarding it. The ordeal is known to have existed, and
still to exist, and it is understood to be a ceremony so advanced
that but few members of a tribe ever attain to it.

As far as the latest signs may be read at present, it is probable
that this final rite was held in a place apart, a more sacred chapel,
as it were, of the Temple of Biamee, and that recent discovery
has revealed that sacred chapel of the Barrang degree.

The position of it is about a quarter of a mile from the
Boranore and near the head of a gully that leads picturesquely
down to chasms and jungle clad gorges.

Across a ravine from the Boranore is a cliffy terrace, the edge
of which, at one point is a large and slightly sloping space of rock,
fairly flat. It is this terrace space that seems to have been the
Barrang chapel.

The whole of the flat rock is covered with aboriginal carvings.
That is not unusual, there are many rock carvings about this
district. But this has features which, so far as is known, have
not been found elsewhere. They have a curious and twofold
significance; first on the debated theory that the Australian
blacks are sun worshippers, and second, on the fact that these
primitive people seem to possess some knowledge of certain
aspects of Freemasonry.

Regarding the latter, various significant circumstances are
gradually accumulating.

It is on record that early explorers coming upon tribes that
had never before seen a white man, were greeted by signs, not
simple but complex, which are peculiar to the craft. That was
the first circumstance.

Another is contained in an incident accidentally and secretly
witnessed some fifty years ago. It is somewhat digressional from
the sacred Valley of Biamee, but is distinctly relevant, both from
the point of view of masonic lore and of sun-worship.

' From the top of the hill overlooking Scrubby Creek, near
Rockhampton, the afternoon silence was broken by a torrent of
words, like a malediction. Dismounting and tying my horse to a

tree, I crept to the top of the hill. Prostrate in two rows, facing the setting sun, was a host of aborigines. In the front line, at the base of the hill, were the old and young warriors. In front of each his weapons and shield. Twenty yards distant were the lubras and children, their black bodies glistening in the rays as they lay there in the mysterious quiet. At short intervals one of the old warriors spoke with intense fervour, his voice rising to a crescendo pitch.

As the last rays were fading, each of these took up a spear and rose, standing erect and motionless, the spear pointing to the setting sun. As by a common impulse the lubras and children walked quietly towards the camp. At a signal from an old warrior the young men lifted their weapons and passed into the scrub.

The climax was dramatic and impressive. Dropping the spears, the veterans raised their hands above their heads three times, and in absolute silence bowed their bodies thrice. They then took up their weapons and departed in single file.

That night, at the same place, a Kaipara corroboree was held, at which only the old and the young warriors were present.

The position of the Kaipara ground was near the entrance to ' Caithness Park,' and a careful examination of the place gave us a clue, as two trees had the sacred marks.'

That is the second circumstance. A third, of interest to members of the fraternity, was revealed when the Boranore, in the Sacred Valley of Baimee, was discovered, with its ceremonial basins in line East and West, and the mundoe, or ghost steps, going South, the number of true steps on the Boranore being *seven*.

There are thus three widely different items of evidence all pointing in the one direction. A fourth is contained in certain features of the most recent discovery in the same locality. These are portions of the carvings, which are numerous and varied.

Among the more commonplace designs are the kangaroo, evidently the totem of the Kamilrois, or of that section of the tribe, since, like a similar carving on the Bora rock across the ravine, there are two parallel lines, the infallible totem sign, across the base of the tail. There are also wallabies, lizards, a burrawa or brush turkey, a heart, a warratah with a long stem, a beautifully formed lyre-bird, or at least its tail, and various other animals of general interest.

Besides the ordinary ones there are features of special interest. One is a boomerang with the apex pointing towards the south, and another is a triangle, also with its apex pointing towards the South.

In the centre of the rock is a large oblong basin. Like the three ceremonial basins on the Bora rock, its direction is East and West. It can safely be said that this excavation was made to fit the body of a man averaging six feet, and it looks like a grave or the representation of a grave, made for a serious religious ceremony.

It might be mentioned that similar rock graves exist on the Burdekin in North Queensland.

Another carving of note is on the slope of the rock facing across the ravine toward the Boranore. It represents some curious and grotesque creature that would seem to have a kinship, though it is more complicated in design, to the carving of Biamee, god of the Kamilrois, on the Boranore. An important point of resemblance between the two is the head, each having several rays (or antennae) projecting from the top of it.

The fifth item, and in a way the most interesting of all, is an unmistakable representation of the rising sun. It is circular and well formed, with thirteen rays extending in a semi-circle from one side of it, their general direction being towards the West, as would be the case of a native looking eastward towards the beams of the rising sun. So far as is known, this is the first time a sun has been found, though many carvings are extant representing the moon.

This sacred area was obviously for some different, and undoubtedly more advanced ceremony than the Boranore across the ravine. The more detailed figures of Biamee supports this conclusion and there is every reason to believe that it would be the sacred chapel for the Barrang degree, with its last and most sacred revelation of the Turroine ordeal.

The figure of the rising sun, since it occurs nowhere else, is a still more definite indication as to this being a chapel apart, and in that rare sign may be the last secret. It is possible that, to the tribesmen who failed to reach the final rite of the Barrang the strange figure with the rays or antennae, at the top of its head would remain for ever the mysterious god, Biamee. But the chosen tribesmen, initiated at last to the most sacred mystery of all, would learn the meaning of those rays, would behold them amplified and simplified in that design of the rising sun, and would learn the final, grand secret that the great god Biamee, after all, was none other than the all-potent Sun.

It is possible and probable. If it be so, from what dim past of straight sun-worship must the Australian blacks have derived their relic of religion ? And because so many signs and ceremonies are woven into it that have a meaning to students of masonic lore, a strange and alluring vista of conjecture is opened, suggesting that the two utterly remote and dissociate mysteries in part have sprung from the same primordial source. It is certainly significant that the figure of Biamee is in the East, the exact position where a W.M. sits, who represents the " Sun at Dawn."

There is, moreover, a curious legend of a hero called Yoone-cara, who set out towards the land of the Setting Sun in order to visit his great ancestor, Biamee. He had to traverse three dangerous areas where attempts were made to stop his progress. Finally, he crossed a great marsh by a bridge made of a tree trunk and reached a beautiful valley, where he found Biamee in his cave. He was kindly received by the daughter of his great ancestor and given a meal, after which Biamee talked with him and sent him back again, adding that he was and should ever remain the only man who returned alive from the land of Biamee.[1]

In this legend we seem to have the origin of the degree which related what befell men after death, and it is in striking analogy with the main features of the Syrian rite as revealed by Lucian.

One of the signs used by these high grade initiates is the sn. of Rev. of the R.A. In addition there is a special ceremony of initiation for the making of a medicine man. As these men preside as Masters in the ceremonies through which the boys pass, it is clear that in a sense this " degree " corresponds to that of an I.M. Before giving it, however, we will consider a few more examples of the Australian Death and Resurrection rites, which will enable us to obtain a clearer mental picture of these ceremonies.

THE GRAVE AND TREE

The Coast Murring tribe of New South Wales perform the following ceremony. First of all the medicine man knocks out a tooth of each initiate, using for that purpose a *chisel* and *hammer*. Perhaps, therefore, the use of these instruments in a masonic lodge was not, originally, merely because they were tools used by operative masons, but, like the 24-inch gauge, because they had a definite part in the ceremony. An eye-witness described these rites as follows:—

At about 11 a.m. the initiated men prepared the ground by digging a grave. Then sheets of bark were beaten out into fibre and from this cloaks were made for six men who were entirely enveloped in them from the crowns of their heads to the soles of their feet, thus completely covering their faces. Four of them were tied to a rope, which was fastened to the backs of their heads, and each man carried two pieces of bark in his hands. The other two men were not fastened to the first four but hobbled along leaning on sticks as if bent and old.

Then another man[a] lay down in the grave on his back with his hands crossed on his chest and held upright thereon a small tree. The roots rested on his body and the top rose several feet above the level of the top of the grave. The latter was then covered in with sticks, leaves and plants, thus burying the man.

---

1.   For full details see Ward, " The Hung Society," Vol. II.
(a)   Thus making *Seven* in all. A perfect Lodge.

All being thus ready, the initiates were led to the brink of the grave and a man who belonged to the " *Eagle* " Totem sat on a tree trunk at the head of the grave singing a mournful dirge. Slowly there appeared out of the bush the two old medicine men, followed by the other four.   They had come in search of the grave of a " supposedly " dead medicine man, i.e., a Master.   It was now *midday*, and as the procession reached the sacred ground it broke into a solemn invocation to Daramulin, a mysterious spirit who is supposed to slay the initiates and then bring them back to life again.

Suddenly the tree began to sway from side to side.   The procession which had reached the grave began to dance wildly and when excitement had reached its height the " dead " man threw out the tree and bursting from the grave began to dance in the grave itself, at the same time pointing to certain magic articles which he held in his mouth and which he was supposed to have received from the great Daramulin.[1]

The tree is evidently supposed to enshrine the soul of the dead man, and is in striking analogy with the " sprig " of Acacia.   The grouping together of the men in the procession is similar to the way in which in the U.S.A. candidates have to journey round the room in the R.A. ceremony.

Similar rites occur among most, if not all, the Australian tribes.   Thus the Toonghi pretend that the youths are slain by the spirit Thuremlin, who subsequently restores them to life.   His voice is simulated by the use of the bull-roarer.[2]

This mythical spirit is the same as Daramulun, who appears to be the Thunder and Rain spirit.   It should be remembered that Vishnu has as his emblem the triangle of water, while the rain God in New Guinea makes a certain significant sign.[c]

Among the Ualaroi it is said that the initiates are slain by a ghost which ultimately restores them to life.[3]

The Arunta tribe say that a spirit named Twanyirika[4] enters into the bodies of the boys as soon as they have been circumcised and carries them away into the forest, ultimately restoring them to the tribe when the wound is healed.   This variant is important. It shows that the boy is supposed to die when he is circumcised and later be reborn.   Now, if the great Mother had received her full rights the boy would like Attis, have died and, like him, have been ultimately reborn.

---

1.   A. W. Howitt, " Native Tribes of South East Australia," pp. 554-56.
2.   A. L. P. Cameron, " Notes on some Tribes of New South Wales." Journal of the Anthropological Institute, XIV.   (1885), pp. 357 sq.
3.   A. W. Howitt, " On Australian Medicine Men "—Journal of the Anthropological Inst. XVI. (1887) pp. 47 sq.
4.   B. Spencer and F. J. Gillen, " Native Tribes of Central Australia," p. 246.
(a)   See illus. op. p. 332 in " Freemasonry and the Ancient Gods."

Among the Unmatjera the uninitiated believe that the boys are slain by Twanyirika and ultimately restored to life,[1] and the same belief is held by the Urabunna tribes who call the spirit Witurna. When we approach New Guinea we find that the beliefs on this point approach nearer and nearer to those held in that island.[2] The spirit becomes a monster who eats or swallows the initiate and then spews him forth again. Tribes who hold this view are the Binbinga and the Anula.[3]

Let us now consider the " Chair Degree " of a Medicine Man. These men declare that they are carried off by the spirits, slain, disembowelled and new spirit intestines placed in them by the ghosts. The usual place of initiation for this rite is a cave, and the victims return in a dazed state, due, undoubtedly, to the severe mauling they have to undergo. There is also, probably, a certain amount of play acting in their pretended ignorance as to their past life, for they are supposed to be " new born." They have to pretend, however, that they recognise no one, not even their wives, till they have been reintroduced to them by the presiding medicine man.

Among the Arunta of Alice Springs the would-be medicine man, and future Master of the " Lodge," enters a cave which is inhabited by spirits and leads to the realms of the dead. This place is said to be a veritable earthly paradise, and reminds us strongly of the place where, according to the legend of Yoonacara, Biamee dwells. The candidate lies down in the entrance and passes into a heavy sleep. Then one of his ancestral spirits comes up to him and drives a " spirit " spear through the back of his neck, and through his tongue, so as to make it cleave to the roof of his mouth. He then drives the spear through the victim's head, entering at one ear and passing out at the other. This blow " kills him," and the spirit carries away his body to Paradise, cuts it open, replaces his old physical intestines by new spirit ones, and then restores him to life.[4]

No doubt the " spirits " are represented by disguised medicine men, and undoubtedly a sharp instrument is driven through the tongue of the candidate, for a hole in the tongue, big enough to insert one's little finger, is the " badge " of a duly installed medicine man. The wound probably represents the sacrifice of a part of the tongue to the spirits, and it is interesting to note that Horus, who represents the risen, or reborn, Osiris, is depicted making a curious sign. I have two bronze statues of the god making this sign, which consists in the one case of laying the finger on the lips as if implying secrecy, and in the other of pointing with

1. B. Spencer and F. J. Gillen, " Northern Tribes of Central Australia,"
        pp. 342 sq., 498.
2. Ibid. 498.
3. Ibid. pp. 366 sq., 373 and 501.
4. B. Spencer & F. J. Gillen, " Native Tribes of Central Australia," pp. 523.

the thumb just beneath the tip of the chin as if suggesting driving a sharp instrument up through the tongue in order to pin it to the roof of the mouth.

Such a sacrifice might in time develop into a penalty which would be exacted from any initiate who dared to break the obligation of secrecy and reveal what happens " beyond the grave." In like manner the spear driven through the ears would naturally explain the meaning of such a sign as pointing at the ear, and a peculiar sign found in many initiation rites in which the candidate places his right hand on his left shoulder or in line with his ear. A good example of this occurs on the Mexican vase found at Chama.[1] Some of these rites involve the sacrifice of a finger or the joint of the finger, evidently a substitute for cutting off the whole hand, and so my readers will realise that the fees claimed from initiates in Australia are remarkably heavy. Another strange ceremony consists in walking under an arch of boomerangs over a mound made to represent a man, who seems to be stretched out as if on a S. Andrew's cross.[2]

Among the natives of Melville Island[3] the following features are of especial interest. Several boys and a girl were initiated together. The candidates were bathed by the older men first, later the men went in procession round the " ground " and when doing so held their left hand in a peculiar way as if shading their eyes from the light (although it was raining). Presently the boys and the girl were all pushed into a little hut, when a body of men represented a hostile tribe and attacked the hut with much vigour, and pretended to slay the initiates, including the girl. Next followed a tug of war with a pole, in which the " dead " initiates joined. Then one of the initiates was led round the fire. Next day a party set out to search for the now missing initiates, including the girl, who were found hidden under a pile of bushes at the foot of a tree. The searchers expressed the greatest amazement at finding them there.

The above details are especially interesting. We have the ceremonial " baptism," as among the Essenes and the Operative Masons. We have a peculiar sign, the attack on the candidates by a band of villains, death, the dragging of the soul through the underworld as by a rope, a journey on foot through the " Underworld," i.e., round the fire, and the raising of the dead initiates whose presence is revealed by the " Pulling up " of a bush. The close association of the rite with the vegetation cult is shown by the fact that " yams " play a very important part in the ceremony, which is supposed to result in a greater supply being produced by the soil. The initiation of the girl shows that here

1. See Ward, " Freemasonry and the Ancient Gods," pp. 334.
2. See Ibid. op. p. 354.
3. B. Spencer, " Native tribes of the Northern Territory " (1914), pp. 69-109.

we have a primitive mixed rite of death and resurrection, a most unusual feature, but one which is widespread in this area. It should also be noted that the initiates are invested with certain ceremonial collars at various points in the ceremony.

This rite, therefore, not only depicts the death of the candidate, but also what befalls him in the Underworld previous to his resurrection. No doubt in a sense he represents the spirit of the Yam.

At the initiation of a boy in the Port Essington tribe there are at least two degrees. In the first degree the initiate has to wear a special girdle, reminding us of the girdle used in the Dervish rites, and a kind of cable-tow, with a long end hanging down his back. In this, some of the men who are taking part fall down as if dead, are covered with bushes, and ultimately rise up again. The second degree is less interesting to us and can be ignored. [1]

Among the Kakadu there are no less than five degrees, namely: (1) Jamba, (2) Ober, (3) Jungoan, (4) Kulori, and (5) Muraian, in which latter only comparatively old men can take part.

(1) In JAMBA the boys are ceremonially bathed, then their heads are covered: they are later allowed to see light. Then a taboo is laid on certain foods and the boys are sent into the bush. Many months later they are fetched back. The Master of the ceremony strikes on a hollow tree log called " Jamba," and the majority of the men who are hidden under piles of grass whistle. The boys, whose eyes are now covered, cannot make out what the noise is. Then they are allowed to see, but warned that what they see is secret. Next follows a kind of " charge " wherein the boys are told to keep various things secret and in return are informed that they now have certain privileges. Then the buried men rise up and dance round the ground. Next day the boys are invested with special armlets and girdles.

(2) OBER. Messengers bearing a special wand go out and summon members of neighbouring camps to the ceremony. This degree deals with legends of the ancestors, a snake dance, and the like.

(3) JUNGOAN consists of various ceremonies intended to ensure good hunting. In one, two men who pretend to be kangaroos, are knocked on the head and symbolically killed. No doubt, in this ceremony we have the counterpart to the killing of the vegetation god, but here applied to this spirit of animal life.

(4) KULORI deals with Yams, which the natives call kulori. The initiates are laid on their backs, covered with slices of yam, and then ceremonially raised from the ground by the arm. After this they are placed in a special hut made of boughs, and must remain in these for the rest of the day. While there, songs about

1. Spencer, Ibid. pp. 116 sq.

the yam and other foods are sung, but the natives themselves do
not know the meaning of the words they sing, so old are the songs.
This ceremony is clearly the same as that held by the Melville
Island tribe,[1] but is worn down and has lost several interesting
dramatic touches, such as the attack on the initiates. The
covering in with yams and the raising of the boys shows that the
death and resurrection of the yam spirit is represented.

(5) MURAIAN. This is the final and most important ceremony of the whole series, and corresponds somewhat to the final
ceremony of the Arunta, which is called Engwura, but the details
do not bear directly on our subject.

During many of these ceremonies when the boy initiate is in
seclusion in the bush he may not speak even to his guardian, save
by signs.[2] Herein we find the origin of the sign language, which
still survives in a very elaborate form among the initiates of the
Hung Society in China.

Among the Worgait tribe, after a boy has been circumcised,
he is told he must no longer let a woman see his private parts, and
a sort of bag or loop is made for the penis, which is fastened to his
waist belt. This incident shows the origin of the modern sense of
modesty. The women must not be allowed to perceive the trick
which has been played on the Great Mother lest they betray the
fact. Also it suggests the origin of the ceremonial bestowal of an
apron on initiates in other rites. The little bag containing the
penek which is bestowed on a Dervish initiate is half-way in
evolution between the two " garments." Interesting and important as the Australian ceremonies are, we can devote no
further space to them, and will now cross to New Guinea.

NEW GUINEA—INSIDE THE MONSTER

A glance at the illustration opposite p. 114 in " Freemasonry
and the Ancient Gods," which depicts the dancing belt and
bull-roarer conferred on a man who has taken his third degree in
New Guinea, will prove instructive. The Dancing Belt, replacing
the humble loop of the Australian savage, is obviously approaching very near to a ceremonial apron, while the emphasis laid on
the navel suggests the origin of the point within the circle, which
among more evolved races becomes the symbol of the sun, and
ultimately of the Supreme Being. Its association with a certain
sign in Masonry thus becomes intelligible.

Among the tribes of New Guinea who dwell round Huon
Gulf and Finsch Bay there is a pretence that the initiates are
swallowed by a monster, and·that the wound caused by circumcision is the result of a scratch given by the beast as he spits them
up again. With these rites are associated the use of flutes, whose

1. B. Spencer, " Native Tribes of Northern Australia," pp. 121 sq.
2. Ibid. p. 168.

importance in the Tammuz rites has already been noted. As I
have already given a fair number of details of these ceremonies
earlier in this book, a short reference must suffice.

Among the Kai a special hut is erected in the forest which is
made to resemble a hideous monster named Ngosa (Grandfather),
and the initiates have to enter the mouth of this creature whose
teeth are represented by bull-roarers held aloft by men, while
other men in its belly simulate its roar by whirling bull-roarers.
While inside the hut they are circumcised, and only when the
wound is healed are they symbolically vomited forth. Even
then they have to keep their eyes closed for a time and to pretend
not to understand when their elders speak to them.

The earth monster which swallows them up reminds us of
mediæval frescoes representing Hell, or the Underworld, where it
is depicted as a monster swallowing human beings.

When a man really dies among the Kai, it is believed that his
soul enters the Underworld, the entrance to which is a certain
ghost cavern, west of the Sattelberg, where it is judged by a king
of the Underworld, Tulumeng.[1] Here, then, we see a direct
relation between the initiation rites and the beliefs as to what
befalls a man after death. It is also significant that most of these
New Guinea tribes sacrifice men at the consecration of a new
" Club house."

Among the Tugeri it is a great giant who kills the initiates
and then restores them to life, instead of a monster, but in all cases
the underlying idea is that the boy is slain as a *boy* and raised a
man. Perhaps some of the mediæval legends of the master
slaying his apprentice were not real murders, but similar ceremonies by which the boy was made a Master Mason.

FIJI

In Fiji the ceremony is most dramatic and is held in a sacred
enclosure of oblong shape, formed of low stone walls, but open to
the sky, called Nanga, which was dedicated to the ancestral
spirits. Here the Yams play an important part, indicating the
close connection between these initiatory rites and the spirit of
vegetation. Yams were regularly placed in these Nanga as
offerings and so were the foreskins of the initiates, the significance
of which custom must by now be clear to my readers. They were
the substitutes given to Mother Earth in place of the whole member. The Nanga had always an inner Sanctum Sanctorum and
the initiation took place at the beginning of the Fijian new year,
which was in October-November.[2] As a preparation, the heads

1.   Frazer, " Balder the Beautiful " II. pp. 239 sq.
2.   Rev. L. Fison, " The Nanga or Sandstone Enclosures of Wainimala,
      Fiji,"—Journal of the Anthropological Inst. XIV. (1885), pp. 20 sq.
      B. Thomson, " The Fijians " (London, 1908) pp. 146 sq.

of the candidates were shaved and their beards plucked out. For four days in succession they went in solemn procession to the Temple and made offerings to the ancestral spirits. When they came on the fifth day they found on the floor a row of " dead " men, whose bodies had been ripped open so that their bowels protruded and blood was everywhere. At the further end sat the high priest, and towards him the candidates had to crawl on hands and knees across the " bleeding " corpses. This done, they paused in a row in front of him. Suddenly he shouted a command and the corpses sprang to their feet and rushed to the river where they bathed.

Then the high priest rose and began a ceremonial dance during which he repeatedly called out, " Where are the people of my enclosure ? Are they gone to Tonga Levu ? Are they gone to the deep sea ? "

In response a solemn chant was heard, at first far away in the distance, but drawing rapidly nearer and nearer, and the dead men, thus restored to life, marched back from the river clean and garlanded with flowers, singing a sacred hymn. They drew up in a line in front of the candidates, and then followed the sacramental meal. Four ancients of the highest degree entered. The first bore a cooked yam wrapped in leaves so that he should not touch it with his hands. The second carried pork, similarly protected. The third held a cup full of water, wrapped round with a native cloth. The fourth carried a napkin of similar material. Each novice partook of a morsel of the yam and pork, drank a little water, and had his mouth wiped with the napkin. Does not this ceremony remind some of my readers of a similar one ? Finally, the High Priest imposed on the initiates inviolable secrecy and warned them of the vengeance of the gods if they failed therein. My readers may be glad to learn that the intestines and blood were those of pigs, not men !

In many other Islands of the Pacific there are ceremonies of death and resurrection. In Rook Island the boys are supposed to be swallowed by a demon, Marsaba, and in New Britain there is a definite society called the Duk-Duk. The Master, or Tubian, strikes the boy a hard blow on the head with a cane, which is supposed to kill him. Now the Tubian, although actually a man, is supposed to be female, and thus once more we see that it is the Great Mother who destroys the initiates. The Tubian, however, brings them to life again and they are supposed to be born anew from " her." [1]

In Halmahera, an island of New Guinea, there seems to be no ceremony of death, but its place is taken by one of re-birth.

1.   R. Parkinson, " Im Bismarck Archipel " (Leipsic, 1887).   pp. 129-134.
     Rev. G. Brown, " Journal of the Royal Geog. Soc." XLVII. (1887)
        pp. 148 sq. id. R.S. IX.   (1887) pp. 17.
     H. M. Romilly, ed. (1887) pp. 11 sq.
     W. Powell, " Wanderings in a Wild Country," pp. 60 sq.

This includes smearing the boys all over with red water at the
" third cock crow," which is supposed to represent the blood
shed at a birth. The boys then run into the forest and hide
behind trees. The Master of the Ceremony follows after and
knocks three times on each tree behind which the boys are hiding.
The boys do not return, however, till evening, when they bathe
and then may eat.[1]

The association of three knocks with a ceremony of re-birth is
certainly interesting. In Easter Island certain hieroglyphs have
been found on which are figures of men making the same sign as
that shown on the New Guinea dancing belt, and also another
curious sign found among the Yaos, and elsewhere, which means
Preserve.[2]   The ceremonies of death and resurrection which lead
to initiation into the famous Kakian Society in Ceram are perhaps the most curious of all.[3]

This is a regular secret society and its lodge is an oblong
building in the depth of the jungle. It is so built as to exclude
all light. The initiates are led thither blindfold and each has
two men in charge of him. When all are assembled the Master
summons the demons, and at once an appalling noise, made by
trumpets, is heard. The women and children think this is the
shrieking of the demons, and amid this din the members and
officers of the Society enter followed by the initiates, one by one.

As each vanishes from the sight of his relations the sound as
of chopping is heard, and a terrible scream rends the air. Then a
sword or spear, dripping with blood, is thrust through the roof of
the house, signifying that the boy has been beheaded. As soon as
the instrument of death appears the women begin to weep for the
murdered children, who, actually, at that moment, are being
thrust into an opening which looks like the mouth of a crocodile,
or sometimes like a cassowary's beak. It is then said that the
demon has swallowed them. They sit in the shed for nine days,
while almost the whole time they hear the continual clashing of
swords and the braying of trumpets, in short, a very dramatic
representation of the sounds of Hell. They are also tattooed
with the sign of the cross, which has not been imported from
Christianity.[c]

The Master, using a trumpet to simulate the voice of the
demons, warns them that they must never disclose the secrets of
their initiation under the penalty of death. Afterwards they are
told the traditions and the moral code of the community.

---

1.   J. G. F. Reidel, " Guella und Tobolenesen, Zeitschift für Ethnologie "
        XVII. (1885). pp. 81 sq.
2.   See " Freemasonry and the Ancient Gods," by Ward, op. p. 112.
3.   Frazer, " Balder the Beautiful," Vol. II. p. 248.
      J. G. F. Reidel, " De sluik-en knoesharigi passen tusschin Selebes en
        Papua " (The Hague, 1886). pp. 107-111.
(a) In Scotland, masonic Kts. T. are similarly tattooed on the wrist. I have
      seen more than one thus marked.

Meanwhile their relations are at home weeping and wailing, but after a day or two, messengers arrive, spent and mudbespattered, who are supposed to have come from the Underworld, and announce that the demons have agreed to restore the lads to life. These messengers are the same men as those who had previously acted as their guides, and thus their duties correspond exactly with those of the Deacons in Masonry.

On the *tenth* day the boys come forth again into the daylight, each bearing a staff, which is regarded as evidence that they have passed through the underworld, therein reminding us of the Caducus of Mercury, and of the wands given in the R.A. The candidates have to pretend that they are like young children and do not even know how to eat properly.

AFRICA

Let us now pass to Africa which abounds in secret societies and initiation rites. When a boy is circumcised in British East Africa he makes the same sign as that on the New Guinea belt.[1] Among the Bondeis, a tribe who live in Tanganyika, opposite Pemba, the boy is figuratively slain with a sword, and the entrails of a fowl are placed on his belly to make it appear as if he had been disembowelled.[2] My readers should here call to mind the way in which the unfortunate slave in the Philippines was sacrificed to ensure a good harvest. The Akikuyu of British East Africa make boys go through a pretence of being reborn from their own mothers.[3] When we turn to Central Africa we find a great number of interesting examples.

The Bushongo, who inhabit the Belgian Congo, had a most interesting ceremony. The supreme chief, who bore the title of God on earth (Chembe Kunji),[4] at intervals sent the boys who had reached puberty into the jungle to be initiated. For several nights during the dark hours the initiated men marched round the camp where they were, whirling bull-roarers, which noise the boys thought was the roaring of ghosts. After a month the first " point " took place. The men dug a trench 10 feet deep and roofed it over with sticks and earth, thus forming a tunnel of considerable length. At intervals four niches were cut in the walls of this tunnel in which men, suitably disguised, were stationed.

The first was draped in a leopard skin, the second as a warrior, with a knife in his hand, the third represented a smith, with a furnace and red hot irons, and the last wore an ape's mask and

1. See illus. op. p. 106, " Freemasonry and the Ancient Gods."
2. Rev. G. Dale, " An Account of the Principal Customs and Habits of the Natives inhabiting the Border Country."—Journal of the Anthrop. Inst., XXV. (1896). p. 189.
3. Frazer, " Balder the Beautiful," II., p. 262.
4. E. Torday et T. A. Joyce, " Les Bushongo (Brussels, 1910). p. 53.

held a knife.   These beings threatened and terrified the candidates as they made their way through the dark tunnel and out on the further side.

So far we see that the boys have been carried off into the jungle and hear the howling of ghosts.   This means that the uninitiated think that they have been carried off and slain by the ghosts.   The tunnel clearly represents the journey through the underworld, or Hades and the passing of four gates therein, which are properly guarded.   This feature appears in many more civilised rites, such as that jeered at by Lucian, and even in the R.O.S., though perhaps some members do not realise it.

The second point is somewhat similar.   A low tunnel, only three feet deep, is made, and sticks are stuck into it which project through the roof, and at the end is a bowl full of goats' blood. The master tells the candidates that they must crawl along this tunnel on hands and knees.   With the memory of what befell them in the first tunnel they are naturally loth to do so, and the Master himself volunteers to go first and show them the way.

He crawls along and his progress can be followed by the candidates from the way in which the tops of the protruding sticks wobble.   When he reaches the end he smears the blood all over himself, but the candidates cannot see this, and so when he crawls out covered with blood and sinks down on his face apparently dead, they think he has really died from the effects.   Furthermore, the initiated men declare that the Master is indeed dead and solemnly carry him away.   The boys are then ordered to do likewise, but in abject terror they beg to be excused, and after a stormy scene it is agreed that they shall be excused on paying a ransom of so many cowrie shells.

The third point takes place a month later, but, though very dramatic, is really a test of courage and not a " Resurrection rite." [1]

It is, however, the secret societies which are of most interest to us.   The Poro of Sierra used to carry off men and initiate them in the jungle.   They were said to have been reborn from a devil, and the playing of flutes formed an important element in the ceremonies.   Candidates had to swear a tremendous oath not to divulge the secrets of the Society and learned a secret language. Anyone attempting to spy on the lodge was slain.   Women were not admitted.   Initiates afterwards wore a girdle of twisted fern. [2]

THE SOOSOOS OF SENEGAMBIA have a society of the same

1.   E. Torday et T. A. Joyce, " Les Bushongo " (Brussels, 1910).   p. 82 sq.
2.   John Matthews, " A Voyage to the River Sierra Leone."   (London, 1791).   p. 82.
      T. J. Alldridge, " The Sherbro and its Hinterland."   (London, 1901). p. 124 sq.

kind which the natives actually compare to Freemasonry. It is called Semo, has terrific oaths and a secret language. The initiate is supposed to have his throat cut and to remain dead for some time, but in due course is raised to life and admitted to a full participation in the secrets of the Order. [1]

In the Lower Congo there are not only puberty rites but several secret societies, two of which are especially important. These admit only adults, and while one, Nkimba, is restricted to men, the other Ndembo, is a mixed society and may be regarded as the primitive type from which such rites as those of Isis and Eleusis evolved.

The Nkimba Guild seems to have a definite place also as a primitive form of Trade Guild, for the members are specifically told they must help a brother in trade and also if in any difficulty. Our information about the exact ceremonies is very meagre, but those desiring to enter must whirl round and round in the market place like dancing Dervishes till they drop in a swoon. They are then supposed to be dead and are picked up and carried into the jungle by members of the Guild, ostensibly to be buried. In reality they are taken to the Lodge house and there initiated. They are taught a secret language and thereafter have a special dress, and usually are whitened with pipeclay. Sometimes instead of whirling, a drug is used to cause the swoon. [2]

The Ndembo Lodge [2] was opened on special occasions when, for example, there was an outbreak of disease, and the object of entering it was to obtain a new body free from disease or chance of infection. Barren women entered in order to obtain a new body which would enable them to bring forth children.

Ndembo means " delivered from the influence of evil or sorcery " and another name used for the society is Nsi A Fwa, which means " The country of the dead."

Candidates whirled themselves round till they swooned and were then carried by the Ndembo members present to a house in the jungle, where they were supposed to remain dead for six months. At the end of this time it was said that they had rotted all away except one bone, which was ostentatiously shown to any enquiring relations. They were then brought back to life in a new body and when restored to their relations behaved like overgrown infants, knew nothing and acted most unreasonably. They had a " baby language " of their own and had to relearn everything. There were three chief officers in Ndembo and they opened the Lodge with quite an elaborate prayer or invocation to the spirits.

1. Thos. Winterbottom, " An Account of the Native Africans in the Neighbourhood of Sierra Leone " (London, 1803). pp. 137 sq.
2. Dr. Bentley, " Pioneering in the Congo." Vol. I. pp. 282 sq.
    J. H. Weeks, " Among the Primitive Bakonga," pp. 172 sq.

THE THREE CHIEF OFFICERS IN A NDEMBO LODGE

There are five grades and three degrees in a Ndembo Lodge—
1. The Master.
2. The Officers.
3. The old members, initiated at a previous meeting.
4. Initiates who come voluntarily.
5. Initiates who are impressed.

The three degrees are represented by Nos. 3, 4 and 5, but the officers and Master also constitute, according to Mr. C. L. Claridge[1] two distinct grades.

It must be remembered that a Ndembo Lodge is usually opened to avert some outbreak of disease, or other disaster, which has overtaken the whole community, and if enough volunteers do not come forward the old members (Grade 3) do not hesitate to impress additional candidates by knocking them on the head and carrying them unconscious into the Lodge. In addition to the Master there are two particularly important officers who, with the Master, seem to approximate to the position held by the three Principals in a R.A. Chapter rather than to the W.M., S.W. and J.W. in a Craft Lodge. This fact is indicated by the prayer which is recited by these three before they attempt to open Lodge.

It is addressed to the fetish Nkita, the Demons of Destruction, who distort and twist things and are considered responsible for plagues, etc.

It begins thus:—" O, living mystery, Nkita of Destruction, shells[a] which never turn their faces upward. O Priest where is the remedy ? I was in trouble, seize upon all outsiders.[b] . . . . O, Nlaza, do not cripple me. I am thy child with the freedom of the family[c] (diavulunga, diavulunga) . . . . I, innocent with nothing to confess. Since you would destroy me, you destroy your own little animal . . . . I am the maker of the Lodge (Masamba), O Ndembo, I am Ndundu, the wrestler. I am Mvemba of Ndundu who gives birth to monsters.

You are Mfuma (the hollow in trees) where pigs die, where goats die as peace offerings, where the pig is the coverer of secrets (sins), where fowls are as plentiful as their feathers (i.e., as offerings). O Nkumbu and Ngazi! O lubonga lua ngazi! Though your chair become small as if dead, we will sit on it a hundred

---

1. C. Cyril Claridge. " Wild Bush Tribes of Tropical Africa."
(a) The evil spirits, Nkita, (a plural word) are supposed to live in shells and unless the mouth of these can be found it is impossible to destroy the spirits or drive them away from their dens.
(b) i.e. impress outsiders and compel them to come into the secret society because Nkita will not harm those who are members thereof, and thus the plague will be stayed.
(c) The principals remind the Nkita that they are blood brothers and so they cannot ignore their appeal or harm them.

times with blessings.   I shall not sleep hungry in trusting Mvemba and Nlaza.   Here I conclude.   Let Kkita be exalted.   It is Imvemba. . . . . ."[1]

Mr. Claridge elsewhere in his book points out the striking similarity which exists between the ancient Babylonian beliefs and those of the Congo natives, and in this prayer there is more than a superficial resemblance in phrases to certain parts of the Babylonian version of the legend of the Deluge. Mr. Claridge says that each of the three repeats this prayer kneeling, with his hands behind his back; he simplifies and explains its purpose thus:[2]

" The three mentioned have suffered or are suffering some misfortune, which necessitates Ndembo being opened for their benefit. They are guilty before the Nkita (spirits). To remove this guilt and the misfortune, they appeal to the Nkita. The first thing is to kill a goat—a peace offering, the guilt bearer— Nkombo a Maboko. After this they are entitled to plead their innocence. They implore the Nkita to stay their anger. They have already suffered. Is it not enough ? Is it the will of the *Nkita* to destroy them outright ? *Mvemba* and *Nlaza* are rich, powerful, abounding in blessings. Why not compel all without to come in and trust so mighty a union in whom repose a hundred blessings ? "

It should be noted that all prayers and offerings made by the Congo native are addressed either to the powers of evil or to the fairies and elemental spirits who preside over the elements, forests, etc., and sometimes, apparently, to the spirits of the dead,—never to God. Yet, they believe that there is a God, the Creator, good and kind, loving and just, only since He will never do them any ill they do not trouble to worship Him.

Before leaving Africa it seems desirable to give in outline a summary of one of the most important rites of initiation of a boy into manhood, which clearly conveys a symbolic death and resurrection. We will therefore conclude this section with an account of the Yao rites which has not previously appeared in print elsewhere.

The Yao Rites

The Wa Yao, a Bantu tribe inhabiting a large area to the East of Lake Nyasa, still observe annually their ancient initiation ceremonies (*unyago*). These rites have been studied by Major Sanderson, Medical Officer of Health for Zomba, Nyasaland, who, I may mention, has not only been accepted by these natives as an initiate, but has been admitted into the jealously guarded order of *Amichila* or " Masters of the Ceremonies."

---

1.   C. C. Claridge, " The Wild Bush Tribes of Tropical Africa." p. 284.
2.   Ibid. p. 285.

Major Sanderson intends to publish a monograph on these rites on account of their anthropological interest, but he has kindly furnished me with the following notes and allowed me to use some of his illustrations as additional proof of the contention that our masonic rites are descended from the initiatory ceremonies of our savage ancestors.

He writes:—

"It is, of course, impossible to describe adequately even a part of the ceremonies in a few words, as they are most elaborate and occupy a period of about two months. Masonically, the rites observed on the last day are of most interest.

When all the boys are healed (after circumcision) the Amichila (Master of the Ceremonies) and his assistants prepare a series of drawings (inyago); these are drawn on the ground with specially prepared flour, after having been carefully modelled in earth. They vary in number, and to a certain extent in character, according to the number of initiates, the amount of material supplied and the skill and inclination of the M.C. Some, however, are never omitted and vary only in the amount of surrounding decoration, and of these the accompanying sketches are specimens: they have been carefully drawn to scale, but as this will probably be altered in reproduction I should mention that the *Namungumi*, for instance, from which I made the sketch was 30 feet long.

The pictures extend in a line, East and West. The first or most Westerly is always *Namungumi* and the last is always the *Ching'undang'unda* mound, the seat of the M.C. in the East. The former represents a water animal with a fish's tail and decorated with mammae, strongly reminiscent of the Egyptian TA-URT; at each side is a human figure with upraised arms, simulating a certain sign. Sometimes next to this, but sometimes towards the eastern end of the line, is the *Crocodile and the Moon*: the situation of this picture is always commented on—that ' this year the moon has risen at Namungumi ' or ' at Ching'unda ' as the case may be. The Crocodile and Moon are always drawn together and the concavity of the crescent is always towards the crocodile's head, which brings to one's mind the ancient Egyptian conception of a crocodile below the horizon, gradually eating away the waning moon. This can hardly be mere coincidence, and may indicate a common origin.

Near the water monster (or ' mother ') is a hole dug to the shape of a man, in which a man lies, covered with a cloth, and answers questions or sings. Sometimes this is replaced by a carefully concealed subterranean chamber in which several men hide for a similar purpose. In either case the picture (or site) is called *Chiuta*, which is not a Yao word, but occurs in neighbouring languages as a name for God, especially as manifested by the rainbow. This figure also has upraised arms. Being struck by this I asked if the figure were always so drawn; the reply was ' Of course, because it is a man. A woman would have the arms down.'

Another picture obviously represents the male and female elements in nature, and is probably constructed as a magical means of conferring fertility on the initiates (compare the constant recurrence of the word ' strength ' in Masonry, especially in association with the phallic emblem of a pillar).

The *Ching'undang'unda* is undoubtedly the replica of the sacred mountain so common in primitive religion; the pole at the apex is noteworthy as it evidently represents a tree. It should be mentioned that the Wa Yao have a tradition that they sprang from a conical hill called Yao, and the resemblance between this word and the name of the Phoenician god Iau, who was, I believe, a mountain god, opens up a fascinating speculation.

Round this mound is a bank about a foot high, and the seat of the M.C. is on the west side of this, distinguished by a special extension of the drawing. Here he marks each initiate on the forehead with sacred flour. The hill is solemnly perambulated, usually seven times, by the initiates, against the sun, as among the Arabs.

Immediately before the initiates, passing from West to East, reach the hill, they have to pass through a fire and between two poles—obviously a purificatory ceremony.

Through the whole of the ceremonies on this day the boys are covered from head to foot with cloaks made of bark-cloth, rendering them quite unrecognizable.

In conclusion I should mention that on the first day, during the very solemn rite of planting the lupanda, the centre of the ceremonies, on the proper preparation of which the success of the whole *unyago* depends,—the M.C. makes the h........g s....n with one arm, the other hand being placed on the ground at the foot of the *lupanda*[a] mound."

The above account has been given verbatim and I must express my gratitude to Major Sanderson for giving me this information in advance of the publication of his work; not every anthropologist would have been so courteous. When Major Sanderson's monograph appears, it will be worthy of careful perusal, for it will contain many additional details.

(1)   We find the H.S. of a F.C. and the sign of G. & D.

(*a*)   This is the pole on the artificial hill and if it should fall down during any part of the ceremony it is believed that the initiates will die.

associated here in Africa, just as we have shown them to be in the hieroglyphics of Easter Island, and they are also found in Central America. The Dervishes likewise use the same pair of signs. Thus we see that this pair can be traced in association right round the world. This is most significant.

(2) The "tracing boards" are most important. If we take the essential four and the mound, we obtain a summary, as it were, of our three Craft degrees and of the journey through the Underworld.

Thus the tracing board which depicts the Vesica Piscis and the Phallus, corresponds in some measure with the first degree, or degree of birth.

The Water-Mother is clearly similar to the Preserver, who is the God of Water, hence Life. The Crocodile and the Moon are also probably connected with the degree of Life, while the grave can have but one original meaning, namely, that the God died and yet lives and answers us, and therefore we may hope to survive death. The importance of the appeal made to the Water Mother by the little figures, who appear to be cut in half, and the sign made by the " grave " will not be lost on my readers.

(3) The journey round the Sacred Mountain, reverse way to the Sun, reminds us of the R.O.S., and of the fact that the " Manes " go W.S.E.N. and shows that the initiates are supposed to be dead and are gradually ascending from the " earth plane " towards heaven and the abode of the Gods.

(4) The purification by fire and the two pillars, will interest not only all Masons but even more, all Rosicrucians. It also calls to mind various fire ceremonies, more especially those among the Australian bushman.

(5) The pole on the top of the mound cannot fail to remind us of the " Tree " on Mount Calvary, and the tree of the Attis rites.

Thus we see that in these primitive rites in Nyasaland we have an epitome of all the Mysteries, and of our own Free-masonry, under which latter name I specifically include certain of the " Higher Degrees."

(6) With regard to Major Sanderson's statement that the figures in the " Water-Mother Tracing Board " and the " Grave " were men because the arms were up, whereas if they had been women they would have been by the side, I would draw my readers' attention to the fact that in British East Africa when the boy comes for circumcision his arms are held in the peculiarly strained position depicted in the Yao pictures. What, however, bears strongly on this point is that the girls at puberty have a somewhat similar operation performed on them, but the girl lies flat on her back with her arms by her side. Hence the Wa Yao's answer—" If it had been a woman, the arms would be

by the side "—is significant, though probably they themselves no longer understand the real reason.

NORTH AMERICA

Among the Red Indians there are still numerous traces of death and resurrection rites, and in former days these were far more widespread than they are now.[1] It is well known, moreover, that they have a complete sign language by means of which tribes who cannot speak each other's language can, nevertheless, carry on quite a lengthy conversation. In addition they have certain secret and " sacred " signs connected with their initiation rites which would instantly be recognised by a mason. Among these are the lion's grip and 5 points, two signs of the Rose Croix, a sign of the I.M., and others.

Among the Dacotas the ceremony is as follows:—The candidate is given a vapour bath for four days and is then led to the appointed spot and stands upright, while behind him is an older man. The medicine man or Master approaches him holding the medicine bag in his hand and points at " a painted spot on the breast of the candidate, at which the *tonwan* (magic influence) is discharged." At this the man behind him gives the candidate a push and he falls down " dead " and is covered with blankets. Those present dance round the corpse chanting, the master pulls off the blanket, then, " chewing a piece of bone of the Onktehi, spits it over him and he begins to show signs of returning life." Finally the victim spits out of his mouth a small shell, which is carefully caught in a bag, and he is then restored to life and acknowledged a member of the Society of Medicine Men.[2]

Similar rites occur among the Niska Indians of British Columbia and when a man is being initiated into a certain secret society, the Olala, the members pretend to kill him with their knives. Really, however, they cut off the head of a dummy while he slips quietly away. The headless dummy is then solemnly burnt while the women wail and mourn for the " dead " man. For a year the initiate remains hidden in the forest, at the end of which period he re-enters the village riding on an artificial animal.[3]

Among the Toukaway Indians of Texas the initiate is buried in a " grave " and dug up and restored to life by a pack of men disguised as wolves.[4]

1. Frazer, " Balder the Beautiful," Vol. II. p. 268.
   H. R. Schoolcraft, " Indian Tribes of the United States," III., 287 and V. 430.
2. G. H. Pond, " Dakota Superstitions," Collections of the Minnesota Historical Society for the year 1867 (St. Paul, 1867). pp. 35 sq.
3. Franz Boaz in tenth Report of the North-western Tribes of Canada, pp. 49 sq., 58 sq.
4. H. R. Schoolcraft, " Indian Tribes of the United States." (Philadelphia, 1853-56). V. 683.

The most interesting of all these ceremonies, however, is that of the Carrier Indians, when they initiate a man into the " Darding Knife " totem. A lance is so arranged that its steel tip, if pressed, instead of remaining firm, slides back into the shaft. The candidate having previously filled his mouth with blood, a member presses the lance against his bare breast which seems to enter his body up to the shaft. He falls to the floor as if dead, and from his mouth pours forth blood which makes it appear as if he has really been stabbed.

One of the members then begins to chant a magic hymn, under whose influence the " dead man " is slowly revived.[1]

In view of these rites my readers should bear in mind the fact that in the 16th century the Mexicans still sacrificed men as representatives of the gods. Among them was one who represented Quetzalcoatl, the god who wore ears of corn in his hair, and most closely corresponds with the Preserver in other lands. Many curious legends are told concerning this god, who, according to one account, was slain by three of the other gods. He also fought against a great giant who wounded him in the foot near to a fall of water, and in " Freemasonry and the Ancient Gods " is an illustration depicting him at the moment he was wounded, wearing maize in his hair and making the sign of Preservation.[2] After his death he rose again and ascended into heaven, where he reigns in that bright morning star, Venus, whose coming heralds the dawn. He also made the sign of despair which we so often find associated with the Dying God.[3] It is, therefore, a significant fact that every year a man was chosen forty days before the date of the festival to represent this god and was clothed in his regalia, which included a sceptre shaped like a sickle. He was first bathed in a lake and then robed in the royal and divine robes. At the end of his forty days he was slain by having his heart torn from his body, which latter the worshippers subsequently ate.[4]

When we turn to North America we find definite traces of similar sacrifices, but perhaps it is from the legends we obtain the clearest evidence of their original meaning. Most of my readers know Longfellow's great poem, " Hiawatha." Although the poet has embroidered the story and incorporated into it legends which originally were entirely separate, the framework is old and genuine, and was derived mainly from two works by H. R. Schoolcraft (1793-1864), " The Algic Researches " and " History of the Indian Tribes."

In this epic, Hiawatha is a hero who helped the Redskins to

1. A. G. Morice, " Notes, Archæological, industrial and sociological, on the Western Denes," Transactions of the Canadian Institute IV. (1892-3) pp. 203 sq.
2. Ward, " Freemasonry and the Ancient Gods," op. p. 110.
3. See Ibid. p. 110.
4. J. de Acosta, " The Natural and Moral History of the Indies." (Hakluyt Society, London, 1880). Vol. II. pp. 384-386.

master the forces of nature and taught them how to grow maize. In order to acquire this secret, he wrestled four times with Mondamin, the Spirit of the Maize, and slew and buried him. In due course, from the grave came up a green shoot which developed into the maize. In this story there is no hint that Hiawatha is a " villain," nay, he is the bestower of blessings on his people in that he slew the maize spirit. Moreover, although they play no part in the slaying of Mondamin, it is noticeable that Hiawatha has two intimate friends and that in one of his adventures he was swallowed in his bark canoe by a huge fish, and yet came forth alive. In his struggle with Pau-Puk-Keewis, the latter, like Taliesen, migrates from body to body. Finally Hiawatha departs in his boat towards the West, sailing into the sunset, like Baldur:—

With facts like these before us, can we have any doubt that among the Red Indians their resurrection rites are intimately blended with the slaying of the God of Vegetation or Fertility ?

AMONG CIVILISED RACES

In the rites of Isis we know from the accounts of Appulius that the candidate passed through the similitude of death.[1]

In the Orphic mysteries we know that the death and resurrection of Dionysius was dramatically enacted by the Cretans,[2] while in the Eleusinian mysteries there was the drama of Ceres searching for her lost daughter, which is but another form of the Death and Resurrection rite.

In the Mithraic rites we have definite evidence that the pretence of slaying a man[3] formed the central theme of the ceremonies, while, of course, the central feature of the Attic cult was a dramatic representation of the death and resurrection of Attis, which took place at the Hilaria, and to which we have already referred.[4]

We thus see that initiation rites of death and resurrection are world-wide and, whatever may have been their origin, as men evolved the opportunity offered thereby to the more spiritual minded was too obvious to be missed. Thus in time, they developed into a means of teaching the sure and certain hope of the Resurrection, and supplied an opportunity for inculcating the most exalted moral teaching.

The strangest fact, to my mind, which emerges from the study of primitive religious beliefs is that the particular religion of the day seldom proclaims a higher moral code than that already

1. Apulius " Metamorphosis."
2. Firmicus Maternus. De Errore, p. 84.
3. Franz Cumont, " Textes et Monuments figures relatifs aux mysteres de Mithra," (Brussels, 1896), and " Commodus." 9.
4. S. R. Farnell, " Cults of the Greek States " (1906) III. 299 sq.

held by the worshippers.   If anything, it perpetuates barbaric customs which are clearly repugnant to the higher conceptions of right and wrong which are gradually evolving.   Thus, after having performed a series of most ghastly human sacrifices, terminating with a cannibalistic feast, the priests of Ancient Mexico would solemnly preach a sermon inculcating a most exalted moral code.   They laid it down that their flock must be kind and charitable, must lead a humble, quiet life, most abhor evil and cling to the good, finally warning them of the doom of the wicked hereafter, while painting in glowing terms the joys of Paradise.[1]

Where did the Mexican priest learn such moral lessons ? Not from the ghastly ceremony in which he had just taken part. Does it not show that the Supreme Master of All does send down messages of light to even his most backward children, and thereby leads them on from stage to stage of True Knowledge ?

1.   Frazer, " The Scapegoat," p. 299.

CHAPTER XXI

CEREMONIES OF RE-BIRTH

We have seen that Divine Kings were regularly slain and that their souls were transferred to the body of a successor. The manner in which this transference was brought about is of particular interest to Freemasons, and I therefore append examples drawn from various countries on which but little comment should be necessary.

Among the Nias, a tribe who inhabit the East Indies, the son of a dying chief must suck in his father's last breath.[1] Among the Indians of Florida, if a woman dies while giving birth to a child the latter is held over her face so as to catch her departing soul.[2] Even the Romans had a similar practice, for when a friend was dying they caught his last breath in their mouth,[3] and a similar practice survived in Lancashire as late as 1882.[4] As it is to Lancashire that we owe the survival of many interesting Masonic degrees this last fact is striking, for it is obvious that the way in which a cand. is r. in our 3,° necessitates a similar process.

In Uganda, a priest had to drink out of the skull of the dead King, and this act transferred to him the royal soul. It was believed that henceforth from time to time the dead King spake through this priest into whom he had entered.[5] This custom reminds us of a former custom among the Masonic Order of Knights Templar where the candidate had to drink from a skull.

The Hausa people of Northern Nigeria have many customs reminiscent of Freemasonry, among which is the use of the Lion's Grip and the f.p.o.f. In the Hausa kingdom of Daura the old king was regularly put to death as soon as he showed symptoms of declining health, and his successor had ceremonially to step over his corpse.[6] Now in a certain Provincial Lodge a similar custom prevails in a certain Craft degree. This way of encouraging a soul to be reborn is exceedingly widespread. Thus the Huron Indians consider that a child who dies should have as early

---

1. Frazer, " The Dying God." 3rd ed., p. 199.
2. D. G. Brinton, " Myths of the New World." (New York, 1876), pp. 270.
3. Servius on " Virgil Aen." IV. p. 685.
4. Q. Harland and T. T. Wilkinson, " Lancashire Folklore." (1882). pp. 7. sq.
5. Frazer, Ibid. p. 201, quoting the Rev. J. Roscoe.
6. Frazer, " Totemism and Exogamy." II. 608.

an opportunity of being reborn as possible, so they do not bury young children as they do adults, but place them in a hole near a path, so that the spirit may re-enter the womb of a woman who chances to pass near by.[1]

The same idea is found among the tribes of the Lower Congo, who bury the body of a young child near its mother's hut hoping that its soul will soon re-enter her womb and be reborn, for they believe that " the only new thing about a child is its body. The spirit is old and formerly belonged to some deceased person, or it may have the spirit of a living person." In the latter case the living person will soon die since he has lost his soul.[2]

In the Northern Congo, a Belgian Official one day found a Bangala woman digging a hole in the road. He was inclined to stop her, till her husband explained the reason. She wanted to raise the body of her firstborn in order that his soul might enter into her and she might once more become a mother. At length she uncovered the skeleton, and *raising it in her arms, embraced it*, humbly begging the dead child to enter into her again. I am glad to say the Official did not even smile at the sad little drama.[3]

In Uganda the Bagishu bury the corpse of anyone whom they desire reborn in their household close under the eaves.[4] In Northern India infants are buried under the threshold of the huts so that they may be reborn in their former mothers,[5] and the same custom is found throughout many other areas of India. In every case it is deliberately done to facilitate an early re-birth.

Moreover, while the Hindoos burn adults who die, they make a rule of burying infants, because, as the little ones have had so short a life on earth, they feel that they ought to have a chance of returning again as quickly as possible.[6]

There are cases on record in India of a barren woman murdering a male child in order that its soul might enter into her. To make sure that this would happen the woman usually bathed over the body of the child, or in its blood.[7]

We thus see that the idea of slaying a Priest-king in order that his soul may enter into another human body, perhaps into

1. " Relations des Jesuits." (1636), p. 130, reprinted Quebec, 1858.
2. Rev. John H. Weeks, " Notes on some Customs of the Lower Congo People." Folklore. XIX (1908) p. 422.
3. Th. Masui, " Guide de la Section de l'Etat Indépendent du Congo à l'Exposition de Bruxelles—Tervueren en 1897." (Brussels, 1897). pp. 113. sq.
4. J. B. Purvis, " Through Uganda to Mount Elgon." (London, 1909) pp. 302 sq.
5. W. Crooke, " Natives of Northern India." (London, 1907) p. 202.
6. Frazer, " Adonis, Attis, Osiris." 3rd ed., I. p. 94 sq.
7. W. Crooke, " Natives of Northern India," p. 202.
    " Census of India " (1901). Vol. xvii. " Punjab." Part I. pp. 213 sq.

that of his actual murderer, is in conformity with primitive ideas on re-incarnation and re-birth.

We have records, however, of an extraordinarily interesting ceremony which was regularly performed by the Red Skin tribe of Attinoindarons when they wished to transfer the soul of a dead warrior of outstanding merit to a living man, and so enable the tribe to retain his services. After a short time had elapsed from the death of the hero, they chose the best man in the tribe and then, " all standing up, except him who is to be resuscitated, to whom they give the name of the deceased, and all letting their hands down very low, they pretend to lift him up from the earth, intending by that to signify that they draw the great personage deceased from the grave and restore him to live in the person of the other, who stands up and, after great acclamation of the people, receives the presents which the bystanders offer him." Henceforth this man loses his old name and bears that of the dead hero. A similar ceremony also took place among the Hurons.[1]

But the real key to our problem lies hidden in the humble sprig of acacia. We have seen that among the Jews a bough was used to transfer the soul of the dead Tammuz to his successor. Primitive races hold that after burial the soul of a dead man enters into a plant, which usually grows from or near the grave, and that it waits in that·plant for a convenient opportunity to re-enter mortal life, by entering into the womb of a woman in the form of a tiny embryo. This belief is widespread in Australia and New Guinea, but it is by no means confined to these primitive races. The Baganda in like manner believe that the souls of the dead enter into trees, particularly into the banana tree, so much so that if the purple blossom of a banana happens to fall on the head of an unmarried woman she thinks that, despite her unmarried state, she will bring forth a child.[2] Many other races think that by eating a fruit in which a spirit is lodged a woman may become pregnant. For example, among the South Slavs a barren woman will go to the grave of one who died pregnant and beg to be given that which lies in her womb. She will then eat some of the grass from the grave.[3]

We find, however, that the doctrine of the transmigration of souls into plants was widespread among far more civilised races. Among the Greeks it was particularly strong, and as this race adopted the modified cult of Adonis a few examples from their legends may be of interest.

Apollo, unfortunately, accidentally killed his friend Hyacin-

1. J. F. Lafitau, " Moeurs des sauvages ameriquains." (Paris, 1724). II. 434.
2. Rev. J. Roscoe, " The Baganda." (1911). pp. 126 sq.
3. F. S. Krauss, " Sitte und Branuch de Sud-Slaven." (Vienna, 1885). p. 531.

thus, and having failed to restore him to life changed him into
the flower named Hyacinth.   Another friend of his accidentally
killed one of Apollo's stags and this sacrilege so troubled him
that he pined away and died, whereupon Apollo changed him
into a Cypress. [1]

Apollo loved the maiden Daphne, who fled from him, and
just as Apollo was on the point of capturing her she prayed to the
gods for aid, who changed her into a laurel bush. [2]

Helios, the Sun, at first loved Clytie, but afterwards forsook
her for Leucothea, whom her father, Onchamus, king of the
Eastern lands, buried alive as punishment.   Helios, after trying
to restore her to life, sprinkled her grave with nectar, and immediately there sprang up a bush of frankincense.   Clytie, unable
to regain the love of Helios threw herself on her back on the
ground and refused to move.   For nine days she turned her face
as the sun sped across the sky, hoping that he would relent, till
on the tenth her limbs became rooted to the spot and she was
changed into a sun-flower. [3]

In this story my readers should note that the king who slew
Leucothea was King of the Eastern lands, and remember the
point of the compass where Hiram met his fate.

Many more examples could be given, but instead we will
conclude this section with an account of what happened to
Aeneas.   He landed in Thrace and was about to found a city
when he tried to pluck " a green-leafed sapling " and the broken
bough dropped blood.   He tore a second sapling from the soil,
and again it bled.   Yet a third time he tugged at another bough,
whereupon a voice cried out from the ground and said that it
was the spirit of Polydorus, who had been murdered, which was
speaking.   This man had been murdered by the King of Thrace
and secretly buried in this spot. [4]

The similarity between this legend and that associated with
the sprig of acacia has been noted by several masonic writers,
some going so far as to say that the masonic legend must have
been copied direct from this one.   There is nothing, however, to
justify the assumption.   What these writers did not realise is
that primitive man, as we have seen, habitually thought that the
souls of the dead entered into the trees or plants which grew from
their graves.   If, then, a man had been murdered was it surprising
that his ghost should tell the fact from the tree ?

Even in England a similar belief was once held, and is clearly
brought out in the following folk song, which is regularly taught
to-day as a folk game to children in schools.

---

1.   E. M. Berens, " Myths and Legends of Ancient Greece and Rome."
       p. 73.
2.   Ibid. p. 74.
3.   Ibid. pp. 63-64.
4.   Virgil Aen. III. 1. 119.

OLD ROGER IS DEAD[1]

Old Roger is dead and he lies in his grave,
Lies in his grave, lies in his grave,
Old Roger is dead and he lies in his grave,
Hey ! hi ! lies in his grave.

They planted an apple tree over his head,
Over his head, over his head,
They planted an apple tree over his head,
Hey ! hi ! over his head.

The apples they grew and they dropped off the tree,
Dropped off the tree, dropped off the tree,
The apples they grew and they dropped off the tree,
Hey ! hi ! dropped off the tree.

There came an old woman who picked them all up,
Picked them all up, picked them all up,
There came an old woman who picked them all up,
Hey ! hi ! picked them all up.

Old Roger got up and he gave her a knock,
Gave her a knock, gave her a knock,
Old Roger got up and he gave her a knock,
Hey! hi ! gave her a knock.

This made the old woman go lippety-lop,
Lippety-lop, lippety-lop,
This made the old woman go lippety-lop,
Hey ! hi ! lippety-lop.

The old man's soul had passed into the apple tree and was particularly deposited in its fruit, the apples, but why did he jump up out of his grave and beat the old woman ? Clearly the reason was that being old she could not bring forth a child, and so, by taking the apples to which his embryo soul clung, she was depriving him of the opportunity of re-birth. Had she been a young woman who was capable of bearing a child I trow, he would not have driven her away from the grave.

In the entry of Taliesen into the witch we see the same principle. When she swallowed the grain she swallowed his soul, and therefore became pregnant. As previously shown the wicked wife in the Egyptian story of the two brothers became pregnant when a chip of the acacia tree entered her mouth, and the son she bore was the younger brother, whose soul had temporarily rested in the acacia tree and who by this accident was able to gain re-birth.

In the story of Osiris, Isis cuts down the Tamarisk and

---

1. Mrs. F. Kirk, " Old English Games and Physical Exercises."

recovers therefrom the body of Osiris, and ultimately restores to that body the soul of the god which had returned to the tree.

In the case of Tammuz, and later of Hiram, the divine soul of the dead man was transferred to his successor by plucking up the branch, or by sniffing it, the essential factor in either case being physical contact with the tree into which the soul had migrated.   Probably in the Hiramic legend originally the plucked acacia spoke and revealed the tragedy, just as the bush did to Virgil, but the 18th century revisors may have thought that this was " too far-fetched " and so gave the " practical " explanation we now have.   In this way the original idea became obscured, for the plucking of the acacia did not cause the discovery of the crime, but enabled the soul of the dead god to be transferred to a new human body.

From what has been written above it will be clear that the doctrine of re-incarnation is not, as many suppose, peculiar to the Hindoos and Buddhists.   On the contrary, it is universally accepted by all primitive people, and was held by most of the nations of the classical period.   Among the Australian blacks it is one of the few beliefs about which they are perfectly definite, and they even go so far as to identify living people as re-incarnations of dead members of the tribe.   Nor is this identification restricted to their own race; on the contrary, many white men have been considerably embarrassed by being " recognised " as the dead relative of some humble Australian black.

The late Sir George Grey tells a moving story of his own identification by a very dirty, old, black woman, who claimed him as her own dead son.   The old woman hobbled up to the party of explorers crying, " Yes, yes, in truth it is him," threw her arms round him, and sobbed with joy at having re-discovered her long dead son.   She then kissed him on the cheeks and introduced his black sister and brothers.   Finally there came up an old man, the woman's husband, who considered that he was the father of Sir George. What followed deserves to be given in Sir George's own words.

" My brothers and father came up and embraced me after their manner,—that is, they threw their arms round my waist, placed their right knee against my right knee, and their breast against my breast, and held me in this way for several minutes." He concludes with the words, " I feel firmly convinced that she really believed I was her son, whose first thought on return to earth had been to revisit his old mother."[1]

We may smile at the old, black woman if we like, but can we definitely say she was wrong ?   Whence we come and whither we go is still largely a mystery, so let us copy the kindly attitude of Sir George and do nothing to hurt the feelings of others on this problem, even if we do not agree with them.

---

1.   George Grey, " Journals of two Expeditions of Discovery in North West and Western Australia." (London, 1841).   I. 301-303.

CHAPTER XXII

THE SURVIVAL OF THE OLD ADONIS SYMBOLS

It is truly amazing to find how the old Adonis symbols have survived in modern Speculative Freemasonry. It would not be difficult to explain the presence of one or two of them, but when we find the vast number of symbols and incidents which we know to be part of the Adonis cult, and which are even to-day venerated by us, few can doubt that they have come down to us direct from the original source.

Let us take, for example, the double-headed Eagle of the Kadosh. We have seen that this emblem is sculptured at Boghaz-Keui, bearing on its back two goddesses, who form part of the procession of the Dying God. It is, of course, easy to say that the 33rd degree derived it via Frederick the Great, from the Hapsburg double eagle. That this in turn was taken over from the Crusaders, who copied it from the Seljuk Sultans, who originally adopted it because they saw it carved on the ruins of Hittite buildings. All this sounds plausible enough, but it quite fails to explain why Frederick should foist into a Masonic degree the crest of his enemies the Hapsburgs. For note, it is not the single-headed eagle of the Roman Empire, but this double-headed Hittite symbol which is the badge of the Supreme Council. Neither does it explain why this double-headed eagle should be worn by the Knights *Kadosh*, or 30th degree.

Kadosh is a Syrian word meaning " sacred," and was, as we have seen, the title of the sacred men and women dedicated to Astarte and Tammuz, the equivalent of the Galli of Cybele. These men were viewed with disfavour by the zealous monotheistic worshippers of Jehovah and were expelled from the Temple by King Josiah, therefore to orthodox Jewish tradition they were anathema. Yet we have their name given to a body of Masons, whose emblem is the same as that on which the twin goddesses ride in the rock temple of the Dying God at Boghaz-Keui.

The combination of name and symbol is thus perfectly correct, and we are driven to the conclusion that they have both descended together to us, not that they were fortuitously brought together by Frederick the Great in the 18th century. Indeed, it is very doubtful whether Frederick ever had any prominent part in moulding even the present form of the A. and A. Rite, whose organisation appears to be derived from French, rather than from German, sources, although much of the material is undoubtedly far older than the date when the degrees were arranged into their present series.

In like manner we find the origin of the " Eagle's Claw," and the " Lion's Grip " in this vast rock-hewn temple at Boghaz-Keui. The Eagle's Claw obviously links up with that double-headed eagle, while the lion's grip is derived from the lion form of the god Tammuz, the son of the lion-goddess, Astarte. At Boghaz-Keui we have seen the god in both his animal and human form, and can therefore understand how it was that the lion god who was slain and rose again could, by his lion grip, draw forth the soul of his priest from his mangled body, and raise him to life eternal. There is no need to go to Egypt and force a somewhat fanciful connection with the sign Leo for the origin of our use of the name. It is true that Ra was known as the god in the lion form, but it was not he, but the jackal god, Anubis, assisted by Horus, who raised Osiris. It seems more probable that the Egyptians borrowed this grip from the Syrian cult than that the reverse process took place, although in view of its wide distribution among races who knew neither Egypt nor Syria, such as the Red Indians and the Australian Blacks, we must be on our guard against hastily assuming that either of these great religious centres borrowed from the other on this point. It is just as likely that in Egypt and Syria alike it evolved independently from a more primitive form of Initiation.

The title, however, is clearly associated with Tammuz, the lion god, and not with Anubis, the jackal god of Egypt. One thing is quite obvious, the name of the lion grip cannot be derived from the way in which a lion seizes its prey, and this shows that it must be derived from the time when a lion-man enacted the part of the raiser. It should be noted that on a vase found at Chama, Mexico, one of the chief officers who is advancing to instruct a candidate wears the skin of a jaguar, the emblem of Quetzalcoatl, who in Mexico represents the Dying God. Neither can we overlook the fact that, according to legends, Vishnu, the dying god in India, once assumed the lion form. So far as the name of the Eagle's grip is concerned, this might have originated from a supposed similarity to the manner in which an eagle grips its prey, but in view of the presence of the double-headed eagle at Boghaz-Keui it seems more probable that it is derived from that symbolical bird. We must not forget the eagle which is flying up above the head of the Babylonian god who is descending into the Underworld.

At first sight all our working tools appear to owe their presence in our ceremonies to their use by masons, but a closer study of the subject makes it seem very doubtful whether they really originated in that way. The fact that they were mason's tools no doubt helped to perpetuate them in the lodge long after their origin had been forgotten, and led to their number being increased so as to produce, as far as possible, a complete set, but as to origin the following facts are suggestive of a much greater antiquity.

We have seen that the Australian blacks use a chisel and

hammer with which to knock out a tooth of a candidate during initiation, one tooth being thus sacrificed to save the others. These blacks do no building even with wood, and yet we can truthfully say that the gavel and chisel are the working tools of such a " lodge." Even the custom of knocking to call to order finds its counterpart in the Jamba ceremony described on page 206. The hollow log which gives its name to the degree being repeatedly struck by the Master.

The square was the emblem of Nabu, the architect god of the Babylonians. His square is itself somewhat peculiar and consists of a right angled triangle, 3 x 4 x 5.[1] In other words, the old Operative secret of the three rods. Now it was this god, as represented by the High Priest, who descended into the Underworld to rescue therefrom Marduk, impersonated by the King of Babylon.[2] May it not be that this is the true origin of the square ? The square in any case has been widely recognised as the emblem of justice, and in the Egyptian papyri the judges in the Underworld are depicted sitting on squares. Perhaps, therefore, the descent of Nabu to rescue Marduk implies the descent of the just judge to try him, and that the god having been wrongfully detained was acquitted and released by Nabu.

As our ceremonies are derived from Syria this suggestion deserves careful consideration.

As to the twenty-four inch gauge, the explanation of its meaning now given is extremely weak, for you to not use a foot rule to measure time. The original purpose was undoubtedly to measure the candidate or his shadow, this done, the measure was thought to attach to itself some of the life principle of the candidate, and if it was subsequently destroyed or buried underneath the foundation of the building, the man thus measured, according to popular beliefs, would die. The measure was thus intended to catch the soul or life of the candidate and hold it hostage for his fidelity. A similar measure also occurs in the ritual of the Hung Society, which lays no claim to consist of masons, and we thus see that four characteristic Masonic tools have an origin quite distinct from their use as working tools. Even the pencil is but a substitute for the pen of the recording god. It is not confined to the pen of Thoth, so well known to all students of the Egyptian Mysteries, but is found also in the ritual of the Hung Society.

The two pillars we have traced back to Syria, and have shown that the description of them as given in the ritual is nearer the truth than that which now stands in the Bible. We have seen that they were merely gigantic phalli, and that examples existed outside at least two of the great temples of Astarte, namely, those at Paphos and Hierapolis. Of the latter we are specifically told by Lucian that the pillars were hollow so that a priest could

---

1. For illustration see the Babylonian Legend of Creation. Brit. Mus.
2. See page 28.

twice a year climb up inside them. Josephus tells us, moreover, that a similar phallus or pillar stood in the temple of Melcarth in Tyre.[1] There can thus be no doubt as to their original meaning, and whence they were derived. The suggestion that they represent the two pole stars may be dismissed at once, for there is no South Pole Star at all. My readers may wonder why two phalli were required. The phallus symbolises birth or re-birth, and the twin phalli arranged on either side of the door at the East end of the temple of Solomon represent the pillars of the dawn, through which the risen Tammuz must pass. The fact that these pillars were phalli symbolises the re-birth or resurrection of the god.

The three villains apparently do not appear in the Syrian legends, but neither do they in that of Osiris. He was slain by Set, and some seventy-two others. In Mexico, we find, however, that it was three gods who plotted the downfall of Quetzalcoatl, and Hiawatha, who slew the corn spirit, had two intimate companions, although these do not appear to have taken part in the actual killing. We may therefore suspect that in the similar Syrian legends of the Dying God there were originally three persons mainly responsible. Maybe at a later period, when the influence of the Stellar cult of Babylon had increased, the former mob was replaced by three specific characters, representing the three Winter signs of the Zodiac. It is more likely, however, that we have here a blending of the Moon cult with its three moonless nights: the three days spent by Jonah and by other initiates inside the monster point clearly enough to these three nights. When we remember that in our ceremonies there were originally fifteen conspirators, that is half a lunar month, it seems more probable that the three who did not repent represent the three dark nights, and that the twelve who did repent represent the twelve nights of the waning moon. The three villains would thus represent the three nights when the moon is invisible, after which she reappears once more.

I need hardly remind my readers that around the vegetation god have gathered myths which did not originally belong to him, but to the moon and even to the sun. Among primitive savages the fertility of the soil is supposed to *increase* with the waxing and *decrease* with the waning moon, therefore the blending of ideas thus indicated is perfectly natural. If then there should be three persons who took part in the slaying of the old priest-king, the representative of the god of vegetation, who were they ? It will be remembered that Hiawatha and his friends were not regarded as villains, but that, on the contrary, the slaying of the maize god by the former was considered a meritorious act. Neither were the three Mexican gods who brought about the downfall of Quetzalcoatl regarded as villains, although in that

---

1.   Josephus, Against Apion I. 18. where he calls it the temple of Jupiter.

legend our sympathies are enlisted on behalf of the victim. The Mexican religion seems to have been rapidly evolving when it was cut short by the Spaniards, and had it been left to itself there is no doubt that the three gods within a few centuries would have become villains.

Therefore we cannot help suspecting that originally these men, on whom fell the duty of slaying Hiram Abiff, were not three workmen, but the greatest and most illustrious persons present. It would be an insult to the god if the body he deigned to inhabit should be destroyed by mere ordinary mortals. None but kings, and if possible priest-kings, could perform this great sacrificial act. If Hiram was a consecration sacrifice, we know from the accounts in the Bible that King Solomon himself offered burnt offerings in the middle of the Court, i.e., at the centre. In other words, the victims were burnt to ashes at the centre, and although the Bible is very careful to say[1] that the victims were beasts, from what we have already seen we can have little doubt that at least one of them was a man.

I therefore suggest that Solomon, King of Israel, Hiram, King of Tyre, and Adoniram, Priest-king of Aphaca in Lebanon had the onorous, painful, yet sacred duty of freeing the divine soul of Abibaal, or Hiram Abiff, and of Consecrating the temple with his blood. It may be that the fatal stroke was dealt by Adoniram, and that into him entered the divine spirit of Hiram Abiff, for this would explain why Adoniram is distinguished from the others by the title Adon, i.e., Lord God, and also why he has become regarded as the successor of Hiram Abiff. Indeed, the ceremony as performed in a lodge contradicts the traditional history, for it is not ordinary members of the Lodge, but its three rulers, who perform a certain task. I shall refer to this point again in a subsequent chapter, for it is important.

In considering this question we must not overlook the fact that the Bible says that Hiram " made an end of doing all the work."[2] This shows that he was slain at the Dedication, and not before it, and does not mean that he was not slain at all, as some have suggested.

We must remember that primitive man does not fear death as do men of to-day: on that point all students are agreed. I think that the old priest-king Hiram Abiff went quite willingly to his fate, glad that his blood should consecrate the great temple which he had supervised for so long, and which had formed his great object in life since the time when the crown of Tyre had passed to his son. I believe that he went more gladly to his death than did his three royal friends to the sad, but sacred, task, which, by releasing his soul from its worn-out body, enabled it to ascend to those mansions whence all goodness emanates.

1. I Kings, 8. 64.
2. Ibid. 8. 40.

It will not be forgotten that when a greater than Hiram Abiff went to His Death there were three Rulers who sat in Judgment upon Him.   The High Priest, who among the Jews at that date was a kind of King, Herod, and Pontius Pilate.   We have seen that those who compassed His death seemed deliberately to have followed the procedure which occurred at the dramatic representation of the slaying of Tammuz, and we can hardly doubt that the three rulers who therein played their part did so in imitation of the ritual of Tammuz.   With such striking similarities before us between Hiram Abiff and Christ is it surprising that many Masons regard the story as an allegory of the Great Master ?

That three villains should later replace the three kings in the Hiramic legend is natural enough.   As more humane ideas developed men came to regard the sacrifice of men as abominable, and in order to purge the reputation of the great king of Israel and his allies, substitutes would have to be found.   Yet we who can see clearer than they who made the change can acquit Solomon of any evil in the matter.   He did but do what was customary, and I think that in Ecclesiastes we see the great soul of Solomon haunted by the tragic events in which custom had compelled him to play his part.

CHAPTER XXIII

THE SONS OF THE WIDOW

At first sight it seems strange that Masons should call
themselves, " Sons of the Widow," apparently because of the
" accidental " circumstances that Hiram is said to be the son of
a widow. It seems too unimportant a fact to have given a sub-
title to the Order, but therein is a hint that at one time the fact
was recognised as being of supreme importance.

I have already shown that Tammuz must be the son of a
widow, since originally the very act of union which begot the son
resulted in the death of the father. The son in his turn dies in
the act of begetting a successor, and so in early times the living
incarnation of the god is always the actual son of the dead representative of the god.

This title survived not only among Masons, but in the Graal
legends where Perceval is called the " Son of the Widow Lady,"
and it would be possible to compile quite a list of " Questing
Heroes," who are similarly called " Sons of the Widow." Perhaps, however, the most striking fact of all is that the Manichees
were known by this title. Now this gnostic sect was organised by
a Persian named Mani, who tried to amalgamate the old Dualist
cult of Persia, the Astarte cult of Syria and Christianity. The
Dualist tendency of the Templars has already been shown,
particularly as symbolised by their black and white banner and
the crest of two knights on one horse. Most of the sects of
Syria at the time of the Crusades, whether Mahomedan or
Christian were also strongly Dualistic.

Among these gnostics Astarte becomes disguised under the
names of Sophia or Achamoth.[1] She is said to have fallen, and
the Saviour replaces Tammuz and descends in order to rescue her,
and with her mankind. In these cults transmigration played an
important part in purifying the soul, and there is considerable
play made with the planets, stars and angelic beings. There is
no doubt that these gnostic sects, especially that founded by
Mani, had a far greater influence on the Templars and on Masonry
than most students seem to have realised, and traces of their
teaching may still be found in Freemasonry to-day.

Therefore, historically, the title " Sons of the Widow " is of
twofold importance. Firstly, it confirms the view that our hero
represents Tammuz or Adonis, and secondly, it suggests a connection between Freemasonry and Manicheism. In like manner

1. Rev. F. W. Russell, D.D., " Religious Thought and Heresy in the
   Middle Ages." p. 553.

235

the avowedly Templar Graal legends used the title for their chief hero, and this indicates a similar connection. As Manicheism was merely an attempt to unite the old Syrian fertility cult with Christianity, we see a still further strengthening of the link which unites both Masonry and Templary with Syria.

As every initiate in Freemasonry represents Hiram, and so Tammuz, it naturally follows that in taking on his character the initiate takes also the title of " Son of the Widow," the widow being originally Astarte, and later Astarte disguised as the fallen Sophia. In this latter form the candidate then becomes the representative of the Saviour whom the Gnostics, like the orthodox Christians, considered to be Christ. Thus in the course of years, and by a perfectly natural process of religious evolution, it comes about that it is to-day quite legitimate to regard the candidate as the humble representative of Christ, and the teaching of Masonry to be a mystic allegory of the development of the Christ spirit within us.

Viewed in this light the ceremonies of initiation take on a deeper and a holier meaning. They are no longer a worn down survival of the Savage Magical ceremonies of a barbarous Semitic race, but a Mystery, teaching the profound lesson that every man must sacrifice himself mystically and spiritually as Christ did actually, and only so can each and all of us hope to reach the Light and attain Union with the Source of our being.

We thus see the meaning of the peculiar manner in which the cand. is admitted to the Lodge and led to the altar. He comes as a willing sacrifice, and the p....s in each degree emphasise the same lesson. Just as Christ sacrificed himself, so must every cand., and in the 3° the manner of advancing from W. to E. emphasises the manner in which Christ died on the cross.

But Christianity, like later Judaism teaches that God does not desire the death of a sinner, but rather that he should repent and live. The sacrifice that God requires is not our body, but the surrender of our wills to His guidance, and it is this, assuredly, that Freemasonry tries to teach us, by word and symbol, if we have but the eyes to see.

If I have read the facts aright, Hiram was not foully slain by scoundrels who desired to extract some secret from him. He went as a willing sacrifice to consecrate with his life the task to which he had devoted his declining years. That task was the building of a temple to the glory of God, and in like manner each Mason is called on to devote his life to the building and consecrating of a temple not made with hands, eternal in the skies. In so far, and in so far only, as he does thus consecrate himself is he justly entitled to be called

" A Son of the Widow "

CHAPTER XXIV

WHY HIRAM REPRESENTS ADONIS AND NOT OSIRIS

There is only one possible alternative to Adonis as the original form of our hero, and this is Osiris, and the reasons why I personally reject the claims of that august personage constitute the main theme of this chapter. Before discussing this question, however, it seems desirable to answer a query which has probably arisen in the mind of more than one of my readers. The query would be worded somewhat as follows:—" Why should not the story as told be correct; why spend hours in digging up the history of Tammuz and trying to identify him with our hero ? "

The story as given is, I consider, manifestly incorrect, for the following reasons:—

1. The object of the scoundrels cannot be as set out therein. They were told by Hiram that the secrets of a M.M. were known to but three in the world, and therefore for reasons already given in chapter 18, they were of no practical use to them.

2. What was the secret they sought ? Speculative Masons say it was a word which in consequence could never henceforth be given. As an allegory this is excellent, but as history it is obviously absurd. Neither does its loss seem to have been of any practical moment, for according to the legend the temple was finished after the crime. Moreover, although the King was so pedantic as to refuse to confer it on another, because he had not a third to assist him in doing so, yet he buried it in a position where it could be subsequently discovered, perhaps by non-Masons.

Operative Masons declare that the secret was a certain trade secret, but if so, why must every aspirant to learn that secret, i.e., every Third M.M. designate (or ruler), be dramatically sl. in order that his successor may receive it ? I suggest herein we get the key. The lost word is a synonym for the Divine Soul of Tammuz, which could only be transferred to his successor by the death of the body of its former owner, but if so the man who inherited the Office, and with it the Divine Soul, should surely do the slaying, as was the case at Nemi. No doubt this was so originally, but when the killing grew to be regarded as murder, the idea that any of those who took part therein could benefit by the crime became repugnant, hence the appearance of the three villains.

From the practical standpoint, a genuine trade secret does appear to be a greater temptation than a method of proof which none could apply, and to that extent the Operative story is more plausible. But plausible is exactly the word. The square of the

Babylonian Architect god Nabu was formed by three rods which made a right angled triangle, and with that fact before us to prove its general acceptance as the badge of an architect, can we possibly believe that among all that mass of workmen employed on the temple only three men, and those men kings, knew such a necessary secret ?   Had the story been that the villains were caught by Hiram spying on him and the others when using the rods, it would have been possible to consider it seriously.

Against these obviously late versions of the legend we have a mass of significant facts.

1.   The widespread nature of the cult of Tammuz in the very district where the tragedy occurred.

2.   The peculiar nature of the names of the men employed.

3.   The fact that an ear of corn is the real meaning of one of the pass w....s, and that we find this symbol associated with several other mystery rites of death and resurrection in neighbouring lands, viz., at Eleusis in Greece, and in Egypt, etc.

4.   The widespread practice of a human Consecration Sacrifice.

5.   The manner in which the cands. are led into Lodge shows that they are meant to represent a sacrifice.

6.   The p....s are all forms of carrying out such sacrifices.

7.   The sprig of acacia shows how the soul was transferred.

8.   The fact that there still existed both public and secret rites of Tammuz hundreds of years later, rites which actually took place in the Temple.

9.   That in these Rites a drama of death and a bough played a significant part.

10.   That the site of the Temple had been the site of a place sacred to Adonis, and that after finishing this Temple Solomon built one to Astarte close beside it.

11.   That Hiram of Tyre was a god-man, representative of Adonis, and so was Adoniram.

12.   The well attested fact that such God-men and priest-kings had to die violent deaths.

13.   That the father of Hiram of Tyre called himself, not by a personal name, but Abibaal, father of the God, i.e., Hiram, and that the architect called himself the father of Hiram.

14.   The path which the architect trod formed the red cross of consecration and the representatives of such vegetation gods were hung on crosses or trees.

Many other points have already been mentioned, but sufficient have now been given to show that while the traditional form of the legend makes the reason for the crime inadequate, the reason for the sacrifice of a priest-king, was, according to current beliefs, overwhelming.

Now let us turn to Osiris.   The glamour of Egypt seems to dazzle the eyes of many able scholars, and it is time to look at things calmly, in the cold light of reason. The world is full of representatives of the Dying God, almost all of whom seem to have evolved from a spirit of vegetation, and as men became agriculturalists this spirit grew to be regarded as the god of corn. The very widespread nature of this " fertility cult " is of great advantage to the anthropologist, since it enables him to piece together the fragmentary nature of the records of what took place in various races at different epochs, and helps him to understand the underlying principles behind certain ceremonies. At this point in our research, however, it is necessary to isolate what is universal in all these cults, and what is peculiar to each, and it is just here that Egypt fails to make good her claim.

Osiris and Tammuz are both gods of corn, and so a certain superficial resemblance between the two may be expected, but can we be sure that Osiris himself is indigenous to Egypt ? Thirty years ago the question would doubtless have been answered promptly in the affirmative, but to-day archæologists are beginning to have their doubts. There seems, indeed, to be an increasing stream of evidence to show that Osiris was originally Semitic, and was brought to the Nile by Semitic invaders in days before the first Dynasty. What is clear about Egypt is that a very definite tone was given to her religion at a very early date, and this, once adopted, persisted to the end.

In Syria, on the other hand, the fertility cult developed on its own lines, and despite a certain amount of interchange of culture remained quite distinct down to the fall of Rome. Moreover, whereas Egypt and Osiris passed into the limbo of forgotten things, Astarte and her cult continued to exercise a profound influence on both Islam and Christianity up to the end of the Crusades. Although the last stronghold of Osiris, Philae, had fallen by the 6th century, and the ancient faith had perished, we find in the 10th century A.D. Tammuz under the name of Tâ-uz was still lamented annually in Syria.

We have seen, moreover, that this cult was firmly established in Rome, under the name of Cybele, in 200 B.C., and survived till the time of the conversion of the Empire, having thus ample opportunity to become incorporated in the Rites of the Roman Collegia, whereas the Isis cult only gained a foothold in the time of the Cæsars.

Above all, our tradition links us with Syria and not with Egypt, in every point and detail, save one fragment of a word in the Arch, and we cannot thus arbitrarily, and without showing good reasons, brush aside so important a part of the tradition just to suit ourselves. Can any of my readers point out anything in the Craft degrees which is found in Egypt and not in the Syrian cult ? I doubt it.

We find in Egypt nothing to represent the Kadosh or the double-headed Eagle, which we can trace in the early Hittite remains, and among the Jews themselves the two pillars which correspond, not with the Biblical account, but with those which stood outside the temples at Hierapolis and Paphos, are not the same in shape as the Tat or the Obelisk of Egypt. On the other hand, the hawk which plays so prominent a part on the Egyptian cult, as representing Isis, and so forth, does not appear in Masonry, where the only bird is that significant double-headed eagle.

The gavel of the Master is the axe of Sandan; why then compare it with the hieroglyphic which means "Neter," or "God," in Egypt ? Osiris did not bear the axe, but the flail, which plays no part in Masonry. Most significant of all is the fact that the forty-two Judges nowhere appear with us. This was one of the central themes of the Egyptian cult, yet, like Syria, we have no trace of it. Elaborate ceremonies associated with the making of the mummy are the very foundation of the cult of Osiris, but there is no trace of them in our ritual. On the other hand the Syrians did not mummify their dead. In short, I suggest that scholars have tried to identify Hiram with Osiris because they had to hand a very complete account of the Egyptian ceremonies and knew little about the resurrection cult of Syria. All the points of similarity between the two cults may be freely admitted. They may even have been borrowed from each other, but the outstanding fact is that nowhere can we find any masonic features in the Egyptian cult which we cannot trace in the Syrian cult, whereas we do find Masonic features in the latter which are not in the Egyptian. Most important of all are these two facts. (1) Our tradition avowedly comes from Syria and not from Egypt, which is not even mentioned by name. (2) There is a continuous line of connection between the old cult of Syria and the Middle Ages, whereas the Egyptian tradition was completely cut off in the 6th century A.D.

If we turn to the High Grades we find the position is the same. Lucian describes three sets of foes who have to be overcome in the belly of the whale, and in the R.O.S. there are three Guardians to be passed before the traveller enters the tower of refreshment. There are three veils in the Excellent Master, and there are three rooms in the Rose Croix. If we compare these simple divisions with the complex Underworld of Egypt we see at once that here also our tradition comes from Syria, with its simpler conception, and not from the elaborate system which for thousands of years persisted on the banks of the Nile.

As, however, the whole of this book has shown in detail how various parts of our legend and ritual come from Syria, and has shown moreover that among the sects and secret societies of Syria a parallel system still survives, of which hardly a trace can be found in Egypt to-day, we will now turn to the next chapter, and indicate the connecting lines which link us with Syria: lines which do not lead us to the banks of the Nile.

CHAPTER XXV

THE HISTORICAL DESCENT OF THE ADONIS CULT AND ITS SURVIVAL

The lines which connect the old cult of Tammuz or Adonis with modern Freemasonry have been indicated at various points in this book, but here we will join up the strands.

Firstly, we see that Hiram Abiff was a Consecration Sacrifice at the completion of the Temple, and was offered up because he was a priest-king, who was supposed to enshrine the Divine Soul of the fertility or corn god, Tammuz.

Secondly, this cult of the Dying God threw out offshoots. One branch, that of Cybele and Attis, migrated to Rome 200 years B.C. Another early offshoot gave the name of Dionysius to the fertility god, and reached Greece quite early, passing to Rome in due course, where the god was known as Bacchus. Both of these cults had a secret mystery Rite as well as popular ceremonies.

Thirdly, in Judea itself we have traces of the development of a similar inner mystery, which was denounced by Ezekiel about 580 B.C.

Fourthly, soon after this date the Jews were carried away captive to Babylon, where they must have seen the Babylonian Mystery drama of the Death and Resurrection of Marduk, and also the grim reality of the criminal who for five days reigned as king and then was crucified, or hung on a tree.

Fifthly, the influence of this Babylonian version of the Dying God is shown in the new festival of Purim which the Jews established not long after their return from Captivity. In this Marduk is probably represented by Mordecai, Ishtar, by Esther, and the criminal king, by Haman. It was customary to hang figures of Haman on a tree or cross, and that the Jews did sometimes use a cross is shown by the fact that the later Christian Emperors forbade them to hang the figure on a cross, as the Christians considered it was done in mockery of the crucifixion. Often they afterwards burnt the figure of Haman, a custom which survived in Germany up to the end of the 18th century. The original fertility nature of this feast is proved by the licentious and drunken nature of the festival, in which the women exchanged clothes with the men, a procedure forbidden by the Mosaic code. [1]

Sixthly, the Jews had a mysterious fertility god, Sabazius, in the 2nd century B.C., a fact which was made the excuse for expelling the first Jews who came to Rome.

Seventhly, during the same period we hear for the first time of the Essenes, who seem to have been a reformed sect of the fertility cult, and worked a secret Mystery Rite which has certain affinities with Masonry, and survived until the 4th century A.D.

---

1. Frazer, " The Scapegoat," pp. 360 sq.

Eighthly, meanwhile the old cult of Tammuz was adopted and modified by the Greeks, who renamed the god Adonis, and by them it was spread far and wide throughout the Roman Empire. It even invaded Egypt and competed with the cult of Osiris, surviving at Alexandria well into the 5th century A.D.

Ninthly, we thus find that during the opening years of the Christian era the Roman Collegia of Architects had all around them Mystery Cults of Death and Resurrection derived from the old cult of Tammuz. · We know from their " tracing board " that they worked a ritual of death and resurrection, and there is further confirmation of that fact in a stone sculpture on their Temple at Pompeii.   Here we can see square, compasses, hammer, chisel, and other working tools, and in addition a down turned funerary urn, a well-known symbol for death.¹   These men painted the H.S. of a F.C. on one of their frescoes, and decorated the walls of their Temple at Pompeii with the interlaced triangle.

Tenthly, one of their lodges survived the downfall of Rome at Comacina, and became the ancestor of the Comacine Masons of the early Middle Ages.

Eleventhly, the Comacines sculptured the H.S. of a F.C. at Ravello, at Coire Cathedral and at Peterborough, and at Coire they also sculptured the S. of G. and D. and a s....n of the Rose Croix.   From them are descended the modern Freemasons.

There is, however, a second line of connection which no doubt strengthened the definitely Semitic side of our ritual towards the close of the Comacine period and infused new life into it.   This came via certain semi-Gnostic sects, and through the Templars. The Tammuz cult itself was still alive and active in the 10th century A.D. in Syria, and about that period a number of heretical Mahomedan sects arose.   All of these had as a characteristic feature the incarnation of the Divine Spirit in the leader of the Order, and secret Rites of initiation.   There was also a host of Gnostic sects, avowedly Christianised versions of the Tammuz cult, among whom was one, the Manichees, who were called " Sons of the Widow."   These also had secret rites of initiation.

Into this welter of secret societies, all more or less directly derived from the old Syrian fertility cult, burst the Crusaders, who brought back to Europe Syrian architectural forms, such as the pointed arch, and Asiatic customs in dress and manners.

More especially we have seen that the Templars became interlocked with at least one of these secret societies, the Assassins, and ultimately were persecuted because they had a secret rite of initiation which the Church considered heretical.   This rite included a ritual of death and resurrection, and some of its teaching occurs in the Graal legends, where an attempt is made to defend and explain it.

---

1.   Photo in possession of the Author.

In these Graal legends we meet with the annual slaying of a King, the beating of the cross, the spear of Marduk, the head of Adonis, castration, and so forth, while the hero, Perceval, is called " The Son of the Widow." It is clear that most, if not all, the adventures in the Quest take place in the Underworld as the Knights journey towards the Graal castle,—the city of God.

Here, as in Lucian, we meet with the two bridges, one leading into Hell, the other linking Paradise with Heaven, and we suddenly remember that while there are no bridges in the Egyptian Rites, there are in Masonry: examples being in the Red Cross of Babylon, and in the Royal Order of Scotland.

We know that many Masons were serving brothers in the Templar Order, and find that there is a persistent Templar tradition in Masonry, and therefore we cannot ignore this second link with the Adonis cult. The Templars were attacked in 1307, and during the 14th century the international organisation we know as the Comacines collapsed before the rising tide of Nationalism. By 1375 we find the Masons calling themselves by the English name of " Freemason," and about the same date the first of the Ancient Charges begin to appear.

We also find that there was an entirely distinct group of Masons, the Guild Masons, whose modern representatives are the so-called Operatives, and the Trade Unions. The latter still had a truncated ritual in 1834, which they have gradually abandoned, but one or two Operative Lodges still exist which work an interesting ritual wherein the *tragedy* is enacted as *an annual drama*, and not as an initiation ceremony.

The Freemasons were more like the modern architects, and their speciality was Church building, hence their importance declined after the Reformation. Had it not been that they began about 1640 to admit Speculatives in large numbers, they would have died out. Instead they took on a new lease of life, and found new and useful work to do when they organised themselves under Grand Lodge in 1717.

The picture by Guercino now in the possession of the Supreme Royal Arch Chapter of Scotland, shows that this new Grand Lodge did not invent the legend, but merely inherited it. They worked the legend not as a drama, but as an initiation, and in one detail seem to have kept nearer to the form of the original tragedy than have the Operatives, or the traditional history. In the last chapter I gave the reasons why I think that the Master was not slain by three ordinary workmen, but by three Kings, and showed how the ritual of the Speculatives supports this view.

Our long task is ended. Back, back, into the dim red dawn of man we have followed the path which leads to the feet of the Master, and having found him we have journeyed back down the long-drawn ages travelling Westward, till the journey ends

in modern London. When we started our task, like the E.A.
we left the West and went to the East, only to find ourselves in
the presence of a terible tragedy, the sight of a Dying Priest-king
of Adonis, and so as M.M.'s we turned our faces to the West.
Journeying from the East we have followed the steps of the
Master ever Westward, and seen how He has borne the banner of
Masonry across Europe and the ocean, to the furthest shores of
America.

As we pause at the end of our journey, we realise that we
found the secret at the centre, in a hidden vault, beneath the altar
of Sacrifice, in the centre of King Solomon's Temple. But on
our journey we have learnt many invaluable lessons. We have
seen a ghastly magic ceremony transformed in the course of ages
into an allegory of immortality, and the traveller who started as
an anthropologist returns as a mystic, who has found the path of
true initiation.

Since, therefore, Hiram has thus proved himself to be our
guide and conductor, in more senses than one, it seems permissible
to end this work with a question whose solution I will leave to my
readers. The name Hiram seems to be closely connected with the
Greek word Hermes, the Messenger of the Gods, the Conductor
of the Dead through the Underworld, and the symbol of the
higher intelligence. Is it not possible that this connection implies
that the Greeks, who accepted the Orphic teaching long before
the Classical period, who celebrated the Mysteries of Dionysius
and adopted and Hellenised the Cult of Adonis, may have derived
not only the name Hermes, but also the whole conception of that
God from Hiram Abiff? He who in his own divine person had
descended into the Underworld, would be of all men and gods
the best fitted to guide others amid the shadows of that valley
which lies beyond the vale, and yet leads to the Mansions of Bliss.

When next, O reader, you eat a humble slice of bread, pause
for a moment and think what we owe to " an ear of corn." On
the material plane we owe to corn the evolution of all civilisation
in the West. To corn we owe the development of the doctrine of
the Resurrection, the hope which has sustained millions in the
hour of grief, of anguish and of death. For this men have died
bravely and unflinchingly, for this they have toiled unceasingly
throughout their lives. Above all, to this we owe the most
sublime and exalted teaching of the Mysteries, by means whereof
the mystic learns the secret of the journey back to God, from
whence he came.

Then, Brother, the Ear of Corn will not be to you an empty
Shibboleth, but a symbol above all symbols, and you, too, will
understand the deep thrill which passed through the soul of the
initiate at Eleusis when as the crowning act of the Mystery he
was shown

AN EAR OF CORN